INFLATION
ACCOUNTING

INFLATION ACCOUNTING

A Guide for the Accountant and the Financial Analyst

SIDNEY DAVIDSON, Ph.D., CPA
Arthur Young Professor of Accounting
University of Chicago

CLYDE P. STICKNEY, D.B.A., CPA
Associate Professor of Accounting
University of North Carolina at Chapel Hill

ROMAN L. WEIL, Ph.D., CPA, CMA
Mills B. Lane Professor of Industrial Management
Georgia Institute of Technology

McGRAW-HILL BOOK COMPANY
New York   St. Louis   San Francisco   Auckland   Düsseldorf   Johannesburg
Kuala Lumpur   London   Mexico   Montreal   New Delhi   Panama
Paris   São Paulo   Singapore   Sydney   Tokyo   Toronto

Library of Congress Cataloging in Publication Data

Davidson, Sidney, date.
  Inflation accounting.

  Bibliography: p.
  Includes index.
  1. Inflation (Finance) and accounting. I. Stickney,
Clyde P., date, joint author. II. Weil, Roman L.,
joint author. III. Title.
HF5657.D28   658.1'553   75-42210
ISBN 0-07-015478-3

1234567890   KPKP   785432109876

The editors for this book were W. Hodson Mogan and Lynne
Lackenbach, the designer was Elliot Epstein, and the
production supervisor was Teresa F. Leaden. It was set in
Baskerville by University Graphics, Inc.

Printed and bound by The Kingsport Press.

CONTENTS

v

PREFACE

OUR ECONOMY in recent years has experienced steadily rising prices. There is every expectation that price increases will continue. Financial reporting that recognizes this economic fact of life is coming. There are various ways of seeking to reflect this increase in prices in the accounts. Probably the most widely discussed type of reporting is variously known as "financial reporting in units of general purchasing power," "general price level adjusted accounting," or, if you are not fond of it, "PuPu (*Purchasing Power Unit*) accounting." We tend to describe it as *general price level adjusted accounting,* or *GPLA* accounting for short. It has also come to be known as *inflation accounting*—thus the title of this book. Although this usage has become widespread, it is unfortunate in a way because there are at least two ways other than GPLA of accounting for inflation. (They are introduced in Chapter One and described in Chapter Eleven.) Personally, we prefer either of the other methods of accounting for inflation to GPLA accounting. Still, GPLA statements may be coming, and accountants must now learn how to prepare and audit them and financial analysts must now learn how to interpret them. This book is designed to facilitate that learning process.

This book is written for accountants, financial analysts, and other interested readers of financial statements. Part I, Chapters Two through Six, attempts to explain how to prepare GPLA financial statements. Part II, Chapters Seven through Ten, attempts to ready financial analysts and other readers to interpret GPLA financial statements and to estimate what GPLA financial statements will look like for corporations of particular interest to them. (As Chapter Six points out, however, the auditor will find the models in Chapters Eight and Ten useful for deriving checks on client-prepared GPLA financial statements.) Part II is self-contained. The nonaccountant can skim Chapter One and then proceed to Chapter

Seven. Part III, Chapters Eleven and Twelve, explains the alternative methods of inflation accounting, including the advantages and disadvantages of each. This part contains material of interest to both accountants and analysts.

We thank the *Financial Analysts Journal* for permission to revise some material originally published there and its editor, Jack L. Treynor, for helpful advice. John M. MacDonald of Coopers & Lybrand helped us to clarify some of the technical details involved in GPLA accounting. Conversations with Myron J. Gordon of the University of Toronto improved our discussion of the implications of GPLA for public utilities. He disagrees, however, with much of what we say. Angela Falkenstein of Legg Mason Washington Service helped us to refine our estimates of GPLA income for the Dow Jones Industrials. Samy Sidky provided research assistance throughout the stages of our work. Day-Luan Yang, Christine Ciarfalia, and James Skrydlak helped prepare material for the special industry studies in Chapter Nine. Mary Lee Peeler and K. Xenophon Rybowiak prepared the manuscript in all its versions. We thank the National Science Foundation for research support, which enabled us to analyze more companies and industries in Chapter Nine than we had originally planned.

Our greatest debt is to Professor Robert T. Sprouse, who in 1970 wrote, for the *Handbook of Modern Accounting*, a chapter on GPLA accounting that served as a model of clarity and exposition for us in preparing much of the material in our Part I. That we acknowledge our debt to Professor Sprouse in no way implies that he, now a member of the Financial Accounting Standards Board, agrees or, for that matter, disagrees with what we say here.

Sidney Davidson
Clyde P. Stickney
Roman L. Weil

INFLATION
ACCOUNTING

Chapter One

ACCOUNTING ADJUSTMENTS FOR CHANGING PRICES

THE MOST PERSISTENT AND SIGNIFICANT COMPLAINT about accounting in recent years is that it ignores the economic facts of life. Throughout the world, a steady and rapid upward movement in prices has occurred during the last few years. This has probably been the single most important economic phenomenon of the 1970's. Yet this significant fact goes unrecognized today under generally accepted accounting principles throughout the English-speaking world, and is similarly ignored or ineffectually dealt with in the accounting procedures of much of the rest of the world. Changes are coming in accounting and financial reporting. This chapter outlines some of the suggested changes and indicates the major objectives of the most likely change.

Currently, almost all accounting measurements are made in terms of the number of dollars (or other monetary unit) expended for the object of measurement. This is commonly referred to as a "historical cost" measure. For example, if during 1973 a firm acquired a machine for $2,000 cash, the machine would be accounted for 3 years later, during 1976, as having a historical cost of $2,000, and the depreciation of the machine during the year 1976 would be based on that figure. Accounting based on historical cost provides no information about the effects of any price changes—either about changes in all prices affecting the general purchasing power of the dollar or about changes in the specific prices of individual assets being used. The effects of price changes are ultimately reflected in the measurement of income, but the effects are implicitly merged with all the other factors affecting the business enterprise.

METHODS OF ACCOUNTING FOR CHANGING PRICES

Depending on the objectives to be served, there are three principal ways to deal explicitly with changing prices in accounting measurements and to report the effects so isolated:

1. Historical dollar amounts can be adjusted for changes in the general price level.

2. The current prices of specific items can be substituted for the historical dollar amounts.

3. The current prices of specific items, adjusted for changes in the general price level, can be substituted for the historical dollar amounts.

Historical Dollar Amounts Adjusted for Changes in the General Price Level

Historical cost can be stated in terms of either the units of money or of the units of general purchasing power that were expended for the object of measurement. The amounts reported in conventional financial statements are measured in terms of the number of units of money (that is, number of dollars) expended for the object of measurement. An important assumption underlying the use of units of money in accounting measurements is that the size of this measuring unit remains relatively stable over time. In this way, dollars expended at different times can be meaningfully added and subtracted to obtain measures of total assets, total equities, and net income.

The size of the measuring unit has, of course, not remained stable in the United States and in most other countries. As the general level of prices has changed, the purchasing power of the dollar has changed. Dollars spent or received at different times reflect varying amounts of purchasing power. Consequently, the assumption of a stable monetary measuring unit has been violated.

One solution to the accounting problems created by changing prices is to report historical cost in terms of units of general purchasing power, rather than in terms of units of money. That is, the historical amounts of general purchasing power expended can be restated into an equivalent number of dollars of current general purchasing power. In this way, accounting measurements will reflect a uniform measuring unit, dollars of equivalent general purchasing power. The Financial Accounting Standards Board (FASB) has issued a proposed Statement of Financial Accounting Standard that would require, for fiscal years beginning on or after January 1, 1976, the restatement of conventional financial statements for changes in the general purchasing power of the monetary unit and the reporting of certain information from the adjusted statements.[1]

[1] Financial Accounting Standards Board, "Financial Reporting in Units of General Purchasing Power," Proposed Statement of Financial Accounting Standard, Stamford, Connecticut, 1974, para. 31.

These adjustments will require measurements of general purchasing power, but the need for such measurements is neither new nor restricted to accounting. For some time, various agencies of the U.S. federal government have been publishing indexes that measure changes in general price levels. Similar indexes are published in other countries. To the extent that such indexes provide acceptable measures of general price level changes, they can be used in accounting to measure historical costs in terms of units of general purchasing power. For example, assume that during the 3-year period, 1973 to 1976, the general price level in the United States increased about 30 percent, as indicated by the Gross National Product Implicit Price Deflator (GNP Deflator) prepared by the Department of Commerce. The machine acquired in the previous example for $2,000 of 1973 purchasing power could be accounted for 3 years later as having a restated cost of $2,600 of 1976 purchasing power (= $2,000 × 1.30), and the depreciation of the machine during the year 1976 would be based on the latter figure.

It is possible to make the purchasing power measurements of historical cost and depreciation in terms of 1973 dollars (2,000) or 1976 dollars (2,600) or dollars of any other date. If, however, other accounting measurements are to be made in terms of purchasing power and reported together with those for the machine, it is crucial that a common measuring unit be used, especially if the arithmetic operations of addition and subtraction are involved. Because accounting information is intended to be used in making current decisions, it seems reasonable that accounting reports should be stated in terms of current dollars—the terms in which the decision maker is most likely to be thinking. The proposed financial accounting standard of the FASB requires the financial statements to be restated to the general purchasing power of the dollar as of the most recent balance sheet date.[2]

This book is devoted primarily to a discussion of general price level accounting (GPLA). Before considering GPLA further, however, we shall consider briefly two other approaches to accounting for changing prices.

Current Prices of Specific Items

The current prices of individual assets, equities, revenues, and expenses could be used in preparing financial statements. Accounting for the current prices of specific items will not provide the same financial statement results as accounting for historical costs adjusted for changes in the general price level. The prices of specific items, such as the machine acquired during 1973, may change less or change more than the general price level or may even move in the opposite direction. The GNP Deflator

[2]*Ibid.*, para. 36.

reflects the average change in prices of all goods and services produced in the economy. It is unreasonable to expect that the GNP Deflator could provide a meaningful measure of the change in the price of any specific item. To illustrate, assume that during the 3-year period there had been no technological changes affecting the machine acquired during 1973, and that the current price for a new, identical machine on December 31, 1976, was $2,500. In 1976, the machine could be accounted for on the basis of its replacement cost of $2,500, and the depreciation of the machine during the year 1976 would be based on that figure. Accounting for changes in specific prices is discussed more fully in Chapter Eleven.

Current Prices of Specific Items and Adjustments for Changes in the General Price Level

The separate effects of changes in the general price level and changes in specific prices may be accounted for. Perhaps this can be most vividly illustrated by analyzing an investment in marketable securities. Assume that the 1973 acquisition in the example above was a block of listed common stock at a cost of $2,000, that the December 31, 1976, price for the stock was quoted at $2,700, and that the general price level increased 30 percent during the 3-year interim.

At acquisition in 1973, the stock was worth $2,000. For the investor to be equally well off on December 31, 1976, in terms of general purchasing power, the stock must have a value of $2,600 (= $2,000 × 1.30); it is actually worth $2,700. There has been a "real" gain in economic resources held by the investor in the amount of $100 of December 31, 1976, general purchasing power—a holding gain of $100 measured in 1976 dollars. The other $600 is not a real gain in any economic sense; rather, it is the additional number of dollars that must be held on December 31, 1976, merely to maintain the amount of general purchasing power invested during 1973. This third method of accounting for changing prices is also considered more fully in Chapter Eleven.

OBJECTIVES OF GENERAL PRICE LEVEL ACCOUNTING

Money serves two purposes: as a medium of exchange and as a store of value. The value of money is determined by the amount of goods and services for which it can be exchanged. Different amounts of money may be exchanged for identical goods or services at different times; that is, the purchasing power of money changes. Sometime in the past, $1 may have been exchangeable for 1 hour of a particular kind of labor; today, perhaps $4 must be exchanged for 1 hour of the same kind of labor.

Sometime in the past, $1 may have been exchangeable for 10 pounds of aluminum ingot; today, perhaps $1 is exchangeable for only 3 pounds of aluminum ingot. Changes in the prices of labor and aluminum are examples of changes in specific prices. Changes in the general price level are measured by changes in indexes based on aggregations of specific prices and thereby represent average changes in all, or large numbers, of specific prices.

The primary objective of adjusting historical amounts for changes in the general price level is to convert monetary units (for example, dollars) reflecting varying amounts of general purchasing power into a common measuring unit reflecting a uniform amount of general purchasing power for all measurements. This objective is analogous to translating measurements in foreign monetary units, perhaps Canadian dollars or Swiss francs, into their equivalent amounts in U.S. dollars in the process of consolidating the financial position and operations of foreign subsidiaries with the financial position and operations of the U.S. parent corporation.

Adjustments of historical amounts to reflect changes in the general price level are designed to improve accounting measurements in a number of ways that are described in the following sections.

To Make the Results of Arithmetic Operations Using Accounting Measurements More Meaningful

When dollars representing different amounts of general purchasing power are intermingled, the results of arithmetic operations may be difficult to interpret. For example, it may not be meaningful to report that the $10,000 cash on hand today, plus the $20,000 cost of inventory purchased 1 year ago, plus the $80,000 cost of land acquired 20 years ago, plus the $60,000 depreciated cost of equipment purchased during the last 10 years, equals $170,000 of total assets. Although the total of 10,000 U.S. dollars, 20,000 Canadian dollars, 80,000 Swiss francs, and 60,000 Danish kroner is 170,000 monetary units, the sum has little economic significance because the monetary units are not equivalent. Likewise, the general purchasing power of one year's dollar is not equivalent to those of other years.

To Make Interperiod Comparisons More Meaningful

Interperiod comparisons made in monetary units representing different amounts of general purchasing power may be meaningless or misleading. A direct comparison of the sales of Shell Oil measured in Dutch guilders, of British Petroleum measured in British pounds, and of Exxon measured in U.S. dollars would be meaningless; the need for a common measuring unit is obvious. Similarly, in a 10-year comparative summary of the operations of a U.S. corporation, a 30-percent increase in dollars of sales reported during a period when the general price level increased 50 percent may be misleading.

To Improve the Meaning and Measurement of Income

The failure to account for the changing purchasing power of the dollar may distort the measurement of income. The Financial Accounting Standards Board has stated:[3]

> Investors and others often look to the income statement, or to ratios that are based in part on measures of income, for information about the ability of an enterprise to earn a return on its invested capital. In the conventional income statement, revenues are measured in dollars of current, or at least very recent, purchasing power, whereas certain significant expense items are measured in dollars of different purchasing power of earlier periods. Depreciation and cost of goods sold are two of the most commonly cited examples, although the problem arises whenever amounts in the income statement represent expenditures of dollars of different purchasing power. In periods of inflation, depreciation and cost of goods sold tend to be understated in terms of the purchasing power sacrificed to acquire depreciable assets and inventory. Further, information stated in terms of current general purchasing power may indicate that an enterprise's income tax and dividend payout rates are significantly different in terms of units of money and in units of general purchasing power.

To Provide Explicit Information About the Impact of Inflation Across Firms

Within a given country, inflation and deflation affect different firms differently. The effects depend on industry characteristics and management policies. In the absence of adjustments for changes in the general price level, the impact of changes in the general purchasing power of the dollar is necessarily submerged with all the other factors affecting the performance of the firm. Therefore, the user of accounting reports must either assume that all firms are affected similarly or make approximations of the impact of changing price levels on one firm versus another. The Financial Accounting Standards Board has stated:[4]

[3]*Ibid.*, para. 66.

[4]Financial Accounting Standards Board, "Reporting the Effects of General Price-Level Changes in Financial Statements," FASB Discussion Memorandum, Stamford, Connecticut, 1974, p. 8.

Changes in the purchasing power of the dollar affect individual enterprises differently, depending on the amount of the change and the age and composition of the enterprise's assets and equities. For example, during periods of inflation, those who hold monetary assets (cash and receivables in fixed dollar amounts) suffer a loss in purchasing power represented by those monetary assets. On the other hand, in periods of inflation, debtors gain because their liabilities are able to be repaid in dollars having less purchasing power. In periods of deflation, the reverse is true. Conventional financial statements do not report the effects of inflation or deflation on individual enterprises.

SUMMARY OUTLINE OF THIS BOOK

This book is written for both accountants and financial analysts. Part I, Chapters Two through Six, explains the accounting procedures for preparing GPLA financial statements. Part II, Chapters Seven through Ten, seeks to help those interested in financial analysis to interpret GPLA financial statements, and provides estimates of GPLA financial statements for particular corporations. The estimating method described in Part II, particularly Chapters Eight and Ten, will also be useful to auditors in checking GPLA financial statements prepared by clients. Part III, Chapters Eleven and Twelve, explains more fully the alternative methods of accounting for price changes introduced in this chapter and considers the advantages and disadvantages of each. Part III contains material of interest to both accountants and analysts. Each part of the book is virtually self-contained.

PART **I**

FOR THE ACCOUNTANT

Chapter Two

INTRODUCTION TO THE GENERAL PRICE LEVEL ADJUSTMENT PROCEDURE[1]

T HE DEMONSTRATION THAT FOLLOWS in Chapters Three through Five is designed to illustrate the kinds of adjustments required in restating financial statements for changes in the general price level and to identify some of the most significant problems encountered in implementing such adjustments. These are the kinds of adjustments that will be required if the proposed Statement of Financial Accounting Standard of the Financial Accounting Standards Board becomes effective.[2] Other special restatement problems are discussed in Chapter Six. The basic information has been accumulated in the accounts of Demonstrator Corporation in terms of historical numbers of dollars. The comparative balance sheet (Exhibit 2.1), income statement (Exhibit 2.2), and statement of changes in financial position (Exhibit 2.3) summarize the basic historical information.

PRICE INDEXES

In order to provide an element of realism to this illustration, the GNP Implicit Price Deflator for the period 1954 to 1973 has been used for Years 1–20, respectively. This 20-year period includes about 10 years of gradual inflation (approximately 1.9 percent annual inflation from 1954 through 1963) and about 10 years of more significant inflation (approximately 3.7 percent annual inflation from 1964 through 1973).

[1] The material in Chapters Two through Six draws heavily from the chapter, "Adjustments for Changing Prices," in the *Handbook of Modern Accounting,* 2nd ed., edited by Sidney Davidson and Roman L. Weil (New York: McGraw-Hill Book Company), to appear in 1977. The chapter in the first edition (1970) was written by Robert T. Sprouse and has been revised for the second edition by Clyde P. Stickney.

[2] Financial Accounting Standards Board, "Financial Reporting in Units of General Purchasing Power," Proposed Statement of Financial Accounting Standard, Stamford, Connecticut, 1974.

EXHIBIT 2.1

DEMONSTRATOR CORPORATION

Balance Sheet

Historical dollar basis

	December 31	
	Year 20	Year 19
Assets		
Current assets:		
Cash	$ 140,000	$ 120,000
Accounts receivable (net of allowance for uncollectibles)	400,000	380,000
Inventories (at first-in, first-out cost)	520,000	500,000
Prepayments	40,000	50,000
Total current assets	$1,100,000	$1,050,000
Investment in Stock of United, Inc. (at cost)	$ 160,000	$ 160,000
Property, plant, and equipment		
Land	$ 80,000	$ 80,000
Buildings (net of accumulated depreciation)	210,000	220,000
Equipment (net of accumulated depreciation)	550,000	520,000
Total property, plant, and equipment (net)	$ 840,000	$ 820,000
Total assets	$2,100,000	$2,030,000
Liabilities and Stockholders' Equity		
Current Liabilities:		
Trade accounts payable	$ 160,000	$ 210,000
Other current liabilities	40,000	60,000
Total current liabilities	$ 200,000	$ 270,000
Advances on maintenance contracts	30,000	20,000
Sinking fund debentures (6%)	500,000	500,000
Deferred income taxes	20,000	10,000
Total liabilities	$ 750,000	$ 800,000
Stockholders' equity:		
Preferred stock (2,000 shares, 5%, $100 par value, $105 redemption value)	$ 200,000	$ 200,000

EXHIBIT 2.1 Balance Sheet (*Continued*)

	December 31	
	Year 20	Year 19
Common stock (50,000 shares, $1 par value)	50,000	50,000
Additional paid-in capital	400,000	400,000
Retained earnings	700,000	580,000
Total stockholders' equity	$1,350,000	$1,230,000
Total liabilities and stockholders' equity	$2,100,000	$2,030,000

EXHIBIT 2.2

DEMONSTRATOR CORPORATION

Combined Statement of Income and Retained Earnings

For the year ended December 31, Year 20

Historical dollar basis

Revenues and Gains:		
Product sales	$2,578,000	
Earned on maintenance contracts	22,000	
Gain on sale of equipment	40,000	
Total revenues and gains		$2,640,000
Expenses:		
Cost of goods sold	$1,980,000	
Selling, general, and administrative	276,000	
Depreciation	124,000	
Interest	30,000	
Income taxes ,,,,,,,,, ...	100,000	
Total expenses		2,510,000
Net income		$ 130,000
Dividends on preferred stock		10,000
Increase in retained earnings		$ 120,000
Retained earnings, January 1		580,000
Retained earnings, December 31		$ 700,000
Earnings per common share (50,000 shares)		$ 2.40

EXHIBIT 2.3

DEMONSTRATOR CORPORATION

Statement of Changes in Financial Position

For the year ended December 31, Year 20

Historical dollar basis

Sources of working capital:	
Net income	$130,000
Add:	
Depreciation expense	124,000
Increase in deferred income taxes	10,000
Increase in advances on maintenance contracts	10,000
Total	$274,000
Subtract:	
Gain on sale of equipment	40,000
Working capital provided by operations	$234,000
Sale of equipment	56,000
Total sources of working capital	$290,000
Uses of working capital:	
Preferred dividends	$ 10,000
Purchase of equipment	160,000
Total uses of working capital	$170,000
Increase in working capital	$120,000

Analysis of Increases (Decreases) in Working Capital

Cash	$ 20,000
Accounts receivable	20,000
Inventories	20,000
Prepayments	(10,000)
Trade accounts payable	50,000
Other current liabilities	20,000
Increase in working capital	$120,000

GNP Implicit Price Deflator (Year 5 = 100)

Yearly average				Quarter	Quarterly average Year 19	Year 20
Year 1	89.6	Year 11	108.8			
Year 2	90.9	Year 12	110.9			
Year 3	94.0	Year 13	113.9			
Year 4	97.5	Year 14	117.6	1st	144.6	150.0
Year 5	100.0	Year 15	122.3	2nd	145.3	152.6
Year 6	101.6	Year 16	128.2	3rd	146.5	155.7
Year 7	103.3	Year 17	135.2	4th	148.0	158.9
Year 8	104.6	Year 18	141.4			
Year 9	105.8	Year 19	146.1			
Year 10	107.2	Year 20	154.3			

ADJUSTMENT CALCULATIONS

In order to restate the dollars of varying purchasing power reported in financial statements prepared on a historical basis into dollars of uniform purchasing power as of the date of the most recent balance sheet, a series of calculations must be made using an index that reflects changes in the dollar's purchasing power. Given an appropriate index, the historical amount and the date of the historical amount must be known. The historical amount is then multiplied by a fraction, the numerator of which is the index for the most recent balance sheet date and the denominator of which is the index for the date of the historical amount.

For example, the cost of an asset acquired for $10,000 during Year 6 could be restated to an equivalent number of end-of-Year 20 dollars as follows:

$$\frac{\text{Index at end of Year 20}}{\text{Index at date of acquisition (during Year 6)}} \times \$10,000 = \text{cost of asset in terms of end-of-Year 20 dollars}$$

The proposed accounting standard of the FASB requires the GNP Implicit Price Deflator to be used in restating the financial statements.[3] Inasmuch as daily GNP indexes are not available, the index to be used for

[3] *Ibid.,* para. 35.

end-of-year will be the index that measures the average of prices for the last quarter, the latest index available for the year.

Technically, the index at date of acquisition should be used for the denominator. As a practical matter, in the absence of truly rampant inflation during the year of acquisition, satisfactory results may be obtained by using the GNP index for the quarter in which the acquisition took place or even the average index for the year in which the transaction originated.

Using the GNP index, the restatement calculation for the asset acquired during Year 6 for $10,000 is

$$\frac{\text{Index for 4th quarter, Year 20}}{\text{Index for Year 6}} \times \$10,000 = \text{cost of asset in terms of end-of-Year 20 dollars}$$

$$\frac{158.9}{101.6} \times \$10,000 = \$15,640$$

MONETARY VERSUS NONMONETARY ACCOUNTS

In the process of restating historical amounts for changes in the general price level, it is essential to distinguish between (1) those accounts that are automatically stated in current dollars and therefore require no price level adjustments, and (2) those accounts that require price level adjustments in order to be stated in terms of current dollars.

Cash, claims to fixed amounts of cash, and obligations to pay fixed amounts of cash are necessarily measured in current dollars, the number of which is not affected by changes in the general price level. In his pioneering work on the subject of price level adjustments, Henry W. Sweeney labeled such items "money-value assets" and "money-value liabilities," describing the former as "like cash in the fact that they remain rigidly and irrevocably set at previously determined money amounts, irrespective of how the value of the money in which they are measured changes."[4] In the more recent discussions of price level adjustments, these items have generally been referred to as "monetary" items.[5]

All accounts that are not classified as monetary items are considered "nonmonetary" items. Examples of nonmonetary items include merchandise inventory, plant, equipment, and capital stock. All revenues and expenses are also nonmonetary items.

The distinction between monetary and nonmonetary items is critical in

[4]Henry Sweeney, *Stabilized Accounting,* Harper & Brothers, New York, 1936, p. 16. Reissued by Holt, Rinehart and Winston, New York, 1964.

[5]Ralph C. Jones, *Effects of Price Level Changes on Business Income, Capital, and Taxes,* AAA, New York, 1956, p. 9. The FASB's proposed statement also uses the terms "monetary."

preparing GPLA financial statements. Monetary items are automatically stated in dollars of current general purchasing power and therefore require no price level adjustment. However, as these items are held over time and the general price level changes, the holder realizes an increase or decrease in purchasing power. During a period of inflation, a firm that extends credit to customers for sales on account loses purchasing power, because the purchasing power of the dollars received at the time of payment is less than the purchasing power of the dollars at the time of sale. Similarly, a firm that borrows from a bank or other creditor gains purchasing power during inflation, because the purchasing power of the dollars expended at the time of payment is less than the purchasing power of the dollars originally received from the creditor. The calculation of these purchasing power, or monetary, gains and losses is the unique product of GPLA.

Nonmonetary items, on the other hand, are stated in conventional financial statements in terms of the historical number of dollars expended for the item. When preparing GPLA financial statements, nonmonetary items must be restated to an equivalent number of dollars of current general purchasing power.

Refer to the balance sheet of Demonstrator Corporation in Exhibit 2.1. Cash and accounts receivable (net of allowance for uncollectibles) are monetary assets. The remaining assets are nonmonetary because their amounts reflect the historical number of dollars expended and do not represent claims to a fixed number of current or future dollars. Trade accounts payable, other current liabilities, and sinking fund debentures are monetary liabilities. Advances on maintenance contracts is nonmonetary because the liability will be discharged in the future by providing goods and services whose specific prices can change. Deferred income taxes is treated as a nonmonetary item under generally accepted accounting principles. As will be discussed in Chapter Three, however, there is some rationale for considering deferred income taxes as a monetary item. The stockholders' equity accounts are also nonmonetary items. Under some circumstances, to be discussed more fully in Chapter Three, preferred stock is considered a monetary item.

COMPARATIVE STATEMENTS

In preparing price level adjusted comparative financial statements (for example, comparative balance sheets and comparative income statements), the previous period's amounts must always be restated in terms of dollars of current general purchasing power.[6] If adjusted statements have

---

[6] Financial Accounting Standards Board, *op. cit.,* para. 53.

been prepared for the previous year, this restatement can be accomplished by multiplying each amount in the previous period's adjusted statements by the change in the index during the current period. For example, if adjusted statements had been prepared for Demonstrator at the end of Year 19, all amounts in those statements would be measured in dollars whose purchasing power is reflected by the index for the last quarter of Year 19 (that is, 148.0). For comparative statements prepared at the end of Year 20, each amount in the Year-19 statements could then be multiplied by 158.9/148.0 so that all amounts—Year 19 as well as Year 20—would be stated in fourth-quarter, Year-20 dollars. In making price level adjustments for Year 20 then, only Year-20 transactions would need to be analyzed.

The illustration in Chapters Three through Five assumes, however, that Demonstrator has not previously prepared price level adjusted statements. Accordingly, it is necessary to analyze the amounts in each account completely in order to determine the date of their origin. The first time that adjustments are made to uniform dollars will inevitably involve greater effort than that required in subsequent years.

Chapter Three

PREPARING THE GENERAL PRICE LEVEL ADJUSTED BALANCE SHEET

Chapter three illustrates the general price level restatement procedures for the balance sheet accounts most commonly found in published financial statements using the data for Demonstrator Corporation presented in Chapter Two. Demonstrator Corporation's comparative balance sheet for December 31, Year 19 and Year 20, in historical dollars and as restated for general price level changes is shown in Exhibit 3.1. This exhibit appears near the beginning of the chapter for easy reference. Chapter Six discusses additional complexities in restating particular balance sheet accounts.

The objective in adjusting the balance sheet accounts of Demonstrator Corporation is to restate the historical dollar amounts to dollars of general purchasing power at the end of Year 20, the date of the most recent balance sheet. Because a general price level adjusted comparative balance sheet is to be prepared, the amounts in the conventional balance sheet at the end of Year 19 must also be restated to dollars of end-of-Year 20 general purchasing power. The critical distinction between monetary and nonmonetary items is emphasized in the following discussion of the restatement procedures for individual assets and equity accounts.

ASSETS

Cash

The amount of cash held by Demonstrator on December 31, Year 20, is $140,000. Those dollars are necessarily 140,000 December 31, Year 20, dollars. Cash is the quintessential monetary asset; no adjustment is necessary.

In constructing a comparative balance sheet, however, the number of Year-19 dollars held at December 31, Year 19, cannot be compared

EXHIBIT 3.1

DEMONSTRATOR CORPORATION

Comparative Balance Sheet

	Historical dollars December 31		Restated in terms of December 31, Year 20, dollars	
	Year 20	Year 19	Year 20	Year 19
Assets				
Current assets:				
Cash	$ 140,000	$ 120,000	$ 140,000	$ 128,838
Accounts receivable (net of allowance for uncollectibles)	400,000	380,000	400,000	407,986
Inventories (at first-in, first-out cost)	520,000	500,000	520,000	536,824
Prepayments	40,000	50,000	41,307	54,470
Total current assets	$1,100,000	$1,050,000	$1,101,307	$1,128,118
Investment in common stock (at cost)	$ 160,000	$ 160,000	$ 216,190	$ 216,190
Property, plant, and equipment:				
Land	$ 80,000	$ 80,000	$ 141,875	$ 141,875
Buildings (net of accumulated depreciation)	210,000	220,000	367,096	384,577
Equipment (net of accumulated depreciation)	550,000	520,000	689,770	693,840
Total property, plant, and equipment (net)	$ 840,000	$ 820,000	$1,198,741	$1,220,292
Total assets	$2,100,000	$2,030,000	$2,516,238	$2,564,600

directly with the number of Year-20 dollars held today. A Year-19 dollar and a Year-20 dollar represent different amounts of purchasing power. Accordingly, the number of dollars held on December 31, Year 19, must be restated to an equivalent number of Year-20 dollars as follows:

$$\frac{\text{Index at end of Year 20}}{\text{Index at end of Year 19}} \times \frac{\text{dollars of cash at}}{\text{end of Year 19}} = \begin{array}{l}\text{purchasing power held} \\ \text{in cash at end of Year} \\ \text{19 measured in terms of} \\ \text{end-of-Year 20 dollars}\end{array}$$

EXHIBIT 3.1 Comparative Balance Sheet *(Continued)*

	Historical dollars December 31		Restated in terms of December 31, Year 20, dollars	
	Year 20	Year 19	Year 20	Year 19
Liabilities and Stockholders' Equity				
Current liabilities:				
Trade accounts payable	$ 160,000	$ 210,000	$ 160,000	$ 225,466
Other current liabilities	40,000	60,000	40,000	64,419
Total current liabilities	$ 200,000	$ 270,000	$ 200,000	$ 289,885
Advances on maintenance contracts	30,000	20,000	31,242	21,825
Sinking fund debentures (6%)	500,000	500,000	500,000	536,824
Deferred income taxes	20,000	10,000	21,531	11,233
Total liabilities	$ 750,000	$ 800,000	$ 752,773	$ 859,767
Stockholders' equity: Preferred stockholders' equity (2,000 shares, 5%, $100 par value, $105 redemption value)	$ 200,000	$ 200,000	$ 210,000	$ 225,466
Common stockholders' equity (50,000 shares, $1 par value)	1,150,000	1,030,000	1,553,465	1,479,367
Total stockholders' equity	$1,350,000	$1,230,000	$1,763,465	$1,704,833
Total liabilities and stockholders' equity	$2,100,000	$2,030,000	$2,516,238	$2,564,600

$$\frac{158.9}{148.0} \times \$120,000 \qquad = \$128,838$$

This, of course, does not mean that $128,838 was held by Demonstrator at December 31, Year 19; it means that the dollars held as cash by Demonstrator at that date are equivalent to $128,838 of December 31, Year 20, purchasing power. Demonstrator's comparative cash position measured in dollars of identical purchasing power was $140,000 at December 31, Year 20, versus $128,838 at December 31, Year 19.

Receivables

The adjustment procedures for receivables, because they are monetary assets, are the same as for cash. On the latest balance sheet date, Demonstrator had a claim against its customers for $400,000 after deducting an allowance for amounts estimated to be uncollectible. That claim is stated in terms of December 31, Year-20, dollars. Because receivables constitute a monetary asset, no adjustment is necessary. (Note that the allowance for uncollectibles account is a monetary item because the account to which it is a contra account, Accounts Receivable, is a monetary item.)

For a comparative balance sheet, however, an adjustment is required to restate the accounts receivable balance at the end of Year 19 to end-of-Year 20 dollars:

$$158.9/148.0 \times \$380,000 = \$407,986$$

The $380,000 net accounts receivable held by Demonstrator at the end of Year 19 had purchasing power equivalent to $407,986 Year-20 dollars. Demonstrator's comparative accounts receivable position measured in dollars of identical purchasing power was $400,000 at December 31, Year 20, versus $407,986 at December 31, Year 19.

Inventories

Most inventories are measured in terms of historical acquisition cost—the number of dollars expended in the past in obtaining the quantities of inventories now on hand. Inventories are therefore nonmonetary items. If all measurements are to be made in terms of today's dollars, it is necessary to convert the historical dollar cost of inventories into an equivalent number of today's dollars. To do so requires knowing the dates of acquisition and the historical cost, which presents a special problem.

If acquisition costs are specifically identified with items of inventory, as may be the case for an inventory of automobiles, expensive jewelry, or elegant furniture, the date of acquisition of each item and the number of dollars expended for each item provide the basic information required for the price level adjustment. The historical number of dollars is multiplied by a fraction, the numerator of which is the current index and the denominator of which is the index for the date of acquisition.

In the more common case, however, accumulation of specific identification information is impractical; a FIFO, LIFO, or average cost flow assumption is used. The price level adjustment must be consistent with that assumption.

During Year 20, Demonstrator purchased inventory having a cost of $2,000,000; the cost of inventory on hand increased $20,000, from a beginning balance of $500,000 to an ending balance of $520,000; the cost of goods sold was $1,980,000. Based on the FIFO assumption used by Demonstrator, the $520,000 inventory on hand on December 31, Year 20, was the most recent $520,000 acquired.

Some simplifying assumptions about the December 31 inventories are in order. If inventory acquisitions are made more or less continuously throughout the year, it is reasonable to assume that the $520,000 ending inventory, which is about one-fourth of the year's purchases, was acquired during the last quarter of Year 20. Because all amounts in the adjusted statements are being stated in terms of fourth-quarter, Year-20 dollars, no adjustment for inventories purchased during that quarter is necessary.

An adjustment for Demonstrator's December 31, Year 19, inventory is necessary, however, if both inventory amounts are to be reported in dollars of the same purchasing power. The adjustment is made using (in the denominator) the index for the last quarter of Year 19 of 148.0 on the assumption that the $500,000 December 31, Year 19, inventory again represented about one quarter's purchases:

$$158.9/148.0 \times \$500,000 = \$536,824$$

Demonstrator's comparative inventory position measured in December 31, Year-20, dollars was $520,000 at December 31, Year 20, versus $536,824 at December 31, Year 19.

This adjustment was based on the FIFO cost flow assumption and assumed that purchases were spread more or less evenly throughout the year. The adjustment procedure, however, can be adapted to other inventory methods (for example, LIFO) and to situations where purchases are concentrated in certain seasons. The essential data are the approximate date of acquisition applicable to the inventory on hand (which, in the case of LIFO, may be many years ago) and the price level index applicable to that period.

For example, the LIFO cost flow assumption requires records of layers of inventory that are distinguishable on the basis of dates of acquisition. The initial or bottom layer is created in the year LIFO is adopted and, if the physical quantity of inventory increases over time, other layers must be identifiable according to years during which incremental quantities were acquired. Price level adjustments of LIFO inventories require that the historical dollar cost of each layer be adjusted by using the index applicable to the date of acquisition of that layer as the denominator in the adjustment fraction. Illustrations of the restatement procedures for both the LIFO and the weighted average cost flow assumption are presented in Chapters Six, Eight, and Ten.

The general price level restatement of inventories is more complicated when the lower-of-cost-or-market valuation basis is used. These adjustments are discussed in Chapter Six.

Prepayments

Prepayments are nonmonetary assets. As such, they must be restated from the number of dollars expended in making the prepayment to an equivalent number of dollars of purchasing power as of the date of the balance sheet. For example, prepaid insurance, prepaid rent, and prepaid advertising are investments in future service potentials—protection against risk, provision of shelter, and enhancement of sales. None of these items is measured on the basis of the future receipt of a fixed number of dollars. Prepaying rent for a building or a machine is one way of investing in the future service potentials to be derived from the building or machine; outright purchase of the building or the machine is another way of accomplishing essentially the same thing. Prepaid property taxes constitute a nonmonetary asset representing the rights of use and occupancy and the benefits of whatever services may be supplied by the governmental unit that levied the tax. Usually no claim to cash exists; the asset is measured on the basis of a past cash outlay, not a future cash receipt. Inventories of miscellaneous supplies are sometimes also classified as prepayments. These supplies, nonmonetary assets, represent past expenditures for future services to be received from the supplies. It is not possible here to examine every item that might possibly be included in prepayments. Those examined may help clarify the grounds for assessing whether other items are nonmonetary items.

Demonstrator's prepayments at December 31, Year 20, are comprised of two items: miscellaneous supplies that cost $30,000 and prepaid property taxes in the amount of $10,000. The amounts for December 31, Year 19, were $35,000 and $15,000, respectively.

The supplies inventory is assumed to equal approximately one year's purchases, which are made fairly evenly throughout the year. It is impractical to identify individual items with dates of acquisition. Accordingly, the average index for the year is used for the denominator. In effect, this assumes that the beginning inventory of supplies has been used and that the ending inventory accumulated steadily throughout Year 20.

$$\text{Year 20: } 158.9/154.3 \times \$30,000 = \$30,894$$

$$\text{Year 19: } 158.9/146.1 \times \$35,000 = \$38,066$$

If supplies are a significant item, then a cost flow assumption will be required and they can be restated using the adjustment procedure described previously for inventories.

Demonstrator's property taxes are paid during May of each year and amortized over 12 months commencing in June. Five-twelfths of each payment remains unamortized at year's end. Because payments are made during May, the index for the second quarter of each year is used in the denominator.

$$\text{Year 20: } 158.9/152.6 \times \$10,000 = \$10,413$$

$$\text{Year 19: } 158.9/145.3 \times \$15,000 = \$16,404$$

On an adjusted basis, total prepayments at the end of Year 20 amounted to $41,307 (= $30,894 + $10,413) as compared to $54,470 (= $38,066 + $16,404) at the end of Year 19.

Investments

Demonstrator Corporation accounts for its 15-percent investment in the common stock of United, Inc., at cost. The investment was made during Year 14, when United, Inc., was organized.

The account "Investment in Common Stock" represents a nonmonetary asset measured on the basis of the amount of cash invested during Year 14. Accordingly, the following price level adjustment is required:

$$158.9/117.6 \times \$160,000 = \$216,190$$

Because there were no changes in the account during Year 20, this amount applies to both December 31, Year 20, and December 31, Year 19, in the comparative balance sheet.

If Demonstrator owned at least a 20-percent interest in United, Inc., it would account for its investment on the basis of its equity in United's net assets. United's financial statements would also be adjusted for price level changes, and Demonstrator would merely adjust the investment account to the amount of its equity in the adjusted net assets as of December 31, Year 19, and to the amount of its equity in the adjusted net assets as of December 31, Year 20. In the absence of dividends, the change in Demonstrator's equity in United's adjusted net assets during Year 20 would be shown as an income item in Demonstrator's Year-20 adjusted income statement.

It would not be possible for Demonstrator to adjust properly its equity in United's net assets unless United's financial statements were first adjusted for price level changes. The initial investment of $160,000 could be adjusted as above, but annual changes in Demonstrator's equity in United's unadjusted net assets could not be adjusted properly merely by reference to Demonstrator accounts. Such changes would involve a mixture of dollars having a variety of purchasing powers.

The general price level adjustments required when the equity method is used are discussed more fully in Chapter Six.

Property, Plant, and Equipment

Price level adjustments for property, plant, and equipment are straightforward, but because large numbers of items and an equally large number of acquisition dates are likely to be involved, the initial adjustment process may be tedious. Fortunately, once the initial adjustment is made, subsequent year's adjustments are likely to be relatively simple.

Demonstrator purchased its land when the corporation was formed, in Year 1. No other land acquisitions have been made, and none of the original land has been sold. Accordingly, the following adjustment is applicable for both December 31, Year 20, and December 31, Year 19:

$$\text{Land: } 158.9/89.6 \times \$80,000 = \$141,875$$

Demonstrator's building was constructed during Year 1 and occupied early in Year 2 (index = 90.9), at which time payment of the $400,000 cost was made. The building is being depreciated on a straight-line basis over a 40-year period. The adjustments are as follows:

	Dollars of December 31, Year-20, purchasing power
Building at December 31, Year 19	
Cost: $158.9/90.9 \times \$400,000$	$699,230
Accumulated depreciation: $158.9/90.9 \times \$180,000$	314,653
Net book value	$384,577
Building at December 31, Year 20	
Cost: (same as above)	$699,230
Accumulated depreciation: $158.9/90.9 \times \$190,000$	332,134
Net book value	$367,096

Alternatively, the adjusted cost, $699,230, could be divided by the 40-year life to determine the amount of adjusted depreciation for Year 20, $17,481. This amount, in turn, could be added to accumulated depreciation at December 31, Year 19 ($314,653 + $17,481 = $332,134), or subtracted from the net book value at December 31, Year 19 ($384,577 − $17,481 = $367,096). Care must be exercised in using these alternative approaches to be sure that the Building and Accumulated Depreciation accounts at the end of Year 19 are restated to end-of-Year-20 dollars.

The equipment held by Demonstrator on December 31, Year 19, was comprised of items acquired over several years and at the historical costs indicated in Exhibit 3.2. By applying the appropriate adjustment factor to the historical amounts of cost and accumulated depreciation, restatements of those amounts in terms of December 31, Year 20, dollars are obtained.

During July of Year 20, Demonstrator sold the equipment acquired during Year 12 for $56,000 cash. The company follows the practice of taking a half-year's depreciation in the year of acquisition and a half-year's depreciation in the year of sale or other disposition. This equipment was being depreciated on a straight-line basis over a 10-year period; one-half year's depreciation during Year 20 amounted to $4,000. Upon sale, therefore, the net book value of the equipment was $16,000 (cost $80,000 less accumulated depreciation $64,000) and the gain on the sale was $40,000 (all amounts in historical dollars).

Demonstrator acquired new, highly specialized equipment during Sep-

EXHIBIT 3.2

DEMONSTRATOR CORPORATION

Equipment at December 31, Year 19

Year acquired	Stated in historical dollars		Restatement factor	Restated in terms of December 31, Year 20, dollars	
	Cost	Accumulated depreciation		Cost	Accumulated depreciation
Year 9 ...$	260,000	$136,500	158.9/105.8	$ 390,491	$205,008
Year 12 ...	80,000	60,000	158.9/110.9	114,626	85,969
Year 14 ...	470,000	258,500	158.9/117.6	635,059	349,283
Year 17 ...	240,000	75,000	158.9/135.2	282,071	88,147
Totals ..	$1,050,000	$530,000		$1,422,247	$728,407
Net book value	$520,000			$693,840	

tember of Year 20, at a cost of $160,000. For reporting purposes, it was decided to depreciate this equipment on a straight-line basis over a period of 4 years; one-half year's depreciation during Year 20, the year of acquisition, amounted to $20,000.

Exhibit 3.3 shows these two transactions and the depreciation on other items of equipment in historical dollars. Again, by applying the appropriate adjustment factor to the historical amounts of cost and accumulated depreciation, restatements in terms of December 31, Year 20, dollars are obtained.

It should be noted that in future years only the second set of computations need be made. Next year, in a comparative balance sheet prepared for December 31, Year 21, the net book value of equipment at December 31, Year 20, as stated above in December 31, Year 20, dollars can simply be adjusted by applying the fraction:

$$\frac{\text{Fourth quarter, Year-21 index}}{\text{Fourth quarter, Year-20 index}} \times \$689,770 = \begin{array}{l} \text{December 31,} \\ \text{Year 20, net} \\ \text{book value} \\ \text{restated in} \\ \text{terms of} \\ \text{December 31,} \\ \text{Year 21,} \\ \text{dollars} \end{array}$$

LIABILITIES

Current Liabilities

Trade accounts payable and other current liabilities (usually wages and salaries, utilities, and similar items representing services already received but for which payment has not been made) are monetary items directly measured on the basis of a fixed number of dollars required for their settlement. As such, they are automatically stated in terms of current dollars. No adjustments of the December 31, Year 20, balances are necessary. As in the case of cash and receivables, for comparative purposes the Year-19 balances must be restated in terms of current dollars:

Trade accounts payable: 158.9/148.0 × $210,000 = $225,466
Other current liabilities: 158.9/148.0 × $ 60,000 = $ 64,419

Advances on Maintenance Contracts

In some businesses, payments from customers are received in advance of the earning process. The collection of 3-year subscriptions by magazine

EXHIBIT 3.3

DEMONSTRATOR CORPORATION

Equipment at December 31, Year 20

Year acquired	Stated in historical dollars		Restatement factor	Restated in terms of December 31, Year 20, dollars	
	Cost	Accumulated depreciation		Cost	Accumulated depreciation
Year 9	$ 260,000	$149,500	158.9/105.8	$ 390,491	$224,533
Year 14	470,000	305,500	158.9/117.6	635,059	412,789
Year 17	240,000	105,000	158.9/135.2	282,071	123,406
Year 20	160,000	20,000	158.9/155.7	163,288	20,411
Totals	$1,130,000	$580,000		$1,470,909	$781,139
Net book value ..		$550,000			$689,770

publishers, the collection of insurance premiums by insurance companies at the outset of a period of coverage, and the advance collection of rentals by landlords are examples. Such advance collections represent obligations requiring future settlement in goods and services. Measurements are typically made on the basis of the historical amounts of cash received in the past rather than on the basis of the future outlay required for their settlement. Measured in this way, they represent nonmonetary liabilities that require price level adjustments.

Demonstrator sells 2-year maintenance contracts on certain types of the equipment in which it deals, the sales being spread rather evenly throughout the year. About $2,000 of the December 31, Year 19, advances on maintenance contracts balance of $20,000 arose from contracts sold during Year 18. The adjustment is, therefore:

$$
\begin{array}{ll}
\text{Sold during Year 18: } 158.9/141.4 \times \$\ 2,000 = \$\ 2,248 \\
\text{Sold during Year 19: } 158.9/146.1 \times \$18,000 = \underline{\ \ 19,577} \\
\text{Total} \hspace{4.5cm} = \$21,825
\end{array}
$$

Of the total advances on maintenance contracts at December 31, Year 20 of $30,000 about $6,000 arose from Year-19 sales and about $24,000 from Year 20 sales. The adjustment is, therefore;

$$
\begin{array}{ll}
158.9/146.1 \times \$\ 6,000 = \$\ 6,526 \\
158.9/154.3 \times \$24,000 = \underline{\ \ 24,716} \\
\text{Total} \hspace{2.2cm} = \$31,242
\end{array}
$$

On an adjusted basis, total advances on maintenance contracts at the end of Year 20 amounted to $31,242, as compared to $21,825 at the end of Year 19.

Long-Term Debt

Demonstrator's 6-percent sinking fund debentures were issued at par during Year 14 to provide additional working capital and funds for purchase of equipment. Sinking fund payments will commence in Year 23; the debentures mature in Year 33.

The obligation to make periodic interest payments and a principal repayment at maturity is measured in terms of specified numbers of dollars, regardless of changes in the purchasing power of the dollar; the obligation is a monetary item measured directly on the basis of the future amounts of cash to be expended in its settlement. The amount reported in the conventional balance sheet, $500,000, is the present value of those future payments discounted at the rate of 6 percent. No adjustment of the

December 31, Year 20, balance is required. For comparative purposes, the Year-19 balance must be restated to end-of-Year-20 dollars:

$$\text{Year 19: } 158.9/148.0 \times \$500,000 = \$536,824$$

A discount (premium) on bonds payable account would also be a monetary item, because the account to which it is a contra (adjunct) account, Bonds Payable, is a monetary item. An illustration of the restatement procedure for bonds issued at a discount and involving amortization of the bond discount during the year is presented in Chapter Six.

Deferred Income Taxes

The deferred income taxes account reported on the balance sheet by Demonstrator Corporation represents the accumulated number of dollars of tax savings that resulted from the use of accelerated depreciation on certain items of equipment for tax purposes rather than the straight-line depreciation method used for the same items in the financial statements. According to one view, the account represents a monetary liability measured directly on the basis of the number of dollars to be paid in the future when the depreciation allowable for tax purposes is less than the depreciation reported in the financial statements. This view is often described as the "liability" method of interperiod tax allocation. The measurement usually assumes that current tax rates will continue unchanged in the future. Viewed as a monetary liability, no adjustment of the December 31, Year-20, balance would be required. For comparative purposes, the Year-19 balance would be restated in terms of current dollars:

$$158.9/148.0 \times \$10,000 = \$10,736$$

APB Opinion 11[1] adopts the so-called deferred method of interperiod tax allocation. Under this method, deferred income taxes are not considered to constitute a liability for income taxes to be paid in the future. Rather, interperiod tax allocation is treated as "a procedure whereby the tax effects of current timing differences are deferred currently and allocated to income tax expense of future periods when the timing differences reverse. . . . The tax effects of transactions which reduce taxes currently payable are treated as deferred credits." According to this view, deferred income taxes represent an "actual tax reduction in the current

---

[1] Accounting Principles Board, "Accounting for Income Taxes," Opinion No. 11, AICPA, New York, 1967, para. 35.

period" that should not be reflected in the current period's income but rather should be carried forward in the balance sheet as a deferred credit "until released to income when recorded depreciation exceeds tax depreciation." The method is said to emphasize "the income statement rather than the balance sheet, by removing from income the actual tax reduction realized in the current period by reason of tax depreciation exceeding book depreciation."[2]

Under the deferred method, the amount of deferred income taxes is measured on the basis of past tax reductions rather than on the basis of future cash outlays. Following this line of reasoning, the account must be adjusted to reflect the purchasing power saved in the past. In keeping with APB Opinion No. 11, this is the procedure adopted by the FASB in its proposed statement on general price level accounting; deferred taxes are designated as nonmonetary.[3]

Demonstrator's deferred income taxes have accumulated during the past 4 years as indicated in Exhibit 3.4. It is assumed in this illustration that, as of the end of Year 20, there have been no reversals of prior years' timing differences. The restatement procedure for deferred income taxes where reversals have occurred is illustrated in Chapter Six. The adjust-

EXHIBIT 3.4

DEMONSTRATOR CORPORATION

Deferred Income Taxes

Year	Historical dollars	Restatement factor	Restated in terms of December 31, Year 20, dollars
Year 17	$ 2,000	158.9/135.2	$ 2,351
Year 18	5,000	158.9/141.4	5,619
Year 19	3,000	158.9/146.1	3,263
Balance, December 31, Year 19	$10,000		$11,233
Year 20	10,000	158.9/154.3	10,298
Balance, December 31, Year 20	$20,000		$21,531

[2]Paul Grady, "Tax Effect Accounting When Basic Federal Income Tax Rate Changes," *Journal of Accountancy,* April 1964, pp. 25–27.

[3]Financial Accounting Standards Board, "Financial Reporting in Units of General Purchasing Power," Proposed Statement of Financial Accounting Standard, Stamford, Connecticut, 1974, Appendix C.

ment also assumes that income taxes are paid and the savings accrue more or less continuously throughout the year. Viewed as a deferred credit, Demonstrator's deferred income taxes are restated to $21,531 as of December 31, Year 20, as compared to $11,233 as of December 31, Year 19.

As a liability, deferred income taxes would automatically reflect a current measure of the purchasing power represented by the number of dollars estimated to be payable in the future in the settlement of the liability; as a deferred credit, deferred income taxes must be adjusted to reflect a current measure of the purchasing power represented by the number of dollars of actual tax reduction experienced in the past.

STOCKHOLDERS' EQUITY

Price level adjustments of stockholders' equity accounts depend on the nature of the information those accounts are intended to convey. For the most part, distinctions are made between capital stock, additional paid-in capital, and retained earnings in historical dollar financial statements. Admittedly, however, the accounts do not necessarily reflect reliable legal distinctions; for example, the retained earnings account in a consolidated balance sheet has no legal significance because the consolidated enterprise has no legal existence as such.

Alternatively, stockholders' equity (1) could be treated as a single residual amount (the difference between total assets and total liabilities); (2) could consist of two accounts, the fixed amount of preferred stockholders' equity and the residual amount of common stockholders' equity; (3) could consist of accounts that distinguish between paid-in capital and retained earnings; or (4) could consist of some other combination of accounts. In the adjustment process, amounts that are fixed in terms of numbers of dollars (for example, the liquidation value of preferred stockholders' equity) are monetary items that are automatically stated in current dollars; other amounts not so fixed are nonmonetary and must be adjusted.

Preferred Stockholders' Equity

Preferred stock may be either monetary or nonmonetary, depending on the basis used in determining its amount. Preferred stock is usually stated in the conventional balance sheet at the aggregate par value of the number of preferred shares issued and outstanding, or, in the case of no-par shares, at the aggregated stated value of such shares. In this case, preferred stock is a nonmonetary item because the valuation reflects dollars of general purchasing power of the period in which the preferred stock was issued. Preferred stock is sometimes stated at the redemption price or liquidation value of the outstanding shares instead of the aggregate par or stated value. The preferred stock is treated as a monetary item in this case.

In its proposed Statement of Financial Accounting Standard, the Financial Accounting Standards Board stated:[4]

> Nonmonetary preferred stock shall be restated by multiplying its unit-of-money carrying amount by the ratio of the index of general purchasing power at the current balance sheet date to the index of general purchasing power at the date the nonmonetary preferred stock was issued. Preferred stock shall not be restated to an amount in excess of its fixed liquidation price; at such time as preferred stock has been restated to an amount equal to its fixed liquidation price, it shall be classified as a monetary item.

In times of rising prices, this means that preferred stock issued for prices near redemption value will almost always be classified as a monetary item.

Assume that the preferred stock of Demonstrator Corporation was issued during Year 5 at par value and has a redemption value of $105 per share. The aggregate par value of the outstanding preferred stock would be restated as follows:

$$158.9/100.0 \times \$200,000 = \$317,800$$

The general price level adjusted aggregate par value amount exceeds the redemption value of $210,000 (= 2,000 shares × $105). The preferred stock is therefore treated as a monetary item and shown on the end-of-Year 20 balance sheet at $210,000. The December 31, Year 19, amount must be restated for comparative purposes:

$$158.9/148.0 \times \$210,000 = \$225,466$$

Common Stockholders' Equity

As discussed above, the distinctions among the common stock account, the additional paid-in capital account, and the retained earnings account are primarily legal in nature; all are components of the common stockholders' equity. From an economic point of view, the common stockholders' equity is a single, inseparable, residual sum; in preparing price level adjusted financial statements, it is probably best to treat it as such. On this basis, common stockholders' equity is measured as the difference between (1) total adjusted assets and (2) total adjusted liabilities plus preferred stockholders' equity. In the case of Demonstrator Corporation:

[4] *Ibid.,* para. 45.

Year 20: $2,516,238 − ($752,773 + $210,000) = $1,553,465
Year 19: $2,564,600 − ($859,767 + $225,466) = $1,479,367

For the first year in which general price level adjusted financial statements are prepared, it is usually necessary to "plug," as shown above, to
obtain the amount of the common stockholders' equity at the beginning
and end of the period. In subsequent years, however, the common
stockholders' equity at the end of the period can be determined indepen-
dently by adding to the adjusted beginning common stockholders' equity
the adjusted net income, adjusted increases in capital stock accounts, and
other increases in the common stockholders' equity and subtracting
adjusted dividends and other decreases in the common stockholders'
equity during the period.

Should it be considered desirable to separate the amount of common
stockholders' invested (paid-in) capital from retained earnings, the former
may be adjusted for price level changes and the latter treated as the
residual amount. Such a division need not have any legal connotation.
Any further breakdown of invested capital along legal lines into stated
capital and additional paid-in capital components, however, is likely to be
confusing. As financial information, the distinction has no meaning; as
legal information, the amounts of stated capital and additional paid-in
capital are fixed in terms of numbers of dollars. In other words, as legal
information, they are monetary items not requiring price level adjustments. Accordingly, the fixed legal amount of common stock and additional paid-in capital would create a purchasing power gain that would
have to be included in retained earnings. This would imply that part of
common stockholders' equity had a gain at the expense of another part—
a nonsensical result.

Chapter Four

PREPARING THE GENERAL PRICE LEVEL ADJUSTED INCOME STATEMENT

T HIS CHAPTER ILLUSTRATES the general price level restatement procedures for income statement accounts using the data for Demonstrator Corporation presented in Chapter Two. This chapter also
discusses the calculation of the gain or loss on monetary items, an element
of general price level adjusted net income. Exhibit 4.1 shows the income
statement of Demonstrator Corporation in historical dollars and as restated for general price level changes. This exhibit appears near the beginning of the chapter for easy reference.

As with balance sheet accounts, the objective is to state all revenues,
expenses, gains, and losses in terms of dollars of end-of-the-period general
purchasing power. Income statement accounts are nonmonetary items.
Each revenue and expense account must be restated from the historical
number of dollars used in its measurement to an equivalent number of
end-of-Year 20 dollars. For Demonstrator Corporation, the numerator of
the restatement factor is the GNP Deflator for the fourth quarter of Year
20. Particular care must be exercised in selecting the appropriate price
index for the denominator of the restatement factor. Revenues and
expenses can be classified into two groups for purposes of discussing the
appropriate denominator of the restatement factor:

Group 1: Revenues and expenses associated with changes in
monetary assets or monetary liabilities.

Group 2: Revenues and expenses associated with changes in
nonmonetary assets or nonmonetary liabilities.

Revenues and expenses are always nonmonetary accounts. The account
debited when a revenue (expense) account is credited (debited) may be
either a monetary account (Group 1) or a nonmonetary account (Group

EXHIBIT 4.1

DEMONSTRATOR CORPORATION

Income Statement

For the year ended December 31, Year 20

	Historical dollars	Restated in terms of December 31, Year 20, dollars
Revenues and gains:		
Product sales	$2,578,000	$2,654,855
Earned on maintenance contracts	22,000	23,537
Gain on sale of equipment	40,000	34,226
Monetary gain on long-term debt	-0-	36,824
Total revenues and gains	$2,640,000	$2,749,442
Expenses and losses:		
Cost of goods sold	$1,980,000	$2,076,448
Selling, general, and administrative	276,000	287,368
Depreciation	124,000	161,914
Interest	30,000	30,894
Income taxes	100,000	102,981
Monetary loss on net current monetary assets	-0-	20,907
Total expenses and losses	$2,510,000	$2,680,512
Net income	$ 130,000	$ 68,930
Preferred dividends	(10,000)	(10,298)
Monetary gain on preferred stock	-0-	15,466
Net income to common stockholders	$ 120,000	$ 74,098
Earnings per common share (based on 50,000 outstanding shares)	$ 2.40	$ 1.48

2). The nature of this other account is the basis for this classification scheme.

Revenues and expenses in the first group are measured on the conventional income statement in terms of dollars dated sometime during the current reporting period. Most revenues and operating expenses are in this first group. For example, the recognition of sales revenue is associated with an increase in either cash or accounts receivable and is measured in current-period dollars at the time of the sale. The recognition of salary expense is associated with a decrease in cash or an increase in salaries payable and is measured in current-period dollars at the time the labor services are rendered. The appropriate price index in the denominator of the restatement factor for revenues and expenses in this first group is the index for the quarter in which the transaction occurred giving rise to the revenue or expense.

Revenues and expenses in the second group are measured on the conventional income statement in terms of the historical number of dollars used in initially recording the related nonmonetary asset or nonmonetary liability in the accounts. For example, depreciation expense represents an allocation of the historical cost of a depreciable asset acquired sometime in the past. Subscription fee revenue recognized currently may represent a reduction in a nonmonetary liability incurred in the past when the subscription fee was received in advance. The appropriate price index in the denominator of the restatement factor for revenues and expenses in this second group is the index for the period when the related nonmonetary asset was acquired or nonmonetary liability was incurred. It is not appropriate to use the price index during the current period when the revenue or expense is recognized. These items are stated in dollars at the time of the initial nonmonetary asset or nonmonetary liability transaction and not in dollars at the time of the revenue or expense recognition.

The distinction between revenues and expenses in Group 1 and in Group 2 is emphasized in the following discussion of the restatement procedure for individual revenues and expenses.

REVENUES

Revenues from Product Sales (Group 1)

Demonstrator's revenues from product sales are measured in terms of Year-20 dollars and are derived from sales assumed to occur evenly throughout the year. The proposed statement on price level accounting of the Financial Accounting Standards Board recommends that revenues and expenses spread evenly over the year be adjusted using the ratio of the fourth-quarter price level to the year-average price level.[1] Since the

---

[1] Financial Accounting Standards Board, "Financial Reporting in Units of General Purchasing Power," Proposed Statement of Financial Accounting Standard, Stamford, Connecticut, 1974, para. 95.

year-average price level approximates June 30 prices and the fourth-quarter price level centers on November 15 prices, the adjustment is effectively a four-and-one-half-month adjustment rather than a six-month one. To get full half-year adjustment, we suggest an adjustment equal to one-half of the price change from fourth quarter of the previous year to fourth quarter of the current year. The use of the six-month adjustment is discussed more fully in Chapters Six, Eight, and Ten.

Following the Financial Accounting Standards Board's recommendation of a four-and-one-half-month adjustment, the following adjustment is applicable to product sales:

$$158.9/154.3 \times \$2,578,000 = \$2,654,855$$

If sales were seasonal or if the price changes had not been reasonably uniform during the year, it would be preferable to use quarterly sales and quarterly indexes. In the case of Demonstrator for Year 20, the difference would not justify the additional effort.

Revenues Earned on Maintenance Contracts (Group 2)

The restatement of revenues earned on maintenance contracts is shown in Exhibit 4.2. These restatements may be more easily followed if the restatement of the balance sheet account, Advances on Maintenance Contracts, discussed in Chapter Three, is consulted.

The revenues earned on maintenance contracts during Year 20 are derived partially from sales of maintenance contracts during Years 18 and 19 and partially from sales of such contracts during Year 20. The revenues recognized in the conventional income statement during Year 20 from sales of maintenance contracts during Years 18 and 19 are measured

EXHIBIT 4.2

DEMONSTRATOR CORPORATION

Revenues Earned on Maintenance Contracts

Earned in Year 20 on contracts sold during:	Historical dollars	Restatement factor	Restated in terms of December 31, Year 20, dollars
Year 18	$ 2,000	158.9/141.4	$ 2,248
Year 19 ($18,000 − $6,000)	12,000	158.9/146.1	13,051
Year 20 ($32,000 − $24,000)	8,000	158.9/154.3	8,238
Total	$22,000		$23,537

in terms of dollars of those prior years. Because sales of maintenance contracts are assumed to occur evenly over the year, the denominator of the restatement factor is the average price index for Years 18 and 19. The remaining revenues earned during Year 20 arose from maintenance contract sales during Year 20 and are adjusted using the average price index for the current year in the denominator.

EXPENSES

Cost of Goods Sold (Group 2)

The cost of goods sold can be restated in terms of current dollars as follows, utilizing information shown in the inventories adjustment section in Chapter Three.

	December 31, Year 20, dollars
Beginning inventory 158.9/148.0 × $500,000	$ 536,824
Purchases 158.9/154.3 × $2,000,000	2,059,624
Goods available for sale	$2,596,448
Ending inventory (December 31, Year 20)	520,000
Cost of goods sold	$2,076,448

Note that this calculation assumes that the purchases were made evenly throughout the year. To the extent that this is not the case, quarterly purchases with adjustments based on quarterly indexes should be used.

Selling, General, and Administrative Expenses (Groups 1 and 2)

Demonstrator's selling, general, and administrative expenses must be adjusted as shown in Exhibit 4.3.

Supplies are assumed to be acquired evenly over the year. Also, the supplies inventory is assumed to turn over once each year. The cost of supplies included in selling, general, and administrative expenses for Year 20 represents supplies acquired during Year 19. They are therefore restated using the average price index for Year 19.

Property taxes are paid during May of each year and then amortized over 12 months beginning in June. The property taxes applicable to the period January through May of Year 20 are measured in terms of a dollar outlay during May of Year 19. The denominator of the restatement factor

EXHIBIT 4.3

DEMONSTRATOR CORPORATION

Selling, General, and Administrative Expenses

Historical dollars	Expiration of prepayments	December 31, Year 20, dollars
	Supplies (Group 2):	
$ 35,000	December 31, Year 19, adjusted balance (based on assumption that supplies inventory at end of Year 20 is equivalent to Year 20's purchases) 158.9/146.1 × $35,000	$ 38,066
	Property taxes (Group 2):	
15,000	December 31, Year 19, adjusted balance 158.9/145.3 × $15,000	16,404
14,000	Paid in May, Year 20, 158.9/152.6 × $14,000	14,578
	Other operating expenses, assumed to be incurred about evenly throughout the year (Group 1):	
212,000	158.9/154.3 × $212,000	218,320
$276,000	Total	$287,368

is therefore the price index for the second quarter of Year 19. The property taxes applicable to the period June through December of Year 20 are measured in terms of a dollar outlay during May of Year 20. The denominator of the restatement factor is therefore the price index for the second quarter of Year 20. The amortization of prepaid property taxes is similar to the depreciation of building and equipment. In both cases, the expenses are measured on the conventional income statement in terms of a specific past dollar outlay and must be restated to dollars of purchasing power at the end of the current period.

The remaining selling, general, and administrative expenses are assumed to be incurred evenly throughout Year 20. These expenses are measured in terms of average Year-20 dollars and are restated using the average price index for the year in the denominator of the restatement factor.

Note that the *services* from supplies, property taxes, and other operating expenses are received evenly over the year. For purposes of general price level adjustments, however, the denominator of the restatement factor is not based on prices during the period when the services were received but on prices during the period when the dollar amounts of those services were initially measured. For prepayments (for example, supplies and property taxes), the measurement is in terms of dollars at the time of the prepayment. These prepayments fall into Group 2 discussed at the beginning of this chapter. For the other expenses, the measurement is in terms of dollars at the time either when cash was paid or a liability was incurred. These operating expenses, therefore, fall into Group 1.

Depreciation (Group 2)

Demonstrator's adjusted depreciation expense can be calculated directly on the basis of the adjusted costs determined earlier for building and for equipment. The amounts of adjusted depreciation are determined by dividing the adjusted costs by estimated useful lives. These adjustments are shown in Exhibit 4.4.

Interest Expense (Group 1)

Interest accrues evenly throughout the year on the 6-percent sinking fund debentures. The following adjustment is required:

$$158.9/154.3 \times \$30,000 = \$30,894$$

EXHIBIT 4.4

DEMONSTRATOR CORPORATION

Depreciation Expense

Year acquired	Stated in historical dollars		Estimated useful life, years	Restated in terms of December 31, Year 20, dollars	
	Cost	Year-20 depreciation		Cost	Year-20 depreciation
Building:					
Year 2 ..	$400,000	$ 10,000	40	$699,230	$ 17,481
Equipment:					
Year 9 ..	260,000	13,000	20	390,491	19,525
Year 12 ..	80,000	4,000	10*	114,626	5,732*
Year 14 ..	470,000	47,000	10	635,059	63,506
Year 17 ..	240,000	30,000	8	282,071	35,259
Year 20 ..	160,000	20,000	4*	163,288	20,411*
		$124,000			$161,914

*One-half year's depreciation is taken in year of acquisition and one-half in year of disposal.

Note in this case that interest accrues ratably over the year as funds from the borrowing are used, even though a payment is not made until the end of each 6-month period. Because interest expense is measured in terms of dollars of average Year-20 purchasing power (a Group 1 item), it is adjusted using the average price index for the year in the denominator of the restatement factor. The date of the cash payment is not relevant to the restatement of interest expense in this case. The cash payment merely reduces a previously measured liability for accrued interest.

Income Tax Expense (Groups 1 and 2)

The Income Tax Expense account is comprised of amounts accrued during the year of $90,000 (Group 1) plus the increase in deferred income taxes of $10,000 (Group 2) resulting from the use for tax purposes of accelerated depreciation for certain assets that are being depreciated on a straight-line basis for financial statement purposes. The income tax accruals were spread rather evenly throughout the year:

$$158.9/154.3 \times \$100,000 = \$102,981$$

As was the case with interest expense above, income taxes are assumed to accrue ratably over the year and are therefore measured in terms of dollars of average Year 20 purchasing power. The subsequent payment of the current period's income tax liability merely reduces the previously measured liability for accrued income taxes.

GAINS AND LOSSES

Gain on Sale of Equipment

As indicated earlier, during July of Year 20, Demonstrator sold for $56,000 equipment that had a book value of $16,000. The equipment had been acquired in Year 12 at a cost of $80,000; the accumulated depreciation at time of sale was $64,000. The historical gain amounted to $40,000.

The proceeds of the sale, measured in terms of current dollars, were

$$158.9/155.7 \times \$56,000 = \$57,151$$

The book value of the equipment, measured in terms of current dollars, was

$$158.9/110.9 \times \$16,000 = \$22,925$$

Accordingly, the adjusted gain on sale of equipment was

$$\$57,151 - \$22,925 = \$34,226$$

It would be incorrect merely to restate the historical gain for price level changes. The gain reported in the conventional income statement of

$40,000 reflects the matching of current-period dollars for the selling price against Year-12 dollars for the book value of the equipment. The restatement of the net amount of these two elements (that is, the gain) by a single conversion factor would not result in fully reporting the transaction in dollars of end-of-the-period uniform purchasing power. Each element must be separately restated as shown above.

Monetary Gains and Losses

Measurement of the monetary gain or loss[2] experienced by Demonstrator Corporation during Year 20 as a result of the increase in the price level from 148.0 at the end of Year 19 to 158.9 at the end of Year 20 requires the identification of all transactions affecting monetary assets and monetary liabilities during the year. This is an important step. The resulting information is the unique product of general price level adjustments. The effects of inflation (deflation) on the management of monetary working capital and management's policy governing capital structure are explicitly revealed.

This step also provides a check on the accuracy of the adjustment procedures. The reconciliation of the beginning and ending balances of common stockholders' equity provided by adjusted income including monetary gains and losses guarantees that the assumptions and analysis in the adjusted balance sheet are consistent with the assumptions and analysis in the income statement. In the analysis that follows, the calculation of the gain or loss on net monetary working capital and on long-term monetary debt are shown separately.

Gain or Loss on Net Monetary Working Capital. Net monetary working capital refers to the excess of current monetary assets over current monetary liabilities. In the case of Demonstrator:

	December 31	
	Year 20	Year 19
Cash	$140,000	$120,000
Accounts receivable (net)	400,000	380,000
Total current monetary assets	$540,000	$500,000
Trade accounts payable	$160,000	$210,000
Other current liabilities	40,000	60,000
Total current monetary liabilities	$200,000	$270,000
Net monetary working capital	$340,000	$230,000

[2] The exposure draft of the FASB describes these as "general purchasing power gains and losses."

As indicated earlier, Demonstrator's sales and collections of accounts receivable are spread fairly evenly throughout the year. The same is true of its purchases and the incurrence of interest and operating expenses. A few lump-sum cash transactions, however, are inevitable. In the case of Demonstrator, three have been identified:

Second quarter:		
May—payment of property taxes		$(24,000)
Third quarter:		
July—sale of equipment	$ 56,000	
September—purchase of equipment . (160,000)		(104,000)
Net isolated cash outlays		$(128,000)

Net monetary working capital increased by $110,000 (= $340,000 − $230,000) between the beginning and end of the year. Isolated net cash outlays during the year as determined above are $128,000. Therefore, the increase in net monetary working capital from all other transactions, except the isolated cash outlays, must have been $238,000 (= $110,000 + $128,000). The transactions affecting the net monetary working capital accounts during Year 20 are summarized as follows:

Net monetary working capital, December 31, Year 19	$230,000
Plus increase in net monetary working capital during Year 20 ignoring isolated outlays	238,000
Less isolated monetary outlays	(128,000)
Net monetary working capital December 31, Year 20	$340,000

The gain or loss on net monetary working capital can be calculated in three parts: (1) the beginning balance, (2) the change during the period ignoring isolated cash transactions, and (3) the isolated cash transactions.

1. The monetary loss from "rolling forward" the beginning of the year balance in net monetary working capital accounts is $16,939, determined as follows:

$$(158.9/148.0 \times \$230,000) - \$230,000 = \$16,939$$

That is, $246,939 of end-of-Year-20 purchasing power is required to obtain the equivalent of $230,000 of end-of-Year-19 purchasing power. Because the beginning amount of net monetary working capital represents a fixed number of dollars, the increase in the price level during the year results in a loss in purchasing power.

2. In addition, ignoring the isolated cash transactions, the balance of net

monetary working capital increased $238,000 during the year. If we assume that this increase took place steadily as sales, purchases, and accruals of expenses occurred throughout the year, a further loss in purchasing power is involved:

$$(158.9/154.3 \times \$238,000) - \$238,000 = \$7,095$$

3. The isolated cash transactions also must be taken into consideration. The isolated expenditure of $24,000 cash during the second quarter negated any subsequent loss in purchasing power on that amount. Similarly, the isolated net expenditure of $104,000 during the third quarter eliminated any subsequent loss in purchasing power on that amount.

$(158.9/152.6 \times \$\ 24,000) - \$\ 24,000$	$ 990
$(158.9/155.7 \times \$104,000) - \$104,000$	2,137
Negated purchasing power loss on isolated transactions	$3,127

In summary, then, the loss in purchasing power suffered as a result of holding net monetary working capital during Year 20 is the net result of these three components.

Loss on January 1 balance of net monetary working capital	$16,939
Loss on increase in balance during year	7,095
Subtotal	$24,034
Negated loss on isolated transactions	3,127
Year-20 loss on net monetary working capital	$20,907

Other methods of calculating the loss on net monetary working capital can be used. For example, a detailed statement of sources and uses of monetary working capital for the period under consideration can be adjusted item by item. Exhibit 4.5 illustrates this method of calculating the loss on net current monetary assets. Using this method, those sources and uses that occurred continuously throughout the year are adjusted using the average index for the year; the isolated or lump-sum sources and uses are adjusted using the index applicable to the date on which such transactions occurred.

Long-Term Debt. During periods of inflation, a firm that has long-term monetary debt outstanding recognizes a monetary gain. In effect, the debt is repayable in dollars having less purchasing power than

EXHIBIT 4.5

DEMONSTRATOR CORPORATION

Calculation of Monetary Gain or Loss on Net Current Monetary Items

For the year ended December 31, Year 20

	Historical dollars	Restatement factor	Restated in terms of December 31, Year 20 dollars
Balance in net current monetary accounts, January 1	$ 230,000	158.9/148.0	$ 246,939
Increases in net current monetary accounts:			
Sales	$2,578,000	158.9/154.3	$2,654,855
Maintenance contracts sold	32,000	158.9/154.3	32,954
Sale of equipment	56,000	158.9/155.7	57,151
Total increases	$2,666,000		$2,744,960
Decreases in net current monetary accounts:			
Merchandise acquired	$2,000,000	158.9/154.3	$2,059,624
Supplies acquired	30,000	158.9/154.3	30,894
Property taxes paid	24,000	158.9/152.6	24,991
Selling, general, and administrative costs incurred	212,000	158.9/154.3	218,320
Interest accrued	30,000	158.9/154.3	30,894
Income taxes paid	90,000	158.9/154.3	92,683
Dividend declared	10,000	158.9/154.3	10,298
Equipment acquired	160,000	158.9/155.7	163,288
Total decreases	$2,556,000		$2,630,992
Balance in net current monetary accounts, December 31	$ 340,000		$ 360,907
Monetary loss on net current monetary items ($360,907 − $340,000)			$ 20,907

the dollars borrowed in the past. Of course, during periods of deflation, outstanding long-term debt has the opposite effect. Demonstrator borrowed $500,000 upon the issuance of its sinking fund debentures during Year 14, at which time the price level index was 117.6. During the 7 years this debt has been outstanding, Demonstrator has enjoyed a gain in purchasing power of $175,595 computed as follows:

$$(158.9/117.6 \times \$500,000) - \$500,000 = \$175,595$$

This is a gain in the sense that the company would have to repay $675,192 (= 158.9/117.6 × $500,000) current dollars to replace the amount of purchasing power borrowed in Year 14, whereas the obligation calls for a settlement of only $500,000 current dollars.

Demonstrator's gain on outstanding long-term debt during Year 20 was $36,824.

$$(158.9/148.0 \times \$500,000) - \$500,000 = \$36,824$$

The long-term monetary debt may be merged with the calculation involving net monetary working capital, but in so doing, a useful item of information is lost. The management of net monetary working capital tends to be distinctly different from the establishment of corporate policy governing the extent to which financing is by means of long-term debt and by means of stockholders' equity. Also, an important distinction is made in the general price level adjusted statement of changes in financial position between monetary gains and losses on net current monetary assets and on long-term debt. This distinction is discussed in Chapter Five.

If deferred income taxes were accounted for by the liability method, a monetary gain would be recognized as in the case of long-term debt. The effect would be to recognize not only the postponement of income tax payments but also the advantage of paying those postponed taxes in the future with "cheaper" dollars. Under the deferred method, any monetary gain will be recognized only when the accumulated historical amount of deferred income taxes is reduced. The actual number of dollars paid in deferred taxes at that time will be less than the reduction in the adjusted Deferred Income Taxes account. The difference will be the related accumulated monetary gain during the entire deferral period. This being the case, the deferred method might well produce the anomaly of a monetary gain during a period of deflation. The calculation of the monetary gain or loss when deferred income taxes are reduced is discussed more fully in Chapter Six.

Preferred Stock. If preferred stockholders' equity and common stockholders' equity are viewed together as total stockholders' equity, the existence of outstanding preferred stock does not call for any adjustments in measuring net income. On the other hand, in determining the net income attributable to the common stockholders' equity, as distinct from total stockholders' equity, the adjustments for outstanding preferred stock must be considered.

Demonstrator follows the practice of declaring and paying preferred dividends on a quarterly basis. Accordingly, the adjustment for the preferred stock dividend may be accomplished as follows:

$$158.9/154.3 \times \$10,000 = \$10,298$$

Note that dividends on preferred stock, unlike interest expense, do not accrue ratably over time. Preferred stock dividends are not recognized in the accounts until they have been declared. They are therefore measured in dollars at the time of their declaration and not necessarily evenly over the year.

The preferred stockholders' equity in Demonstrator Corporation is fixed in terms of numbers of dollars. As inflation continues, that constant number of dollars represents less and less purchasing power, in a manner identical to outstanding long-term debt. In computing price level adjusted earnings per share of common stock, the common stockholders' monetary gain on outstanding preferred stock must also be taken into consideration. The gain on preferred stock accruing to Demonstrator's common stockholders' equity during Year 20 was

$$(158.9/148.0 \times \$210,000) - \$210,000 = \$15,466$$

Chapter Five

PREPARING THE GENERAL PRICE LEVEL ADJUSTED STATEMENT OF CHANGES IN FINANCIAL POSITION

THE PROPOSED STATEMENT on general price level accounting of the Financial Accounting Standards Board does not require the presentation of information from the general price level adjusted statement of changes in financial position.[1] There may be important differences, however, between the historical dollar amount and the general price level adjusted amount for several items in this statement, particularly in the amount of working capital provided by operations. This chapter describes the procedures for adjusting the statement of changes in financial position. As is the case in preparing the statement of changes in financial position in historical dollars, the adjusted statement is most easily prepared after the restated balance sheet and income statement have been prepared. Exhibit 5.1 shows Demonstrator Corporation's statement of changes in financial position in historical dollars and as restated for general price level changes. This exhibit appears near the beginning of the chapter for easy reference.

WORKING CAPITAL PROVIDED BY OPERATIONS

The calculation of working capital provided by operations begins with the net income amount from the price level adjusted income statement. General price level adjusted net income for Demonstrator Corporation, as shown in Exhibit 4.1, is $68,930.

Several additions to and subtractions from net income are required to

---

[1]Financial Accounting Standards Board, "Financial Reporting in Units of General Purchasing Power," Proposed Statement of Financial Accounting Standard, Stamford, Connecticut, 1974.

EXHIBIT 5.1

DEMONSTRATOR CORPORATION

Statement of Changes in Financial Position

For the year ended, December 31, Year 20

	Historical dollars	Restated in terms of December 31, Year 20, dollars
Sources of working capital:		
Net income	$130,000	$ 68,930
Add:		
Depreciation expense	124,000	161,914
Increase in deferred income taxes	10,000	10,298
Increase in advances on maintenance contracts	10,000	9,417
Total	$274,000	$250,559
Subtract:		
Gain on sale of equipment	40,000	34,226
Monetary gain on long-term debt	-0-	36,824
Working capital provided by operations	$234,000	$179,509
Sale of equipment	56,000	57,151
Total sources of working capital	$290,000	$236,660
Uses of working capital:		
Preferred dividends	$10,000	$ 10,298
Purchase of equipment	160,000	163,288
Total uses of working capital	$170,000	$173,586
Increase in working capital	$120,000	$ 63,074

Analysis of Increases (Decreases) in Working Capital

Cash	$ 20,000	$ 11,162
Accounts receivable	20,000	(7,986)
Inventories	20,000	(16,824)
Prepayments	(10,000)	(13,163)
Trade accounts payable	50,000	65,466
Other current liabilities	20,000	24,419
Increase in working capital	$120,000	$ 63,074

determine working capital provided by operations. The depreciation charge for the period is usually the most significant addback. For Demonstrator Corporation, the historical dollar depreciation charge of $124,000 is restated to $161,914, as shown in Exhibit 4.4. Similarly, an addback to net income is required for the increase in deferred taxes during the period. The addback for Demonstrator Corporation of $10,298 is calculated as follows:

$$158.9/154.3 \times \$10,000 = \$10,298$$

This addback amount is also equal to the change in the price level adjusted Deferred Income Taxes account for the period.

Addbacks of this type would also be made for depletion, amortization of goodwill and other intangible assets, amortization of discount on noncurrent debt, and the minority interest in earnings if these items appear in the conventional income statement. The price level adjusted amounts for these addbacks can generally be determined from the price level adjusted income statement.

An addback to net income is required for maintenance contract transactions by Demonstrator Corporation in calculating price level adjusted working capital provided by operations. This arises because Advances on Maintenance Contracts is viewed as a noncurrent liability and thus is not a working capital item. The revenue recognized from maintenance contracts during Year 20 arose partially from sales of maintenance contracts during Years 18 and 19. Also, cash was received from the sale of maintenance contracts during Year 20 that will not be recognized as revenue until Year 21 or 22. The revenue recognized from maintenance contracts during Year 20 on an accrual basis must therefore be converted to a working capital basis. An analysis of the Advances on Maintenance Contracts account, a noncurrent liability account, for Year 20 appears below.

	Historical dollars	Restated in terms of December 31, Year 20, dollars
Balance, January 1 (Exhibit 3.1) ...	$20,000	$21,825
Plus maintenance contracts sold during Year 20 (Exhibit 4.5)	32,000	32,954
Less revenue recognized from maintenance contracts during Year 20 (Exhibit 4.1)	(22,000)	(23,537)
Balance, December 31 (Exhibit 3.1)	$30,000	$31,242

The conversion of maintenance revenue to a working capital basis requires an addition to general price level adjusted net income of $9,117 (= $32,954 − $23,537).

A similar procedure would be employed for intercorporate investments accounted for using the equity method. The restated equity in the affiliated corporation's earnings for the year would be subtracted and the restated dividends declared would be added to convert to a working capital basis. This conversion would probably require a net subtraction rather than a net addition, because the amount of the equity in current earnings would probably exceed the amount of dividends declared.

Two subtractions from net income are required for Demonstrator Corporation to determine working capital provided by operations. The general price level adjusted gain on the sale of equipment of $34,226 must be subtracted. The proceeds from sales of noncurrent assets are usually classified as nonoperating sources of working capital rather than as operating sources. Another subtraction, which will appear in the general price level adjusted statement but not in the historical-dollar statement, is the monetary gain on long-term debt during periods of inflation. This monetary gain is included in net income but does not provide working capital. This long-term monetary gain must therefore be subtracted. A monetary loss on noncurrent monetary assets during periods of inflation would be an addback rather than a subtraction.

The loss of net monetary working capital of $20,907 need not be added back because the monetary loss resulted in a decrease in working capital. This decrease in working capital is largely attributable to rolling forward the net monetary working capital accounts on January 1, to the general price level on December 31, Year 20. The GPLA beginning net monetary working capital position is larger than that shown on the historical-dollar statements, and in this case, the adjustment of that opening balance is a major explanation of why net monetary working capital did not increase as much on a GPLA basis as it did on an historical-dollar basis.

The monetary gain on preferred stock does not have to be subtracted because the gain produces an intra-stockholders' equity adjustment and is not included in net income.

General price level adjusted working capital provided by operations is $179,509, as compared to $234,000 in historical dollars. The difference of $54,491 between these two amounts is largely explained by the upward restatement of the January 1, Year 20, inventory included in cost of goods sold (= $36,824) and the monetary loss from rolling forward the beginning of the year amount of net monetary working capital (= $16,939). The significance of general price level adjusted working capital provided by operations in interpreting GPLA financial statements is discussed in Chapter Ten.

OTHER SOURCES OF WORKING CAPITAL

The sale of equipment resulted in an increase in working capital of $56,000 in historical dollars. This amount is restated as follows:

$$158.9/155.7 \times \$56,000 = \$57,151$$

Similar adjustments would be made for working capital provided by issuing noncurrent debt and capital stock.

OTHER USES OF WORKING CAPITAL

The working capital used for preferred stock dividends is restated as follows:

$$158.9/154.3 \times \$10,000 = \$10,298$$

The working capital used in acquiring equipment must also be restated:

$$158.9/155.7 \times \$160,000 = \$163,288$$

Similar adjustments would be made for working capital used in redeeming bonds and acquiring treasury stock.

ANALYSIS OF CHANGES IN WORKING CAPITAL ACCOUNTS

The change in each working capital account shown in the lower portion of Exhibit 5.1 is obtained directly from the general price level adjusted comparative balance sheet in Exhibit 3.1.

Chapter Six

GENERAL PRICE LEVEL ADJUSTMENTS—SOME COMPLEXITIES

THE ILLUSTRATION OF THE RESTATEMENT PROCEDURES for Demonstrator Corporation in Chapters Two through Five was purposefully kept simple in order to demonstrate the basic approach of general price level accounting. This chapter discusses some complexities that might be encountered in restating certain items in the financial statements. Consideration is also given to several problems in using price indexes.

ASSETS

Cash and Temporary Investments

A monetary asset is a claim to a fixed number of dollars, the amount of which is not affected by changes in the general price level. Cash on hand as well as in demand, time, and certificates of deposit are monetary items if they are denominated in U.S. dollars. Similar items denominated in foreign currencies are nonmonetary. Their U.S. dollar equivalent amounts are not fixed, but can change as exchange rates change The restatement procedure for these items is discussed later in this chapter when the consolidation of foreign subsidiaries is considered.

The monetary versus nonmonetary classification of temporary investments in securities depends on whether the firm will receive a fixed number of dollars at the time the securities are sold or redeemed. Temporary investments in U.S. Treasury Bills and similar short-term securities are likely to be monetary items. Most temporary investments in corporate bonds and common stock are likely to be nonmonetary items, because the receipt of a fixed number of dollars at the time of sale or redemption is not assured. These latter items should be restated for cumulative inflation since the bonds or common stock were acquired. If the restated acquisition cost exceeds market price, a write-down to market may be required at the end of each period. The guideline used to determine whether a write-down is required in the restated financial statements is the same as in the historical-dollar financial statements. Accounting Research Bulletin No. 43 states that "in the case of marketable securities where market value is less than cost by a substantial amount and it is evident that the decline in market value is not due to a mere temporary condition, the amount to be included as a current asset should not exceed the market value."[1] Market value will be less than restated cost whenever the market price of an individual security rises less rapidly than the general price level.

We discuss the restatement procedures for long-term investments in intercorporate securities later in this chapter.

Receivables

Accounts and notes receivable are monetary items, because a fixed number of dollars will be received at the time of payment. Contra-receivables accounts, such as allowance for uncollectible accounts, allowance for sales discounts, returns and allowances, and notes receivable discounted are likewise monetary accounts, because the accounts to which they are contra are monetary items.

In the income statement, the restatement of the periodic provision for uncollectible accounts, returns, and allowances under the allowance method depends on the method used in determining the amount of the periodic provision in the conventional financial statements. If the provision is based on a percentage of sales, it should be adjusted using the same restatement factor as is used to adjust sales revenue for the period. These provisions are viewed as immediate reductions in the *amount* of revenue recognized. If the periodic provision is based on an aging of the end-of-the-period amount of accounts receivable, the provision made against

---

[1] American Institute of Certified Public Accountants, *Accounting Research Bulletin No. 43*, New York, 1953, chap. 3, para. 9. The notion that a current decline in market price is due to a temporary condition is inconsistent with the evidence that capital markets are efficient. In an efficient capital market, current market prices reflect the present value of anticipated future cash flows given all publicly available information. If information is publicly available concerning the favorable events expected to reverse the "temporary decline," then the effects of these favorable events are already reflected in market prices. It is possible that information about the favorable events is not publicly available (that is, inside information), in which case it may not be reflected in current market prices, suggesting a market inefficiency. We think that accountants should not base their anticipations on inside information, and we therefore conclude that for accounting purposes all market price declines are not due to temporary conditions.

earnings is already stated in dollars of end-of-the-year purchasing power and no restatement is necessary. These provisions are viewed as reductions in the amount of accounts receivable.[2]

Installment accounts receivable and the related deferred gross profit account present unusual restatement problems. Installment accounts receivable is a monetary account, because it represents a claim to a fixed number of dollars. The deferred gross profit account, even though classified as a contra-account to installment accounts receivable, is a non-monetary item. It must be restated for cumulative inflation since the time of the installment sale. Likewise, the portion of the deferred gross profit that is recognized as income each period as cash payments are received must be restated for cumulative inflation since the time of sale.

To illustrate the restatement of deferred gross profit, assume that an equipment retailer acquires a machine on January 1, 1976, for $800. The general price index on this date is assumed to be 100 in this illustration. The machine is sold on December 31, 1976, at a price of $1,000. The general price index on this date is 110. The gross profit on the sale in historical dollars and as restated for general price level changes are determined as follows:

	Historical dollars	Dollars of December 31, 1976, purchasing power
Selling price— historical dollars	$1,000	
—adjusted dollars ($1,000 × 110/110)		$1,000
Acquisition cost— historical dollars	800	
—adjusted dollars ($800 × 110/100).		880
Gross profit	$ 200	$ 120

Assume that income is recognized using the installment method and that $400 is collected on December 31, 1977. The general price index on this date is 125. The deferred gross profit recognized in historical dollars and restated dollars is determined as follows:

[2]When the direct charge-off method of accounting for uncollectible accounts is used, the charge against earnings is for a specific customer's account measured in dollars at the time of the sale. Accordingly, the amount charged off must be restated for cumulative inflation since the sale took place.

Historical dollars: $400/$1,000 × $200	$80.00
Restated dollars: ($400/$1,000 × $120) × 125/110	$54.54

Note one important point. It is incorrect merely to restate the historical-dollar realized gross profit of $80 for general price changes. The historical-dollar gross profit on the sale is the result of matching a selling price and an acquisition cost measured in dollars of different general purchasing powers. This gross profit must first be redetermined in dollars of uniform purchasing power before any restatements can be made. Hence, separate records must be kept of gross profit amounts in historical dollars and restated dollars when the installment method is used.

Inventories

Manufactured Inventories. The demonstration in Chapters Two through Five assumed that all inventories were purchased. For manufacturing companies, the adjustment procedure is bound to be somewhat more complicated. It may be convenient to adjust manufacturing companies' inventories according to the three components as they would appear in a statement of cost of goods manufactured: materials, labor, and overhead.

Adjustments of overhead costs are likely to be the most difficult, and they may also be the most significant. Many overhead costs involve current cash outlays (for example, utilities, indirect labor, salaries of factory administrators). These overhead costs can generally be adjusted in the same manner as direct labor. Other overhead costs involve amortization of previous cash outlays (for example, depreciation of building and equipment). The adjustment of depreciation charges on buildings and equipment for a manufacturing firm is no different from the adjustment of depreciation expense described in the demonstration for a nonmanufacturing firm. Here, as in other cases, the crucial data are the date of acquisition and the price level index applicable to that date.

Some inventory items may be stated at the standard cost of manufacturing the items. If the cost standards used in valuing the inventory reflect end-of-the-period prices, then the items are already stated in current dollars and no adjustment is required. If, however, the cost standards used are significantly out of date or if manufacturing cost variances are partially allocated to units in ending inventory, then the valuation of the units is probably closer to acquisition cost in historical dollars. In this case, price level adjustments of the ending inventory are required.

Measurements Based on Current Market Prices. Monetary items are automatically stated in current dollars and therefore require no restatement. Certain nonmonetary items may also be stated in current dollars and require no restatement. For example, certain products in the agricultural and natural resource industries are frequently measured at their net realizable values (that is, the number of dollars that could be received if the inventory items were sold currently) rather than at their historical costs. Because these inventory items are already stated in terms of current prices, no price level adjustment is necessary. If, instead, these items were stated at acquisition cost, a price level restatement would be necessary. The need for price level adjustments, therefore, is determined by the measurement procedure employed rather than by the inherent nature of the item itself.

Even though price level adjustments are not required for assets measured at current market prices or net realizable values, it is important to distinguish such assets from monetary assets. Monetary assets represent claims to a fixed number of dollars; therefore, holding them necessarily gives rise to measurable monetary gains (deflation) and losses (inflation). Whether gains or losses result from holding nonmonetary assets, however they may be measured, depends on the movement of the prices of those specific assets relative to changes in the general price level.

Cost or Market, Whichever Is Lower. The well-established accounting practice of writing down inventories whenever their historical costs are greater than current market value applies to accounts whose historical amounts have been adjusted for changes in the general price level. For example, *Accounting Research Bulletin No. 43*[3] requires that a loss be recognized "whenever the utility of goods is impaired by damage, deterioration, obsolescence, changes in price levels, or other causes. The measurement of such losses is accomplished by applying the rule of pricing inventories at cost or market, whichever is lower."

These requirements apply whether the measurements of cost are made in terms of historical numbers of dollars or in terms of invested purchasing power stated in current dollars. For example, the Financial Accounting Standards Board has stated:[4]

> Those nonmonetary assets that are stated in unit-of-money financial statements at the lower of cost or market (for example, inventory and

[3]*Accounting Research Bulletin No. 43, op. cit.,* chap. 4, para. 8.

[4]Financial Accounting Standards Board, "Financial Reporting in Units of General Purchasing Power," Proposed Statement of Financial Accounting Standard, Stamford, Connecticut, 1974, para. 42.

some investments) shall be stated, in terms of units of general purchasing power, at the lower of (a) the unit-of-money cost of the asset restated to units of current general purchasing power ... or (b) market. If (a) is greater than (b), the restated cost shall be written down in the general purchasing power financial statements just as would be done in the unit-of-money financial statements. The amount of the write-down shall be included in determining general purchasing power net income in the same manner as it would be in determining unit-of-money net income.

The following example illustrates the application of the lower of cost or market rule:[5]

Assume inventory that was purchased for $100 in 19X1 (general price level index = 100) has a market value of $90 at the end of 19X2 (index = 110). A $10 write-down to market would be reflected in the 19X2 unit-of-money income statement, and the inventory would be carried at $90 in the unit-of-money balance sheet. The cost of the inventory restated for changes in the general purchasing power of the dollar is $(X2)110 (= $100 × 110/100). [$(X2)110 is the convenient notation used by the FASB to indicate 110 dollars of general purchasing power dated 19X2.] Applying the lower-of-cost-or-market rule just as was done in the unit-of-money financial statements results in a $(X2)20 write-down to market in the 19X2 general purchasing power income statement (most likely as part of cost of goods sold), and the inventory would be carried at $(X2)90 in the general purchasing power balance sheet. The cost of an asset will sometimes be written down for purposes of reporting in units of general purchasing power even though no write-down was required for purposes of reporting in units of money. If the market value of the inventory at the end of 19X2 in the previous example had been $105 (rather than $90), there would have been no write-down in the unit-of-money financial statements. A write-down from the restated cost of $(X2)110 to market value of $(X2)105 would nonetheless be required in the general purchasing power financial statements.

If the price of an inventory item increases less rapidly than the general price level, then a write-down to market will be required in the general price level adjusted statements. The write-down will usually be reflected in higher cost of goods sold for the period. If the price of the inventory item increases more rapidly than the general price level, then the item will be reported at its restated acquisition cost in the price level adjusted state-

[5]*Ibid.*

ments. No write-up to the higher market value is permitted. If the price of the inventory item increases at the same rate as the general price level, restated acquisition cost and market will be the same.

Inventory Cost Flow Assumption. The restatement procedure for inventories and costs of goods sold depends on the cost flow assumption—FIFO, LIFO, weighted average—that is used.

FIFO. The illustration for Demonstrator Corporation in Chapters Three and Four is based on a FIFO assumption. In that example, the inventory turned over approximately four times each year. The beginning inventory was therefore restated using the price index for the fourth quarter of Year 19. The ending inventory represented approximately 3 months' purchases, so it was already stated in terms of prices during the last quarter of Year 20. Purchases were assumed to take place evenly throughout the year and were restated using the average price change during the year. For purposes of illustrating the restatement of inventory and cost of goods sold under various cost flow assumptions, we shall assume that the ending inventory for Demonstrator Corporation under FIFO was $550,000, instead of $520,000 as illustrated previously. The use of a different ending inventory will simplify the example and make it easier to generalize about the effects of using alternative cost flow assumptions on the restated financial statements.

The determination of cost of goods sold under the FIFO cost flow assumption for Demonstrator Corporation, based on an ending inventory of $550,000, is as follows:

	Dollars of December 31, Year 20, purchasing power
Beginning inventory $500,000 × 158.9/ 148.0	$ 536,824
Purchases $2,000,000 × 158.9/154.3 ..	2,059,624
Goods available for sale	$2,596,448
Less ending inventory	550,000
Cost of goods sold	$2,046,448

LIFO. Now assume that the beginning inventory for Demonstrator Corporation under the LIFO cost flow assumption was $370,000 and consisted of the following layers:

Base layer: Year 1 prices	$100,000
Second layer: Year 8 prices ...	70,000
Third layer: Year 14 prices ...	80,000
Fourth layer: Year 18 prices ..	120,000
Total beginning inventory ..	$370,000

Also assume that a larger number of units were purchased during Year 20 than were sold, and that there was an incremental quantity increase of $10,000.

Under the LIFO cost flow assumption, each layer of the beginning inventory is restated from the price level when the layer was added to the price level at the end of Year 20. The restatement of the beginning inventory is as follows:

	Dollars of December 31, Year 20, purchasing power
Base layer: $100,000 × 158.9/89.6	$177,344
Second layer: $70,000 × 158.9/104.6 ...	106,338
Third layer: $80,000 × 158.9/117.6	108,095
Fourth layer: $120,000 × 158.9/141.4 ...	134,851
Total beginning inventory	$526,628

If a strict LIFO cost flow assumption were followed, the price index for the first quarter of each year rather than the average index for the year would be used to restate the layer added during each year. This refinement is not employed here.

The restatement of the ending inventory is as follows:

	Dollars of December 31, Year 20, purchasing power
LIFO beginning inventory as determined above	$526,628
Fifth layer: $10,000 × 158.9 × 154.3	10,298
Total ending inventory	$536,926

The cost of goods sold under LIFO is determined as follows:

	Dollars of December 31, Year 20, purchasing power
Beginning inventory (see above) ..	$ 526,628
Purchases $2,000,000 × 158.9/154.3	2,059,624
Goods available for sale	$2,586,252
Less ending inventory (see above) .	536,926
Cost of goods sold	$2,049,326

LIFO WITH INVENTORY DECREASE. If a larger number of units were sold during Year 20 than were purchased, there would have been a quantity decrease. Under the LIFO cost flow assumption, the quantity decrease would be reflected as an elimination of one or more of the LIFO layers, beginning with the last layer added in Year 18. Cost of goods available for sale would be the same as shown above. Because the restated amount of ending inventory would have been smaller, cost of goods sold would have been larger.

LIFO WITH LOWER OF COST OR MARKET. To continue the LIFO illustration further, assume that the beginning inventory under LIFO of $370,000 was composed of the layers listed below instead of those assumed previously:

Base layer: Year 1 prices	$200,000
Second layer: Year 8 prices ...	90,000
Third layer: Year 14 prices ...	60,000
Fourth layer: Year 18 prices ..	20,000
Total beginning inventory ..	$370,000

Also assume again that there was an incremental quantity increase under LIFO during Year 20 of $10,000.

The restated cost of the beginning inventory in end-of-Year-19 prices is determined as follows:

	Dollars of December 31, Year 19, purchasing power
Base layer: $200,000 × 148.0/89.6	$330,357
Second layer: $90,000 × 148.0/104.6 ...	127,342
Third layer: $60,000 × 148.0/117.6	75,510
Fourth layer: $20,000 × 148.0/141.4 ...	20,934
Total beginning inventory	$554,143

Given a beginning inventory under FIFO of $500,000 in historical dollars, the restated LIFO beginning inventory of $554,143 determined above appears to be significantly in excess of market value at the end of Year 19. Accordingly, the LIFO beginning inventory would be written down from restated cost to market. Assume that the market value of the beginning inventory is determined to be $505,000. The beginning inventory would be stated at $505,000 in end-of-Year-19 dollars. The general price level adjusted beginning inventory stated in end-of-Year-20 dollars is $542,193 (= $505,000 × 158.9/148.0).

The write-down from restated cost to market under LIFO is likely to be largest during the first year in which GPLA statements are prepared. This initial write-down reflects the cumulative excess of changes in the general price level over changes in the specific prices of inventory items since the LIFO layers were established.

The ending inventory for Year 20 under LIFO will now be composed of two layers. One layer will be the beginning inventory, determined to be $505,000 after applying the lower-of-cost-or-market rule. This layer becomes the base LIFO layer in the general price level financial statements. Thus, the composition of LIFO inventory layers in historical dollars and in restated dollars may be different. The second LIFO layer results from the incremental quantity increase during Year 20 of $10,000. The restated "cost" of the LIFO ending inventory is determined as follows:

	Dollars of December 31, Year 20, purchasing power
Base layer: $505,000 × 158.9/148.0 ...	$542,193
Second layer: $10,000 × 158.9/154.3 ..	10,298
Total ending inventory	$552,491

Note that the base layer is stated in end-of-Year-19 prices and is therefore restated for one full year of price change. The restated cost of the LIFO ending inventory, as was the case with the beginning inventory, appears to be greater than the market value of the ending inventory (ending inventory in historical dollars under FIFO is $550,000). Assume that the market value of the ending inventory is $552,000. The LIFO ending inventory would again be stated at market, because market value is less than restated cost.

Cost of goods sold under lower of LIFO cost or market for Year 20 is determined below:

	December 31, Year 20, dollars
Beginning inventory: $505,000 × 158.9/148.0 .	$ 542,193
Purchases: $2,000,000 × 158.9/154.3	2,059,624
Goods available for sale	$2,601,817
Less ending inventory	552,000
Cost of goods sold	$2,049,817

The restated beginning inventory for Year 21 under LIFO is $552,000. This amount becomes the new LIFO base layer. Note also that any subsequent decreases in inventory quantities will result in a decrease in this Year-20 base layer and not, as in the historical-dollar financial statements, in a decrease in a layer of Year 18 or some earlier year. For general price level accounting purposes, these historical-dollar LIFO layers are eliminated once the ending inventory is written down from restated cost to market. The market value amount becomes the new "cost" and the process of establishing LIFO layers begins over again. A liquidation of a LIFO layer will therefore not increase restated net income as much as it would increase historical-dollar net income, because the "cost" of the liquidated layer will likely be higher on a restated basis than it was on an historical basis.

DOLLAR-VALUE LIFO. The restatement procedures under the dollar-value LIFO method are similar to those under regular LIFO. *Specific* price indexes are used to establish the amount of each layer. Each layer is then restated for general price changes since the layer was established. The lower-of-cost-or-market rule is then applied as illustrated above.

WEIGHTED AVERAGE. The restatement procedure for a weighted-average cost flow assumption is somewhat different from that for a FIFO or LIFO assumption. The costs of units sold and in ending inventory are assumed to come from both beginning inventory and from purchases during the year (that is, cost of goods available for sale).

The cost of units in beginning inventory is based on an average of all purchases of the firm since it began using the weighted-average cost flow assumption. In order to restate the beginning inventory, the average age of units in beginning inventory must be determined. The average age depends on two factors: (1) the percentage of total purchases during the year that remain in ending inventory (an amount related to the rate of inventory turnover), and (2) the rate of growth in purchases. The first of these two factors has a more significant impact on the average age than does the second factor. Exhibit 6.1 presents average ages of inventory items for various percentages of purchases remaining in ending inventory and rates of growth in purchases. Using .80 of a year is a reasonably accurate estimate in this case. That is, the beginning inventory can be assumed to have been acquired about March 14, 292 days (= .80 × 365) prior to the end of the year. The beginning inventory under a weighted-average cost flow assumption can therefore be restated for approximately one-and-three-fourths years of price change.

Purchases during the current year can be restated for one-half year of price change on the assumption that they were made evenly over the current year. Under a weighted-average cost flow assumption, the beginning inventory in historical dollars is assumed to be $485,000 and the ending inventory is $522,000. The cost of goods available for sale of Demonstrator Corporation is determined as follows:

	Dollars of December 31, Year 20, purchasing power
Beginning inventory $485,000 × 158.9/144.6	$ 532,963
Purchases $2,000,000 × 158.9/154.3	2,059,624
Goods available for sale	$2,592,587

The proportion of goods available for sale that are in ending inventory can be determined as follows:

$$\frac{\text{Cost of ending inventory in historical dollars}}{\text{Cost of goods available for sale in historical dollars}} = \frac{\$\ 522,000}{\$2,485,000}$$

$$= 21.00 \text{ percent}$$

EXHIBIT 6.1

AVERAGE AGE IN YEARS OF DOLLARS IN WEIGHTED-AVERAGE BEGINNING INVENTORY

As a Function of Annual Growth Rate (g) in Inventory and the Percentage of Annual Purchases Remaining in Ending Inventory (s)*

Percentage of annual purchases in ending inventory (s)	Annual growth rate (g) in percent per year				
	−10%	0.0%	5%	10%	30%
0.0%...............	.50	.50	.50	.50	.50
0.5	.51	.51	.50	.50	.50
1.0	.51	.51	.51	.51	.51
2.0	.52	.52	.52	.52	.52
3.0	.53	.53	.53	.53	.52
4.0	.55	.54	.54	.54	.53
5.0	.56	.55	.55	.55	.54
6.0	.57	.56	.56	.56	.55
8.0	.60	.59	.58	.58	.57
10.0	.63	.61	.61	.60	.58
12.0	.65	.64	.63	.62	.60
15.0	.70	.68	.67	.66	.63
20.0	.79	.75	.74	.72	.68
25.0	.88	.83	.81	.79	.74
30.0	1.00	.93	.90	.88	.80
40.0	1.30	1.17	1.12	1.07	.94
50.0	1.75	1.50	1.41	1.33	1.13

*The number shown in the body of the table is

$$\frac{1 + g + s}{2(1 + g - s)}$$

As the table indicates, and the formula makes clear, the estimate of the average age is much more sensitive to changes in inventory turnover, represented by changes in s, than it is to changes in rates of growth in inventory, represented by changes in g. The derivation of this formula is omitted because it involves the use of difference equations. The interested reader can derive the formula by noting the following relations. Let P_n represent purchases for inventory in year n and let EI_n represent ending inventory as of year n. Then,

$$EI_n = sP_n + sEI_{n-1} \text{ and } P_n = (1 + g)P_{n-1}$$

Similarly, the proportion of goods available for sale that were sold during the year can be determined as follows:

$$\frac{\text{Cost of goods sold in historical dollars}}{\text{Cost of goods available for sale in historical dollars}} = \frac{\$1,963,000}{\$2,485,000}$$

$$= 79.00 \text{ percent}$$

The restated cost of goods available for sale under the weighted-average method is allocated to units in ending inventory and units sold as follows:

Ending inventory: $\$2,592,587 \times .2100 = \underline{\$\ \ 544,443}$

Cost of goods sold: $\$2,592,587 \times .7900 = \underline{\$2,048,144}$

COMPARISON OF INVENTORY COST FLOW ASSUMPTIONS. The restated amounts of beginning and ending inventory and cost of goods sold for Demonstrator Corporation illustrated in this chapter are summarized in Exhibit 6.2. The following observations can be made about the effects of the cost flow assumption on the restated amounts of inventory and cost of goods sold.

1. When the specific prices of inventory items rise more rapidly than the general price level (Cases 1, 2, and 3), the effect of alternative cost flow assumptions on the restated financial statements is in the same relationship

EXHIBIT 6.2

COMPARISON OF RESTATED BEGINNING AND ENDING INVENTORY AND COST OF GOODS SOLD AMOUNTS FOR VARIOUS COST FLOW ASSUMPTIONS

	Beginning inventory	Ending inventory	Cost of goods sold
Case 1: FIFO	$536,824	$550,000	$2,046,448
Case 2: Weighted average ..	$532,963	$544,443	$2,048,144
Case 3: LIFO (specific prices increased more rapidly than general price level since LIFO layers were established)	$526,628	$536,926	$2,049,326
Case 4: Lower of LIFO cost or market (specific prices increased less rapidly than general price level since LIFO layers were established)	$542,193	$552,000	$2,049,817

as in the conventional financial statements. That is, FIFO produces the largest beginning and ending inventory amounts, followed by weighted average and LIFO. LIFO produces the largest cost of goods sold amounts, followed by weighted average and FIFO.

2. When the specific prices of inventory items rise less rapidly than the general price level (Case 4), inventory items are written down to market at the end of each period. Beginning and ending inventory amounts are approximately the same under each of the cost flow assumptions (lower of FIFO and weighted average cost or market are not illustrated here). Cost of goods sold will therefore also be approximately the same.

Construction in Process. The restatement procedure for the Construction in Process account depends on whether the completed-contract or the percentage-of-completion method is used for recognizing income from the contract.

When the completed-contract method is used, the Construction in Process account accumulates the actual cost incurred on construction projects. The Construction in Process account in this case is essentially the same as the Work in Process account of a manufacturing company. In both cases, the accounts are nonmonetary items. Each element of construction cost must be restated for the change in the general price level since the cost was initially incurred. This restatement is analogous to the restatement of material, labor, and overhead costs in the Work in Process account.

When income is recognized under the percentage-of-completion method, on the other hand, the Construction in Process account is viewed as a receivable and is therefore treated as a monetary item.[6] No restatement is made of the cost elements for changes in the general price level as would be done if the account were considered a nonmonetary item. Instead, a monetary loss is recognized each period on the outstanding receivable.

To illustrate the restatement procedures for the Construction in Process account under both methods, assume that a contract is signed for the construction of a bridge on January 1, Year 19, at a contract price of $2,000,000. Construction costs are incurred evenly over the period of construction as follows: Year 19—$900,000; Year 20—$600,000. The contract is completed on December 31, Year 20, at which time $2,000,000 is received from the customer. The GNP Deflator indexes presented in Chapter Two are used in illustrating the restatement procedures.

First, assume that the completed-contract method is used for recognizing income from the contract. No income is recognized during Year 19, since the contract has not yet been completed. The construction costs of

[6]Financial Accounting Standards Board, *op. cit.,* Appendix C.

$900,000 incurred during Year 19 are accumulated in the Construction in Process account. These costs are shown on the end-of-Year-19 balance sheet at $911,704 (= $900,000 × 148.0/146.1), after being restated for the average general price level change during Year 19.

During Year 20, all of the income from the contract is recognized. Since the contract is completed on December 31, Year 20, the income recognized in historical dollars is the difference between the contract price ($2,000,000) and the accumulated costs incurred ($1,500,000). The income recognized in restated dollars is determined as follows:

	Dollars of December 31, Year 20, purchasing power
Contract price:	
$2,000,000 × 158.9/158.9	$2,000,000
Less costs incurred:	
$900,000 × 158.9/146.1	(978,850)
$600,000 × 158.9/154.3	(617,887)
Restated income from contract	$ 403,263

Now assume that the percentage-of-completion method is used for recognizing income from the contract. Exhibit 6.3 presents the calculations under this method. During Year 19, $900,000 of costs are incurred out of a total of $1,500,000 estimated costs for the entire contract. The contract is therefore estimated to be 60 percent (= $900,000/$1,500,000) complete as of the end of Year 19. The historical-dollar income recognized of $300,000 (= $500,000 × 9/15) must be restated for the average rate of inflation during the year. Unlike the completed-contract method, income under the percentage-of-completion method is assumed to accrue each day as construction work progresses, so one-half year of price change should be used in the restatement factor. A monetary loss of $15,606 is recognized for the increase in the monetary asset during Year 19.

Similar calculations apply to Year 20. The historical-dollar income recognized is restated using the average price change for the period. Monetary losses are recognized from rolling forward the beginning-of-the-period balance in the monetary asset account ($88,378) and for the increase in the monetary asset account during the period ($23,849). The net income (income recognized minus monetary losses incurred) from the contract for the 2-year period stated in end-of-Year-20 dollars is $403,263.

Note that the total restated net income in uniform dollars under the completed-contract method is the same as under the percentage-of-completion method. The difference comes in the timing of the income. The recognition of income is more accelerated under the percentage-of-completion method.

Intercorporate Investments

The monetary versus nonmonetary classification of investments in securities depends on whether the firm will receive a fixed number of dollars at the time the securities are expected to be sold or redeemed. If the receipt of a fixed number of dollars is anticipated, then the investments are monetary items. Otherwise, they are nonmonetary items.

Bonds. Investments in bonds classified as noncurrent assets are more likely to be held until maturity than are those classified as current assets and are, therefore, more likely to be considered monetary items. In determining the classification of convertible bonds, consideration must be given to the probability of conversion into common stock. If conversion is highly probable, then the convertible bonds are nonmonetary assets.

Preferred Stock. Investments in preferred stock are nonmonetary items at the time of acquisition, because the receipt of a fixed number of dollars at the time of a subsequent sale is not assured. The cost of the preferred stock is restated for cumulative inflation since acquisition on subsequent balance sheet dates.

Within a few years after acquisition, the restated cost of the preferred stock will likely exceed its market value. This is because market values of preferred stocks are generally unlikely to rise much above the redemption values of the shares. The proposed statement on price level accounting of the FASB does not indicate whether a lower-of-cost-or-market-type adjustment for the investment in preferred stock is required in this case. We feel that this situation meets the general guidelines for applying the lower-of-cost-or-market method to marketable securities discussed earlier in this chapter. Preferred stock should therefore be written down to market when that amount is less than restated cost.

Common Stock. Investments in common stock are nonmonetary items in virtually all cases. The restatement procedure for investments in common stock depends on (1) whether the cost or equity method is used and (2) whether there is any difference between the cost of the investment and the amount of the net assets underlying the investment. The various restatement possibilities are illustrated in the three examples below.

Case 1. P Company acquired a 15-percent interest in the common stock of S Company on January 1, 1975, for $150,-

EXHIBIT 6.3

RESTATEMENT OF CONSTRUCTION IN PROCESS

Percentage of Completion Method

	Historical dollars	Dollars of December 31, Year 19, purchasing power	Dollars of December 31, Year 20, purchasing power
Year 19			
Income recognized:			
Historical dollars ($500,000 × 9/15)	$300,000		—
Restated dollars ($500,000 × 9.15) × (148.0/146.1)	—	$303,901	—
Monetary loss:			
On increase in receivable for costs incurred ($900,000) and income recognized ($300,000) $1,200,000 − ($1,200,000 × 148.0/146.1) ..	—	(15,606)	—
Year 20			
Income recognized:			
Historical dollars ($500,000 × 6/15)	$200,000	—	—
Restated dollars ($500,000 × 6/15) × (158.9/ 154.3)	—	—	$205,962
Monetary loss:			
On beginning balance in receivable account, $1,200,000 − ($1,200,000 × 158.9/148.0) .	—	—	(88,378)

EXHIBIT 6.3 (*Continued*)

	Historical dollars	Dollars of December 31, Year 19, purchasing power	Dollars of December 31, Year 20, purchasing power
On increase in receivable for costs incurred ($600,000) and income recognized ($200,000) $800,000 − ($800,000 × 158.9/154.3)			(23,849)
Total	$500,000	$288,295	$ 93,735
Restatement of Year 19 income and monetary loss to dollars of end-of-Year 20 purchasing power ($288,295 × 158.9/148.0)	...		309,528
Total restated income and monetary loss from contract	...	...	$403,263

73

000. The net assets of S Company on this date were $1,000,000 in historical dollars and $1,200,000 in general price level restated dollars. During 1975, S Company earned $200,000 in historical dollars and $100,000 in restated dollars. S Company did not declare a dividend during 1975. The general price level increased 8 percent during the year.

The cost method of accounting for the investment is used in this case, because P Company owns less than 20 percent of S Company. The investment is stated at $150,000 in historical dollars at the beginning and end of the year. In restated dollars, the investment is reported at $162,000 (= $150,000 × 1.08). Under the cost method, recognition does not need to be given to any difference between the cost of an investment and the value of the underlying net assets.

> *Case 2.* Assume the same information as in Case 1 except that P Company acquired a 30 percent interest in S Company on January 1, 1975, for $400,000. Any excess of cost over book value acquired is to be amortized over 40 years.

The equity method of accounting for the investment is used in this case, because P Company owns more than 20 percent of S Company. Under the equity method, any difference between the cost of an investment and the book value of the net assets must be amortized. At the date of acquisition, the cost of the investment is greater than both the historical-dollar and the restated-dollar value of the underlying net assets. The excess amounts are calculated as follows:

	Historical dollars	Dollars of January 1, 1975, purchasing power
Cost of the investment ..	$400,000	$400,000
Interest in net assets on January 1, 1975:		
Historical dollars, $1,000,000 × .30	300,000	
Restated dollars, $1,200,000 × .30		360,000
Excess cost	$100,000	$ 40,000

In applying the equity method during 1975, P Company will recognize in the income statement its share of S Company's earnings and amortize the excess cost arising from the acquisition. The calculation of the amounts of S Company's earnings recognized by P Company and the amounts of excess cost amortized during 1975 are shown below in accounting for the change in the Investment in S Company account during the year.

	Historical dollars	Dollars of December 31, 1975, purchasing power
Investment in S Company, January 1, 1975	$400,000	$432,000
Plus P Company's share of S Company's earnings		
$200,000 × .30	60,000	
$100,000 × .30		30,000
Less amortization of excess cost		
$100,000/40	(2,500)	
$40,000/40 × 1.08		(1,080)
Investment in S Company, December 31, 1975	$457,500	$460,920

Case 3. Assume the same information as Case 2 except that the cost of the investment is $320,000.

In this case, there is an excess of cost over historical-dollar book value but an excess of restated-dollar book value over cost. The excess amounts are calculated as follows:

	Historical dollars	Dollars of January 1, 1975, purchasing power
Cost of the investment ...	$320,000	$320,000
Interest in underlying net assets		
$1,000,000 × .30	300,000	
$1,200,000 × .30		360,000
Excess cost (book value) ..	$ 20,000	$(40,000)

The excess historical dollar cost would be amortized in a manner similar to that illustrated for Case 2. Accounting Principles Board Opinion No. 18 requires that any excess of book value over cost be eliminated by writing down the carrying amounts of individual assets and liabilities to their market values. The $40,000 excess of restated book value of the net assets over cost would be eliminated in this manner. The investment would be shown on the restated balance sheet on the date of acquisition at cost, $320,000.

If dividends had been declared during 1975 by S Company, they would be restated to dollars of December 31, 1975, purchasing power. Under the cost method, the restated dividends would be included in net income. Under the equity method, they would be subtracted in determining the December 31, 1975, amount of Investment in S Company.

Other Investments. The monetary versus nonmonetary classification of other noncurrent investments follows the general principles discussed above. Refundable deposits and advances to unconsolidated subsidiaries are monetary items, because they represent claims to a fixed number of dollars. Deposits on purchase contracts are nonmonetary items. They are viewed as partial payments on the nonmonetary assets being acquired. The cash surrender value of life insurance is a receivable to a fixed number of dollars and is therefore a monetary item.

Property, Plant, and Equipment

Chapters Three and Four extensively illustrated the restatement of property, plant, and equipment accounts for Demonstrator Corporation. One additional point is made here.

Price level adjustments of historical amounts invested in items of property, plant, and equipment may also produce measurements that are clearly in excess of their current market values, in which case write-downs might seem to be in order. For example, assume that the land acquired by Demonstrator Corporation in Year 1 for $80,000 is located in an area where land values have not increased substantially during the 20-year period the land has been held. Perhaps recent sales of similar land in the vicinity have been made at about $120,000. Although, in a balance sheet prepared on a historical-dollar basis, Demonstrator's land may be properly reported at a cost of $80,000, it would seem inappropriate to report Demonstrator's land at a price level adjusted cost of $141,875 (= $80,000 × 158.9/89.6) in the December 31, Year 20, adjusted balance sheet. The cost-or-market rule would set an upper limit of $120,000.

The application of the lower-of-cost-or-market rule to noncurrent assets such as property, plant, and equipment is an unsettled issue, even in historical dollar accounting. APB Statement No. 4 states:[7]

> In unusual circumstances, persuasive evidence may exist of impairment of the utility of productive facilities indicative of an inability to recover cost although the facilities have not become worthless. The amount at which those facilities are carried is sometimes reduced to recoverable cost and a loss recorded prior to disposition or expiration of the useful life of the facilities. . . . Noncurrent assets whose market prices have declined are *generally* retained in accounting records at their recorded amounts until they are disposed of or have become worthless.

The statement of the Financial Accounting Standards Board that "the same accounting principles used in preparing unit-of-money financial statements shall be used in preparing financial information stated in units of general purchasing power"[8] might seem to preclude application of the lower-of-cost-or-market rule to property, plant, and equipment in general price level restated accounting reports. We think that such write-downs should be made whenever the restated amount becomes substantially greater than some measure of current value, as it easily can.

Intangibles

Intangible assets typically arise from expenditures of a prior period that are being amortized over some number of future periods. Intangible assets are therefore nonmonetary assets and must be restated for cumulative inflation since the expenditure occurred.

LIABILITIES

Current Liabilities

Most current liabilities, such as accounts, notes, salaries, interest, and dividends payable are monetary items. Chapters Three and Four illustrate the price level accounting treatment of these items using the data for Demonstrator Corporation. Advances received on sales contracts are

---

[7]Accounting Principles Board, "Basic Concepts and Accounting Principles Underlying Financial Statements of Business Enterprises," Statement No. 4, New York, AICPA, October 1970, para. 183 (emphasis added).

[8]Financial Accounting Standards Board, *op. cit.,* para. 34.

nonmonetary items, because the obligation will be satisfied with the delivery of goods or services whose specific prices can fluctuate.

Estimated liabilities arising from warranty, premium, and similar plans are nonmonetary in that they represent obligations to provide goods or services whose prices may fluctuate. As with other nonmonetary items, these items must be restated to the general purchasing power of the dollar on the most recent balance sheet date.

In some cases, the historical-dollar amount of the estimated liability is already stated in current dollars and needs no restatement. For example, the amount shown for estimated warranty claims is often reassessed at the end of each period in light of changing material prices, wage rates, and rate of customers' claims. The end-of-period balance in the liability account is increased or decreased to reflect the estimated future costs of the warranty plan. Under these circumstances, the estimated liability need not be adjusted for price level changes. As was the case with inventory items stated at market prices, estimated liabilities stated at end of the year prices, although they do not require adjustment, are not monetary items. The estimated liability does not represent an obligation to pay a fixed number of dollars. The amount to be paid in the future depends upon changes in the prices of specific goods and services.

Noncurrent Liabilities

Bonds. Long-term bonds are monetary items, representing an obligation to pay a fixed number of dollars at maturity. The proposed statement of the FASB treats all outstanding bonds, including convertible and callable bonds, as monetary items until they are repurchased, converted, called, or redeemed at maturity.

Unamortized premium or discount on bonds payable is also considered a monetary item. The premium or discount is viewed as inseparable from the debt to which it relates. These accounts are similar to the Accumulated Depreciation account in that their purpose is to account for the difference between the current book value of an account and the value at some other date (acquisition cost of equipment, maturity value of bonds).

Exhibit 6.4 illustrates the general price level adjustments made for outstanding bonds issued at a discount. The bonds are 8 percent, semiannual coupon bonds with a $1,000,000 face value. The bonds are issued on January 1, Year 20, to yield 10 percent. The issue price is $828,414. Interest is paid on January 1 and July 1 of each year. The illustration is based on the effective interest method of amortizing the bond discount.

The amounts of semiannual interest expense are restated for the average rate of inflation during each 6-month period. Monetary gains are recognized on the January 1, Year 20, amount in the Bonds Payable

EXHIBIT 6.4

RESTATEMENT OF BONDS PAYABLE ISSUED AT A DISCOUNT

Data for Illustration: On January 1, Year 20, 8 percent, semiannual coupon bonds with a $1,000,000 face value are issued to yield 10 percent on the market. Interest is paid on January 1 and July 1 of each year. The issue price is $828,414.

	Historical dollars	Restatement factor	Dollars of December 31, Year 20, purchasing power
Interest expense (effective interest method):			
First 6 months: .05 × $828,414	$41,421	158.9/151.3[a]	$43,502
Second 6 months: .05 × ($828,414 + $1,421)	41,492	158.9/157.3[b]	41,914
Monetary gains:			
On accrued interest payable			
First 6 months: $40,000 − ($40,000 × 158.9/151.3[a])	—		(2,009)
Second 6 months: $40,000 − ($40,000 × 158.9/157.3[b]) ...	—		(407)
On beginning amount of bonds payable			
$828,414 − ($828,414 × 158.9/148.0)	—		(61,012)
On increase in bonds payable from amortization of bond discount			
First 6 months: $1,421 − ($1,421 × 158.9/151.3[a])	—		(71)
Second 6 months: $1,492 − ($1,492 × 158.9/157.3[b])	—		(15)
Net interest expense and monetary gains	$82,913		$21,902

[a]Denominator index is the average for the first two quarters of Year 20.
[b]Denominator index is the average for the last two quarters of Year 20.

account, on the accrued interest payable during the year, and on the increase in the Bonds Payable account as a result of amortizing the bond discount. Restated interest expense of $85,416 (= $43,502 + $41,914) is larger than interest expense in historical dollars of $82,913 (= $41,421 + $41,492). However, the net of restated interest expense and monetary gains of $21,902 is significantly smaller than historical-dollar interest expense alone. We prefer the method of disclosure in the last column of Exhibit 6.4, where monetary gains on the outstanding debt are netted against restated interest expense. This format emphasizes the real cost to the firm of borrowing. By delaying payment of interest and principal, the firm realizes monetary gains, because the dollars paid have less general purchasing power than the dollars borrowed. The interpretation of the net amount of restated interest expense and monetary gain is discussed more fully in Chapter Ten.

In the general price level restated statement of changes in financial position, an addback to restated net income is required in determining working capital provided by operations for the portion of interest expense attributable to amortization of bond discount. This addback is $2,999 (= $1,421 × 158.9/151.3 + $1,492 × 158.0/157.3). Also, a subtraction from restated net income is required for the monetary gain of $61,012 on the beginning amount of bonds payable and for the gain or the increase in bonds payable of $86 (= $71 + $15).

Using the straight-line rather than the effective interest method of amortizing the bond discount results in a larger interest expense during the early years while the bonds are outstanding. This results from a more rapid rate of amortization of the discount. Interest expense in historical dollars and as restated for general level changes for Year 20 using the straight-line method of amortization is as follows:

	Historical dollars	Restatement factor	Dollars of December 31, Year 20, purchasing power
First 6 months,			
$40,000 + ($171,586/40)	$44,290	158.9/151.3	$46,515
Second 6 months,			
$40,000 + ($171,586/40)	44,290	158.9/157.3	44,741
Total interest expense ..	$88,580		$91,256

The monetary gain on accrued interest payable and on the beginning balance in the Bonds Payable account is the same regardless of whether the effective interest or straight-line method of amortization is used. The monetary gain on the increase in bonds payable due to the discount amortization will be larger under the straight-line method, as shown below:

First 6 months, $4,290 − ($4,290 × 158.9/151.3)	$215
Second 6 months, $4,290 − ($4,290 × 158.9/157.3)	44
Total	$259

The net of restated interest expense and monetary gains using the straight-line method of amortization is summarized below:

	Dollars of December 31, Year 20, purchasing power
Restated interest expense	$91,256
Monetary gain on:	
Accrued interest payable ($2,009 + $407)	(2,416)
Beginning amount of bonds payable .	(61,012)
Increase in bonds payable from amortization	(259)
Net interest expense and monetary gains	$27,569

Now, consider the effect on historical dollar and restated earnings of using the effective interest and straight-line amortization methods:

	Effective interest method	Straight-line method
Interest expense in historical dollars	$82,913	$88,580
Net of interest expense and monetary gain in restated dollars	21,902	27,569
Total	$61,011	$61,011

In both cases, the interest expense in historical dollars is larger than the net of interest expense and monetary gain in restated dollars. However, the excess (that is, $61,011) is independent of the method of amortization used.

The restatement procedure for a premium on bonds payable is the same as that illustrated above for a discount. The restatement procedure for the straight-line method of amortization is similar to that illustrated above except the amount of premium amortized each period will be different.

Leases. Long-term leases capitalized under the financing method are monetary items. To illustrate the restatements for long-term leases, assume that a firm agrees on January 1, Year 20, to lease a machine for 10 years. Lease payments of $10,000 are to be made on December 31 of each year. The firm could borrow funds at an interest rate of 8 percent. The capitalized amount of the lease on January 1, Year 20, is $67,101 (= $10,000 × 6.7101). The price level restatements relating to this lease are shown in Exhibit 6.5. In this illustration, the capitalized property rights shown among the assets are depreciated using the straight-line method. If the double-declining-balance or sum-of-the-years'-digits method were used, depreciation expense both in historical and restated dollars would be larger. Interest expense is computed using the effective interest method and restated using the average price change during the year. Monetary gains are recognized on the interest expenses accruing throughout the year and on the beginning of the period amount of the lease liability.

In subsequent years, depreciation expense will be restated for cumulative inflation since January 1, Year 20, the same as if the equipment had been purchased rather than leased.

If the firm did not capitalize this lease obligation, it would account for the lease using the operating method. In this case, the firm would show a lease expense in historical dollars of $10,000. In restated dollars, lease expense would be $10,298 (= $10,000 × 158.9/154.3). A monetary gain would not be reported each period, because a liability is not recognized on the balance sheet under the operating method.

The restatement procedure for long-term leases is illustrated again in Chapter Ten using data for Sears and UAL (United Airlines).

Deferred Income Taxes. As discussed in Chapter Three, the monetary versus nonmonetary classification of deferred income taxes is controversial. This controversy stems from the differing views as to whether the account is a liability or a deferred credit. The liability proponents argue that the account represents a monetary obligation measured directly on the basis of the number of dollars to be paid in the future when timing differences are reversed and taxable income exceeds book income. The deferred credit proponents view the account as a current tax savings from using different accounting methods for tax and book income, the

EXHIBIT 6.5

GENERAL PRICE LEVEL RESTATEMENTS RELATING TO A CAPITALIZED LEASE

	Historical dollars	Restatement factor	Dollars of December 31, Year 20, purchasing power
Depreciation expense ($67,101/10)	$ 6,710	158.9/148.0	$7,204
Interest expense (.08 × $67,101)	5,368	158.9/154.3	5,528
Monetary gain on:			
Accrued interest payable, $5,368 − ($5,368 × 158.9/154.3)	—		(160)
Beginning amount of the capitalized lease obligation, $67,101 − ($67,101 × 158.9/148.0)..	—		(4,942)
Total	$12,078		$7,630

benefits of which are to be recognized in earnings during future periods. Deferred taxes are measured in dollars of the period of the tax savings and must, according to the deferral viewpoint, be restated to dollars of current general purchasing power. Accounting Principles Board Opinion No. 11 adopted the deferred credit viewpoint. The proposed statement on price level accounting extended this viewpoint by treating deferred income taxes as a nonmonetary item. The Board stated:[9]

> Deferred income taxes are nonmonetary because they represent a past cost savings that will be amortized to income in future periods as a reduction of expenses. Moreover, amounts of income taxes that will ultimately be paid when the timing differences related to the tax credits reverse can change as a result of changes in tax rates or tax laws and depend on future taxable income.

The illustration of the restatement of deferred income taxes for Demonstrator Corporation in Chapter Three was based on two assumptions which are considered more fully in this chapter. It was assumed that (1) the deferred taxes account arose from only one type of timing difference, the use of accelerated depreciation methods for tax purposes and the straight-line method for book purposes, and (2) there were no reversals of timing differences originating in prior periods. Accounting Principles Board Opinion No. 11 requires that recognition be given to reversals of tax effects in the period in which they occur. For this purpose, timing

[9]Financial Accounting Standards Board, *op. cit.,* Appendix C.

differences may be considered individually, or similar differences may be grouped. To illustrate the restatement of deferred taxes when there are reversals of prior tax savings, reconsider the deferred taxes account of Demonstrator Corporation as shown in Exhibit 3.4 and as summarized in Exhibit 6.6. Assume that the deferred taxes account increased by $10,000 during Year 21. This increase reflects a $15,000 increase due to tax timing differences originating in Year 21 and a $5,000 decrease due to reversals of prior years' timing differences. The price index for the fourth quarter of Year 21 is assumed to be 171.6, and the average for Year 21 is assumed to be 166.3. The January 1, Year 21, balance in the deferred taxes account is $20,000 in historical dollars and $23,251 in dollars of December 31, Year 21, purchasing power. The increase in the account due to tax savings originating in Year 21 of $15,000 is restated using the index for the average price change for Year 21 in the denominator. In order to restate the decreases in the account, or reversals, it is necessary to know the year in which the tax savings originated. Two possibilities are illustrated in Exhibit 6.6. First, specific identification is used when the decreases can be traced back to specific provisions for deferred taxes made in prior periods. Second, when such specific identification is impractical, a first-in, first-out assumption can be employed.

In preparing the general price level adjusted statement of changes in financial position for Demonstrator Corporation for Year 20, the increase in deferred taxes was added back to net income to obtain working capital provided by operations. Similarly, the increase in deferred income taxes during Year 21 shown in Exhibit 6.6 of $9,449 for specific identification (= $15,478 − $6,029) and $9,299 for first-in, first-out (= $15,478 − $6,179) would be added to net income to obtain working capital provided by operations.

Deferred Investment Tax Credits. Deferred investment tax credits appear on the balance sheet when a firm selects the deferral rather than flow-through method of accounting for the tax credit. The Deferred Investment Tax Credit account is a nonmonetary item measured in terms of the past tax savings from claiming the credit. The account must be restated each year for cumulative inflation since the credit was claimed. Likewise, the portion of the tax credit recognized in determining earnings each year must be restated for cumulative inflation.

STOCKHOLDERS' EQUITY

The restatement procedures for most stockholders' equity accounts were illustrated in Chapter Three using the data for Demonstrator Corporation. One additional account is discussed briefly here.

EXHIBIT 6.6

RESTATEMENT OF DEFERRED INCOME TAXES

Year	Historical dollars	Restatement factor	Dollars of December 31, Year 21, purchasing power
Year 17	$ 2,000	171.6/135.2	$ 2,538
Year 18	5,000	171.6/141.4	6,068
Year 19	3,000	171.6/146.1	3,524
Year 20	10,000	171.6/154.3	11,121
Total	$20,000		$23,251
Plus increase due to Year 21 timing differences	15,000	171.6/166.3	15,478
Total	$35,000		$38,729
Less decrease assuming specific identification can be made:			
Year 17	$ 1,600	171.6/135.2	$ 2,031
Year 18	1,400	171.6/141.4	1,699
Year 19	1,200	171.6/146.1	1,409
Year 20	800	171.6/154.3	890
Total decrease	$ 5,000		$ 6,029
Balance, December 31, Year 21	$30,000		$32,700
Less decrease assuming first-in, first-out:			
Year 17	$ 2,000	171.6/135.2	$ 2,538
Year 18	3,000	171.6/141.4	3,641
Total decrease	$ 5,000		$ 6,179
Balance, December 31, Year 21	$30,000		$32,550

Treasury stock is a nonmonetary account measured in dollars at the time of its acquisition. The account must be restated each period for cumulative inflation since the time of acquisition. When the treasury stock is sold, the difference between the selling price and restated cost is recognized as an addition to or subtraction from restated common stockholders' equity.

Consolidation of Foreign Subsidiaries

Two possible methods exist for consolidating foreign subsidiaries in price level adjusted financial statements: (1) the accounts of foreign subsidiaries can be adjusted for general price level changes using a price level index for the foreign currency and then the adjusted amounts can be translated into U.S. dollars (adjust-translate method); and (2) the accounts of foreign subsidiaries can be translated into U.S. dollars and then the translated amounts can be adjusted for general price level changes using a price level index for the U.S. (translate-adjust method). If exchange rates between the foreign currency and the U.S. dollar changed continuously and precisely to reflect changes in the relative general purchasing powers of the monetary unit of the two countries involved, then the adjust-translate method and translate-adjust method would produce virtually identical results. Because exchange rates do not always change precisely to reflect changes in relative purchasing powers,[10] the two methods can produce different results. An example may serve to clarify the differences.

Assume that U.S. Domestic Company established a wholly owned Foreign Subsidiary on January 1, Year 1, with an investment of $100,000. The investment was immediately converted into 500,000 units of local currency (LC), the exchange rate being $.20 per LC, or 5LC to $1. The Foreign Subsidiary immediately purchased land for LC800,000, paying LC300,000 in cash and signing a long-term mortgage note for LC500,000. During Year 1, Foreign Subsidiary had no other transactions. The U.S. general price level increased 10 percent and the general price level in the foreign country increased 25 percent during Year 1. At the end of Year 1, however, the exchange rate remained unchanged at $.20 per LC (LC5 to $1). Balance sheets under both methods are shown in Exhibit 6.7.

In preparing financial statements by the adjust-translate method, price level adjusted statements in terms of December 31, Year 1, LC are first constructed using a general price level index for that country. Those price level adjusted statements are then translated from foreign monetary units to dollars at the current exchange rate, in the example at the rate of $.20

[10]Robert Z. Aliber and Clyde P. Stickney, "Accounting Measures of Foreign Exchange Exposure: The Long and Short of It," *The Accounting Review,* January 1975, pp. 44–57.

EXHIBIT 6.7

FOREIGN SUBSIDIARY

Balance Sheet

December 31, Year 1

	Adjust-translate			Translate-adjust		
	Historical LC	Adjusted (25% inflation)	Translated, dollars ($0.20 per LC)	Historical LC	Translated, dollars ($0.20 per LC)	Adjusted, dollars (10% inflation)
Cash	200,000	200,000	$ 40,000	200,000	$ 40,000	$ 40,000
Land	800,000	1,000,000	200,000	800,000	160,000	176,000
	1,000,000	1,200,000	$240,000	1,000,000	$200,000	$216,000
Long-term debt	500,000	500,000	$100,000	500,000	$100,000	$100,000
Stockholders' equity	500,000	700,000	140,000	500,000	100,000	116,000
	1,000,000	1,200,000	$240,000	1,000,000	$200,000	$216,000

Statement of Income and Stockholders' Equity for the Year Ended December 31, Year 1

Monetary loss on net monetary working capital (.25 × LC200,000)	LC(50,000)	(0.10 × $40,000)		$ (4,000)
Monetary gain on long-term debt (.25 × LC500,000)	125,000	(0.10 × $100,000)		10,000
Net income	LC 75,000			$ 6,000
Stockholders' equity, January 1— LC500,000	LC625,000	$100,000		110,000
Stockholders' equity, December 31	LC700,000			$116,000

per LC (LC5 to $1). In preparing financial statements under the translate-adjust method, the historical amounts in the foreign subsidiary's accounts are first translated using appropriate exchange rates. In general, current exchange rates are used for monetary items, and the exchange rates in effect at the historical dates are used for nonmonetary items. The resulting historical amounts stated in numbers of dollars are then adjusted for changes in the U.S. price level since those historical dates.

Each of the two methods has its advantages and disadvantages. The choice must depend on the primary informational objectives to be served. For example, in the adjust-translate balance sheet, land is reported at $200,000. That is the historical amount of foreign purchasing power that was invested in foreign land, translated into December 31, Year 1, dollars based on the current exchange rate; it would take 200,000 December 31, Year 1, dollars to duplicate the foreign purchasing power invested in land. In the translate-adjust balance sheet, land is reported at $176,000. That is the historical amount of U.S. purchasing power that was invested in foreign land, measured in terms of December 31, Year 1, dollars. The $176,000 understates the amount of foreign purchasing power invested in the land and the $200,000 overstates the amount of U.S. purchasing power invested in the land. This phenomenon is the direct result of the failure of exchange rates to equate the purchasing power of the monetary units in question.

If the primary goal is the consistent reporting of historical amounts in terms of U.S. purchasing power, the translate-adjust procedure would seem preferable. On the other hand, if the primary purpose is to reflect the performance of foreign investments in the unique economic environment in which they operate, the adjust-translate procedure would be preferable. The Financial Accounting Standards Board has taken a position favoring the translate-adjust method.[11]

> An objective of general purchasing power accounting is to express all amounts in a single unit of measure, namely, units of general purchasing power of a single currency such as the U.S. dollar. Accordingly, the Board has required that financial statements of foreign branches, subsidiaries, and other investees first be translated into U.S. dollars and then restated for changes in the dollar's general purchasing power. . . . The alternative, restatement for changes in the purchasing power of a foreign currency prior to translation, would result in an intermingling of units of the general purchasing power of the dollar and units of the general purchasing power of a foreign currency and would, therefore, be inconsistent with the objective stated above.

[11]Financial Accounting Standards Board, *op. cit.,* para. 80.

One further problem in consolidating foreign operations in general price level adjusted statements should be noted. In the illustration of the two procedures, the foreign cash and the long-term debt payable in foreign currency were treated as monetary items for purposes of both foreign currency translation and general price level adjustment. Thus, the amounts reported for foreign cash and long-term debt on December 31, Year 1, reflect the exchange rate and U.S. general price level on that date. Monetary gains and losses are recognized on the January 1, Year 1, balances in long-term debt and cash respectively as a result of rolling forward the beginning-of-the-year amounts to the general price level at the end of the year. If the exchange rate had changed during the year, foreign exchange gain and losses would also have been recognized on the beginning of the period amounts of these monetary items.

Treating foreign cash and long-term debt as monetary for purposes of translation is consistent with the stated objective of translation, which requires that foreign statements be translated in a way that the underlying local currency transactions are accounted for the same as though they had been foreign currency transactions of the enterprise originally measured and recorded in dollars rather than in foreign currency.[12] If cash and long-term debt had originally been recorded in dollars, they would be considered monetary items. Likewise, treating translated cash and long-term debt as monetary for purposes of general price level adjustments is consistent with the objective of expressing all amounts in terms of a single unit of measurement, the general purchasing power of the dollar at the end of the period. The translated dollar amounts for cash and long-term debt before adjustment for general price level changes reflect the purchasing power of the dollar at the beginning of Year 1. These amounts must be rolled forward to the purchasing power at the end of the year and monetary gains and losses recognized for the period.

The proposed statement on price level accounting takes the position that foreign currency and claims receivable or payable in foreign currency should be treated as nonmonetary items *for purposes of general price level adjustments*. Monetary items have been defined as cash and claims to cash that are fixed in terms of numbers of U.S. dollars regardless of changes in the general price level. According to this definition, foreign cash, foreign receivables, and foreign payables are not monetary items because their amounts are not fixed in terms of U.S. dollars. The U.S. dollar equivalents

---

[12]Financial Accounting Standards Board, "Accounting for the Translation of Foreign Currency Transactions and Foreign Currency Statements," Statement of Financial Accounting Standard no. 8, Stamford, Connecticut, 1975, para. 9.

of these items change as foreign exchange rates change, that is, as the specific prices of foreign monetary units change.

Consider the effect of treating the cash and long-term debt accounts of Foreign Subisidary as monetary and as nonmonetary items. When these items are treated as monetary, they are stated on the balance sheet at the end of Year 1 at their translated dollar amounts, $40,000 for cash and $100,000 for long-term debt. A net monetary gain of $6,000 is recognized for the year as a result of holding net monetary liabilities while the general price level increased 10 percent. When these items are treated as nonmonetary, their translated dollar amounts are adjusted for the 10-percent increase in the U.S. price level during the year. This adjustment merely converts the historical amounts from dollars of January 1, Year 1, purchasing power, the date when the cash was received and long-term debt was issued, to an equivalent number of December 31, Year 1, dollars.

One result of treating foreign cash, foreign receivables, and foreign liabilities as nonmonetary is that the dollar amounts at which these items are stated on the balance sheet may exceed the dollar equivalent of the foreign amounts involved at the end of the period. Thus, whereas the 200,000 LC could be converted on December 31, Year 1, into $40,000, treating cash as a nonmonetary item results in reporting it at $44,000 (= 200,000 LC × $.20 × 1.10). It seems appropriate under these circumstances to adjust the cash account to its dollar equivalent of $40,000 at year end and reflect the $4,000 difference as a loss in determining net income (a lower-of-cost-or-market-type adjustment). A similar adjustment would be made to reduce the amount shown for long-term debt from $110,000 (= 500,000 LC × $.20 × 1.10) to $100,000. The $10,000 difference would be reflected as a gain in determining net income. These adjustments are implicitly required in the FASB's proposed statement on price level accounting. Because these items are explicitly designated as nonmonetary, these adjustments cannot represent monetary gains or losses. It is not clear, however, whether they represent foreign exchange gains or losses or some other type of gain or loss.

Note that whether foreign cash, foreign receivables, and foreign liabilities are treated as monetary or as nonmonetary, net income for the period, after adjusting cash and long-term debt downward as described above, will be the same. If these items are treated as monetary, a monetary gain of $6,000 will be recognized. If these items are treated as nonmonetary, a gain of $6,000 will be recognized from writing down the restated amounts of cash and long-term debt to an equivalent amount of end-of-the-year dollars. The only difference may be in the designation of the gains and losses (that is, monetary, foreign exchange, or something else). In Chapters Seven through Nine, gains and losses on foreign debt are disclosed separately from monetary gains and losses.

AUDITING GPLA FINANCIAL STATEMENTS

The independent CPA will be required to express an opinion on the GPLA financial statements if publication of such statements becomes a "generally accepted accounting principle." Many audit tests of GPLA statement items can be performed in conjunction with the audit of the item in historical dollars. For example, the amount of restated depreciation expense can be audited in conjunction with the audit of historical-dollar depreciation expense, because much of the same data (that is, acquisition cost, date of acquisition, depreciable life) applies to both the historical- and restated-dollar amounts of depreciation.

The model described in Chapters Eight and Ten for estimating GPLA earnings, financial position, and funds flow may also serve as a useful audit tool. That model permits estimations of restated sales, cost of goods sold, depreciation expense, monetary gain or loss, net income, and amounts for individual balance sheet accounts. Such estimated amounts might be used in assessing the reasonableness of the GPLA restated amounts provided by a firm.

USING THE PRICE INDEX

GPLA accounting requires the use of a price index. The FASB requires that the GNP Deflator be used. There are a surprising number of problems that arise out of the dictum, "Use the GNP Deflator." (Many of these problems would arise whatever price index is used.) This section explores some of these problems and our suggested solutions to them. Four different topics are discussed:

1. What the GNP Deflator measures.

2. How to link and interpolate price index numbers.

3. How to choose the "year-end" number.

4. How to measure prices for one-half year of price change.

The last of these is probably the most important, because nearly all revenues and most expenses except depreciation and cost of goods sold are assumed to occur fairly evenly throughout the year and thus require adjustment for one-half year of price change.[13]

[13]Perhaps we can alert the reader to the importance of this matter by referring to the discussion in Chapter Ten where we show that the various choices for measuring one-half year of price change produced GPLA income amounts for Shell Oil Company for 1974 ranging from $623.4 million to $645.0 million, a variation of about 4 percent of historical-dollar income.

What the GNP Implicit Price Deflator Measures

The U.S. Department of Commerce and the U.S. Department of Labor are continually measuring prices in our economy. These price measurements are then expressed as indexes. Probably the best known of the indexes published by the Department of Labor is the Consumers Price Index (CPI). The major price index of the Department of Commerce is the GNP Implicit Price Deflator. The latter index is the one that has been suggested for use in general price level accounting in all of the major U.S. studies on this subject.

In the GNP Deflator series, the average price of a bundle of goods and services representative of the total output in the economy in the year 1958 is designated 100. (Put more simply, 1958 is the base year in the GNP Deflator series.) The average price of a bundle representative of the output of the year 19XX divided by 1958 prices is the GNP Average Annual Deflator for 19XX. The average price of the representative bundle during the first (or second or third or fourth) quarter of 19XX divided by the 1958 price of that bundle is the GNP Deflator Quarter Average for the first (or second or third or fourth) quarter of 19XX. There are five GNP Deflator numbers published for each year—one for each of the four calendar quarter averages and the annual average.

The annual average for the GNP Deflator for a given year represents an average of prices for the year. If prices change at a uniform rate throughout the year, then that annual average, if a given date has to be chosen, represents June 30 prices more closely than any other date. Similarly, the quarterly average, insofar as it represents prices as of a given date, represents prices for about the midpoint of the quarter. Therefore, the first-quarter average is more representative of February 15 prices than it is of March 31 prices. More important for accounting purposes, the fourth-quarter average is more representative of November 15 prices than it is of December 31 prices. For GPLA accounting purposes, however, the fourth-quarter average GNP Deflator is deemed by the FASB to be the price index as of the end of the calendar year.

Linking and Interpolating Numbers

If prices increase 12 percent in a given year, how much have prices increased in one-half (or one-third) of a year? The best answer to this question is not 6 (or 4) percent. If prices go up 6 percent for two consecutive half-years, then prices have increased by $(1.06 \times 1.06) - 1 = 1.1236 - 1 = 12.36$ percent for the entire year. Compounding of price increases works in just the same way as compound interest. If \$1 is invested at 12 percent compounded semiannually, then it will grow to

$1.1236 at the end of 1 year. At what rate compounded semiannually must $1 be invested to grow to $1.12 exactly? The rate is $\sqrt{1.12} - 1$, or 5.83 percent. If prices increase by 12 percent during a year of uniform price change, then prices must have risen by 5.83 percent during any 6-month period of that year.

In linking and interpolating price changes in the illustrations in Chapters Three through Six, "simple interest" techniques were used. That is, where prices increased 12 percent during the year, the average price change was assumed to be 6 percent. It would have been more correct, however, to use "compound interest" techniques. Thus, if the price increase for one period is 4 percent and for the next period is 5 percent, then the price increase over the two periods is $(1.04 \times 1.05) - 1 = 9.2$ percent, rather than $4 + 5 = 9$ percent. If a certain number should be adjusted for the sum of price changes over several periods, then the price change factors (one plus the individual price change) should be multiplied together and one subtracted from the total.

To determine the price change for one-third of a year when prices increased by 12 percent during the year, the "compound interest" answer is the rate r such that $(1 + r)^3 - 1 = 12$ percent. The r that satisfies this relation is $(1.12)^{1/3} - 1 = 3.85$ percent. In general, to calculate the price change during a fraction of a year equal to X, where X is a number between zero and one, when prices went up by 12 percent during the entire year, then the "compound interest" answer is $(1.12)^X - 1$.

If, as is required for some of the balance sheet inventory adjustments, it is necessary to reduce one price change, say 12 percent, by another, say 5 percent, the "compound interest" answer is not $12 - 5 = 7$ percent, but is $1.12/1.05 - 1 = 6\frac{2}{3}$ percent. That is, $1.06667 \times 1.05 - 1 = 12$ percent.

In linking price index numbers, price changes should not be added. Instead, the price change factors should be multiplied together and one subtracted from the product. In interpolating price index numbers, do not subtract the price changes, but raise the price change factor to a fractional power and subtract one.

Choosing the "Year-End" Number

As indicated earlier, the Commerce Department publishes five GNP Deflator numbers for a year—one for each quarter's average and one for the annual average. The numbers for the GNP Deflator are published monthly in the U.S. Department of Commerce's *Survey of Current Business* and are included each year in the appendixes of the *Economic Report of the President*. These published numbers are subject to constant revision. The accountant, accustomed to following the rules of *APB Opinion No. 20,* is uncomfortable with procedures that require constant changes in num-

EXHIBIT 6.8

A HISTORY OF THE GNP DEFLATOR NUMBER FOR 1973's ANNUAL AVERAGE AND FOURTH-QUARTER 1973 AVERAGE

Source and date	1973 year average	Fourth-quarter 1973 average
Economic Report of the President, February 1, 1974	153.86	158.04
Survey of Current Business		
January 1974	153.86	158.04
February 1974	153.86	158.36
March 1974–May 1974	153.94	158.36
June 1974–December 1974 ..	154.31	158.93
Economic Report of the President, February 4, 1975	154.31	158.93

bers. The changes in the GNP Deflator figures are not large, but they are large enough to affect some of the significant digits that the accountant reports. Exhibit 6.8 shows the history of the GNP Deflator annual average for 1973 and the fourth quarter of 1973.

Although these differences will affect GPLA numbers rounded to the nearest thousand dollars, the differences are not material. Any one published version of the numbers will be suitable for audited financial statements, but the auditor will find the use of different numbers by different individuals frustrating. We suggest that all GPLA statement calculations be based on data in the *Survey of Current Business* dated the month after the end of the company's business year, January for calendar-year companies and, for example, October for September 30 year-end companies. The general rule could, of course, be to use the *Survey of Current Business* data for n months after the close of the business year, where n is any number. In the interest of speedy publication of annual reports, we suggest that n be one.

One-Half Year of Price Change

Most revenues and many expenses, except depreciation and cost of goods sold, are to be adjusted for one-half year of price change. What is one-half year of price change? In APB Statement No. 3 and the FASB Exposure Draft, the answer to this question for a calendar-year company is illustrated as follows:

$$\frac{\text{Fourth-quarter average GNP Deflator}}{\text{Annual average GNP Deflator}}$$

We think there are two things wrong with this answer.

1. Companies with fiscal years that end on a date different from December 31 cannot know what to do because there is no analogue of the Annual Average for them.

2. As we pointed out above, the fourth-quarter average is more representative of November 15 prices than it is of December 31 prices, whereas the annual average represents June 30 prices, if any one day must be chosen. Thus the calculation of "one-half year of price change" suggested is really the calculation of about four and one-half months of price change. That is,

$$\frac{\text{November 15 prices}}{\text{June 30 prices}} - 1 = 4\frac{1}{2} \text{ months of price change}$$

As a substitute, we suggest a measure that represents a full 6 months of price change. The calculation begins with the measure of price change for a full year. There is little question in anyone's mind about how to calculate the rate of price change for a year. Taking a calendar year, for example, the rate of price change for the year is[14]

$$\frac{\text{Fourth-quarter average as of this year}}{\text{Fourth-quarter average as of last year}} - 1$$

---

[14]Even this undisputed calculation is not the best estimate of price change between January 1 and December 31 of a given year. Because the fourth-quarter average represents prices as of November 15 and the first-quarter average represents prices as of about February 15, the best estimate or price change between January 1, 1975, and December 31, 1975, is

$$\sqrt{\frac{\text{Fourth quarter 1975} \times \text{first quarter 1976}}{\text{Fourth quarter 1974} \times \text{first quarter 1975}}} - 1$$

The rate of price increase for 1974, measured by the price change between the fourth quarters of 1973 and 1974, is 11.8 percent; if we use the more exact method of this footnote, it is measured to be 11.3 percent. (These calculations are based on data in the 1975 *Economic Report of the President* for all numbers except the first quarter of 1975. Because that number is not available in the President's Economic Report, it is taken from the April 1975 *Survey of Current Business.*) This refinement probably involves more trouble than it is worth and cannot be used in practice because of the delay in getting the number for the first quarter of "next" year.

To make the following discussion concrete, suppose that the calculation of the price increase for the year shows an increase of 12 percent. Assume the price index data for years 19X0 and 19X1 as shown in Exhibit 6.9. They do not reflect price indexes for any specific year but are chosen to illustrate an annual increase of exactly 12 percent occurring uniformly through the year.

One year of price change would be

$$\frac{112.00}{100.00} - 1 = 12 \text{ percent}$$

The price change for one-half year computed from

$$\frac{\text{Fourth-quarter average}}{\text{Annual average}} - 1$$

would be $112.00/107.34 - 1 = 4.43$ percent. We know that one-half year of price change is 5.83 percent ($= 1.12^{.5} - 1$), which is more than one-third again as large. This is an enormous difference given the uses to which the estimate of one-half year's price change is put in constructing GPLA financial statements.

The preceding analysis emphasizes the importance of using the following formula for computing one-half year of price change for a calendar-year company:

$$\sqrt{\frac{\text{Fourth-quarter average this year}}{\text{Fourth-quarter average last year}}} - 1$$

Put in words, this involves taking the square root of a full year's price change and then subtracting one.[15] The formula for a "geometric mean"

---

[15]This procedure for calculating one-half year of price change is based on the assumption that it is *unit* purchases or sales that occur evenly throughout the year. If *dollar* amounts occur evenly throughout the year, then the best estimate of one-half year's price change is based on a harmonic, not a geometric, mean. Define the following notation: I_0 is the price index for the fourth-quarter average of last year, I_1 is the price index for the first-quarter average of this year, and I_2, I_3, and I_4 represent the price index for the second-, third-, and fourth-quarter averages of this year. Then if dollars flow evenly throughout the year, the dollar total to be adjusted for one-half year's price change should be adjusted by an amount equal to

$$\frac{I_4}{4} \times \left(\frac{1}{\sqrt{I_0 I_1}} + \frac{1}{\sqrt{I_1 I_2}} + \frac{1}{\sqrt{I_2 I_3}} + \frac{1}{\sqrt{I_3 I_4}} \right)$$

EXHIBIT 6.9

HYPOTHETICAL PRICE INDEX DATA TO ILLUSTRATE A YEAR OF PRICE CHANGE AT AN ANNUAL RATE OF 12 PERCENT

Designation of price index	Date	Index number
Fourth quarter, 19X0 ..	November 15, 19X0	100.00
First quarter, 19X1	February 14, 19X1	102.87
Second quarter, 19X1 ..	May 15, 19X1	105.83
Annual average, 19X1 ..	June 30, 19X1	107.34
Third quarter, 19X1 ...	August 15, 19X1	108.87
Fourth quarter, 19X1 ..	November 15, 19X1	112.00

(Footnote 15 continued)

We believe that in most cases, it is units, rather than dollars, that flow evenly throughout the year, so we prefer the geometric mean (or its arithmetic approximation) described in the text to the harmonic mean described here. Where information indicates that dollars, not units, flow evenly, then the harmonic mean better reflects reality.

When sales in units occur evenly throughout the year, but prices increase throughout the year, then the average sales dollar occurs just after midyear, although the average unit is sold at midyear. In principle, then, the total of items that are spread evenly throughout a year when prices increase uniformly throughout the year should be adjusted for less than one-half year of price change. The "error" caused by using one-half year of price change defined as we think it should be defined is small. Let g represent the change in prices during the year:

$$g = \left(\frac{\text{price index fourth quarter this year}}{\text{price index fourth quarter last year}}\right)^{.5} - 1$$

Let $r = \ln_e (1 + g)$. Then, if units flowed evenly throughout the year, the average dollar flowed at time T where

$$T = \frac{\int_0^1 te^{rt}\,dt}{\int_0^1 e^{rt}\,dt} = \frac{r(1 + g) - g}{(gr)}$$

The number T is a fraction between zero and one and measures the fraction of the year elapsed since January 1 until the average dollar flowed. Under these circumstances, the items occurring evenly throughout the year should be adjusted for the fraction $(1 - T)$ of the year's price change. If g is -10 percent per year, then $(1 - T)$ is .509; if g is 0, then $(1 - T)$ is .500; if g is 10 percent per year, then $(1 - T)$ is .491; if g is 50 percent, then $(1 - T)$ is .466. Our procedures, in effect, always use $(1 - T) = .500$ for items spread evenly throughout the year. Even when prices change by 50 percent per year, the average dollar flowed during mid-July, not at July 1, as we assume.

We thank John M. MacDonald of Coopers & Lybrand for calling this problem to our attention and helping us to devise a solution for it.

is approximately modified for companies with business year-ends different from December 31. If that formula seems too complex, the following approximation of one-half year's price change is a relatively satisfactory substitute:

$$.5 \times \left(\frac{\text{fourth quarter this year}}{\text{fourth quarter last year}} - 1\right)$$

This is an arithmetic average and is equivalent to saying that if prices went up by 12 percent during the whole year, then prices went up by 6 percent during one-half year. The arithmetic average is a slight overestimate of the rate of change for one-half year. The amount by which it overestimates, however, is less than the amount by which fourth quarter/annual average underestimates one-half year of price change in times of rising prices. As the rate of price change increases, the arithmetic average becomes a less satisfactory approximation.

Exhibit 6.10 shows the effects over 12 years of measuring one-half year of price change by each of the methods we discuss:[16]

$$(1) \quad \frac{\text{Fourth-quarter average GNP Deflator this year}}{\text{Annual average GNP deflator this year}} - 1$$

$$(2) \quad \left(\frac{\text{Fourth-quarter average GNP Deflator this year}}{\text{Fourth-quarter average GNP Deflator last year}}\right)^{.5} - 1$$

$$(3) \quad .5 \times \left(\frac{\text{Fourth-quarter average GNP Deflator this year}}{\text{Fourth-quarter average GNP Deflator last year}} - 1\right)$$

[16]The thoughtful reader of this section might conceive of using as the measure of one-half year of price change for a calendar year an amount equal to

$$\frac{\text{Fourth-quarter average this year}}{\text{Second-quarter average this year}} - 1$$

or its analogue for business years not ending December 31. Although this measure, because it does measure 6 months of price change, is superior to fourth quarter/annual average, it has the following weakness. The average price change for one-half year is much misstated if the prices did not increase at a fairly uniform rate throughout the year. Consider, to take the extreme example, a year when prices went up by 12 percent in the first half-year and were stable for the second half-year. The procedure of dividing fourth-quarter average by second-quarter average would indicate that the average price increase for a half-year is about zero. Although it is true that prices did not increase in the last half-year, price increase for the average 6-month period during the year was about 6 percent, or 5.83 percent to be more exact.

EXHIBIT 6.10

TABLE OF ADJUSTMENT PERCENTAGES UNDER THREE DIFFERENT MEASURES OF ONE-HALF YEAR OF PRICE CHANGE

(1) Fourth quarter/annual average -1
(2) (Fourth quarter this year/fourth quarter last year)$^{.5}-1$
(3) .5 × (fourth quarter this year/fourth quarter last year-1)

Year	One-half year of price change			Rate of price change for year*
	(1)	(2)	(3)	
1963	0.59%	0.75%	0.75%	1.51%
1964	0.69	0.83	0.83	1.67
1965	0.67	0.91	0.91	1.82
1966	1.19	1.64	1.66	3.32
1967	1.11	1.55	1.56	3.12
1968	1.55	2.20	2.23	4.46
1969	1.81	2.51	2.54	5.09
1970	2.09	2.85	2.89	5.78
1971	0.96	1.66	1.68	3.35
1972	1.26	1.83	1.84	3.69
1973	2.99	3.64	3.71	7.41
1974	4.45	5.73	5.90	11.80

*$\dfrac{\text{Fourth quarter average GNP Deflator this year}}{\text{Fourth quarter average GNP Deflator last year}} - 1.$

Source: *Economic Report of President,* 1975, and *Survey of Current Business,* various issues.

In times of rising prices the measurement in (1) is less than in (2), which is less than in (3). The difference between (2) and (1) is substantially greater than the difference between (3) and (2). In times of declining prices (1) shows a larger rate of price change for one-half year than (2), which in turn shows a larger rate than (3). The faster prices increase, the greater the differences between the measures.

Summary

We suggest that price change for a full year be measured from quarterly averages of the GNP Deflator published in the *Survey of Current Business* dated as of the month following the close of the business year. One-half year of price change should be measured with a geometric mean [(fourth quarter this year/fourth quarter last year)^5 − 1], rather than with the [fourth quarter this year/annual average − 1]. An adequate approximation to the preferred measure of price change for one-half a year is one-half the year's price change; that is, 6 percent when the year's price change is 12 percent. This approximation becomes less satisfactory the more rapid the rate of price change.

II

FOR FINANCIAL ANALYSTS AND OTHER READERS OF FINANCIAL STATEMENTS

Chapter Seven

INTERPRETING THE GENERAL PRICE LEVEL ADJUSTED INCOME STATEMENT[1]

PART II OF THIS BOOK is written for those who want to estimate, audit, or interpret the general price level adjusted (GPLA) financial statements. Inflation affects all items in the financial statements, but primary attention is usually focused on the way inflation affects reported income. Hence, Part II emphasizes the income statement. Much of the material in Part II is designed to aid in forecasting what GPLA income statements will look like for various companies. Analysts may wish to construct GPLA statements before audited GPLA statements are issued, either before GPLA statements are required or for interim periods after they are required for annual reports. Many aspects of accounting are more easily understood if the reader has once prepared accounting statements containing the particular aspect under consideration. And so it is with GPLA financial statements. The analyst may find it useful, when troubled by certain aspects of the GPLA statements, to refer to the appropriate sections in Part I to review the construction of GPLA statements. Auditors will find the estimating procedures in Part II to be useful in deriving numbers to serve as checks on management's GPLA statements.

This chapter introduces and illustrates the five major types of adjustments one will find in GPLA income statements. (Two minor types are also explained.) Chapter Eight explains in detail a procedure that analysts can use to construct estimated GPLA income statements for companies of particular interest to them. Chapter Nine reports and analyzes the results of applying the estimating procedure to the 30 companies in the Dow

---

[1]The material in Chapters Seven through Ten draws heavily from a series of articles by Sidney Davidson and Roman L. Weil, which appeared in the *Financial Analysts Journal* during 1975. See the bibliography for references.

Jones Industrial Index and 44 other large companies, and to the largest firms in several specific industries—steel companies, pharmaceutical companies, automobile and truck manufacturers, and public utilities. Chapter Ten discusses some of the implications of GPLA accounting and illustrates the construction and importance of the estimated GPLA funds statement. It also deals briefly with the GPLA balance sheet. Finally, Chapters Eleven and Twelve, which we have called Part III because it contains information of interest to both practicing accountants and financial analysts, describe and evaluate several ways of accounting for inflation, of which GPLA accounting is just one.

GENERAL PRICE LEVEL ADJUSTED ACCOUNTING

General price level accounting adjusts the recorded historical cost amount of each item disclosed in the conventional financial statements for changes in the general purchasing power of the dollar since the item was first recorded in the accounts. The adjustments rely on an index of the general price level and attempt to show all financial statement items in terms of the purchasing power of the dollar as of the most recent balance sheet date. The Gross National Product (GNP) Implicit Price Deflator is the index of general purchasing power used in the United States to adjust all financial statement items. General price level adjustments do not present market values of individual assets and equities. Rather, they present historical dollars adjusted to dollars of end-of-year purchasing power by the use of a general price index, not specific price indexes.

GENERAL PRICE LEVEL ADJUSTED INCOME STATEMENTS

General price level adjusted income statements differ in essentially five significant, and two, usually less significant, respects from conventional income statements. These seven differences are explained next. They are illustrated in Exhibit 7.1 for the operations of the General Electric Company (GE) for 1974 and in Exhibit 7.2 for the operations of the General Electric Credit Corporation, a wholly owned nonconsolidated subsidiary of GE.

(1) Revenues and Expenses Occurring Fairly Evenly Throughout the Year

Sales and most other revenues, as well as most expenses except cost of goods sold and depreciation, represent services rendered (revenues) and costs expired (expenses) which usually occur fairly evenly throughout the year. To restate these items in terms of dollars of end-of-year general purchasing power, they are adjusted for one-half of the year's general price change. For example, if a $1 sale is made at mid-month each month during the year, then the average sale took place on July 1. To adjust an item stated in July 1 dollars to dollars of December 31 purchasing power requires that the item be adjusted for one-half year of price change. Because the price increase in 1974, as measured by the GNP Deflator, was about 11.8 percent, the price change for half a year was about 5.7 percent.[2] Revenues (except those described in Adjustment 5, below) as well as expenses (except cost of goods sold and depreciation) are increased by 5.7 percent in the adjustment process. Refer to Exhibit 7.1. All items in the income statements are marked with a number keyed to the adjustments described here. Note that "Revenues and other income" and "All other" expenses and deductions are designated adjustment "(1)."

(2) Cost of Goods Sold

With rising prices, cost of goods sold on a price level adjusted basis will be higher than that reported in conventional financial statements. How much higher depends in large part on the cost flow assumption—FIFO, LIFO, or weighted average—used. During periods of rising prices and increasing inventory quantities, the inflation adjustment will be largest for firms using a FIFO flow assumption. The procedures for estimating the cost of goods sold adjustment are described in Chapter Eight. Usually, LIFO companies will have adjusted cost of goods sold that is larger than conventional cost of goods sold by a percentage slightly smaller than one-half year of price change. FIFO companies generally will have adjusted cost of goods sold larger than conventional cost of goods sold by a percentage significantly larger than one-half year of price change but less than a full year of price change.

GE uses a LIFO flow assumption for about 80 percent of its inventory and a FIFO flow assumption for about 20 percent. Our analysis, discussed in Chapter Eight, indicates that this results in an average increase of a little over 6 percent in cost of goods sold in the adjusted income statement. Refer to Exhibit 7.1, Adjustment (2).

[2]The correct method of finding an average of a series of price changes is to use the geometric mean (in this case, $\sqrt{1.118} - 1$, which is about 5.7 percent), rather than an arithmetic mean (in this case, $11.8/2 = 5.9$ percent). Chapters Six and Nine discuss this issue at greater length. Throughout this chapter, items that require adjustment for one-half year of 1974's price change are adjusted by 5.7 percent. Chapter Six also discusses the implications for the adjustment process when dollars, rather than units, are spread evenly throughout the year.

(3) Depreciation

General price level adjusted depreciation is almost always much larger than depreciation as conventionally reported. For most firms, depreciable assets typically are acquired many years before the period being reported on and general price levels have increased substantially since acquisition. The depreciation adjustment reflects a portion (equal to the depreciation rate) of the cumulative change in general prices since the depreciable assets were acquired. [For example, if the depreciation rate for an asset is 10 percent and price levels have increased by 60 percent since that asset

EXHIBIT 7.1

GENERAL ELECTRIC COMPANY

Income Statement for 1974

(Dollar Amounts Shown in Millions)

Adjustment numbers[a]		Historical dollars (shown in annual report)	In 12/31/74 dollars (as estimated)	Percentage change
	Revenues			
(1)	Sales and other income ...	$13,556	$14,334	+5.7%
(5)	Equity method revenue (loss)	43	(24)	−155.8
(6)	Gain on net foreign monetary items	—	1	—
	Total	$13,599	$14,311	+5.2
	Expenses and Deductions			
(2)	Cost of goods sold[b]	$ 9,761	$10,357	+6.1
(3)	Depreciation[c]	376	545	+44.9
(1)	All other expenses	2,853	3,017	+5.7
	Total	$12,990	$13,919	+7.1
	Income before gain on monetary items	$ 608	$ 392	−36.0
(4)	Gain on monetary items[d] ..	—	177	—
	Net income	$ 608	$ 569	−6.4

Footnotes to Exhibit 7.1 appear on pg. 107.

was acquired, then the depreciation adjustment will be 6 percent (= .10 × .60) of the asset's acquisition cost.] Our analysis in Chapter Eight indicates that GE's depreciable assets as of December 31, 1974, were acquired, on average, a little over 6 years before that date. The cumulative increase in general prices over that time has been about 45 percent. The depreciation expense is correspondingly increased for the GPLA income statement.

Of all the adjustments for the GPLA income statement, the one for depreciation is likely to require the most additional analysis if an approximation of current replacement costs is sought. Depreciation charges restated on the GPLA income statement are likely to be the item that departs most significantly from current replacement valuation. Prices of a given firm's specialized depreciable assets can increase substantially more or substantially less rapidly than general prices increase. (For example, the price index for producers' durable goods increased by about 19 percent during the 5 years, 1970–1974, while the GNP Deflator increased by about 26 percent.) Moreover, the percentage increase in the depreciation charge is usually the largest on the GPLA income statement. (The dollar

---

[a] Keyed to description in Chapter Seven.

[b] Ending inventories are 80 percent LIFO, 20 percent FIFO.

[c] Sum-of-the-years'-digit method. Average life of depreciable assets is estimated to be 6.3 years; price index increased by 44.9 percent during the 6.3 years preceding December 31, 1974.

[d] The net monetary liabilities for GE are computed as follows:

	($ in Millions)	
	12/31/74	12/31/73
Monetary Liabilities		
Current liabilities and long-term (domestic) borrowing	$5,068.3	$4,401.3
Monetary Assets		
Cash, receivables (both long- and short-term), customer financing, recoverable costs, government securities, and advances to affiliates	3,430.5	3,031.7
Net Monetary Liabilities	$1,637.8	$1,369.6

The average of net domestic monetary liabilities for the year 1974 was $1,503.7 [= .5 × ($1,637.8 + $1,369.6)] million. The price change for the year was 11.8 percent. GE's gain from being a net debtor during 1974 when prices increased by 11.8 percent was, then, about .118 × $1,503.7 = $177 million. ($117.4 million of this gain is attributable to net *current* liabilities and the rest, $59.6 million, is attributable to net *long-term* monetary items. This information is required for the GPLA funds statement; see Exhibit 10.2.) Foreign debt is treated separately in adjustment (6).

amounts of increase are, however, usually less than that for revenues and cost of goods sold.) The analyst therefore will want to interpret the GPLA depreciation expense with caution.

(4) Gain or Loss on Net Monetary Items

The GPLA income statement explicitly shows the gain for the period in purchasing power captured by a debtor (or the loss suffered by a creditor) during a period of rising price levels. Because most industrial companies are typically net debtors, they will usually show purchasing-power gains from this debt. (The liabilities will be paid off, or discharged, with dollars of smaller general purchasing power than were originally borrowed. The difference between the purchasing power borrowed and that repaid is the gain on a monetary liability during the term of the loan.) During 1974, GE was a net borrower and experienced a purchasing-power gain of about $177 million. The gain from being in a net monetary liability position, although real in an economic sense, does not produce a current flow of cash.

The gain or loss from holding monetary items is in many ways the most meaningful of the general price level adjustments. The interest expense reported in the conventional income statement is the actual cost of borrowing. It depends on the interest rate negotiated at the time of the loan. That interest rate, in turn, depends in part on the lender's and borrower's anticipations about the rate of inflation during the term of the loan. (Interest rates are increased when the lender expects inflation during the term of the loan to erode the purchasing power of the principal. The borrower accepts the higher rate because he or she expects to repay with "cheaper" dollars.) Thus the borrower's conventional income statement shows an interest expense that reflects the inflation expected by both the borrower and the lender. The gain from being in a net monetary liability position in a time of rising prices is, in a real sense, an offset to reported interest expense. It reflects a gain from being a debtor during a period of inflation that both parties to the loan expected. After the fact, who benefited from inflation, the borrower or the lender, depends on whether the actual rate of price increase during the term of the loan differed from the rate anticipated by both parties to the loan at the time it was made. If the actual rate of price increase turns out to be less than the anticipated rate, then the lender benefits. If the actual rate turns out to be greater than the anticipated rate, then the borrower benefits.

(5) Revenue Recognized Under the Equity Method

Most published financial statements are consolidated statements, which report information about a group of affiliated companies essentially as if the group were one company. Many companies, however, have *un*consolidated subsidiaries. On its income statement, conventional or GPLA, the parent shows its proportional share of the income, conventional or GPLA, of the unconsolidated subsidiary. The subsidiary prepares GPLA income statements using the same kinds of adjustments as are described here.

Consolidation Policy. Whether or not a parent company consolidates a given majority-owned subsidiary depends upon the consolidation policy of the parent.[3] If the asset and equity structure of the subsidiary is significantly different from that of the parent, then the subsidiary's financial statements are frequently not consolidated with those of the parent. Instead, the parent uses the equity method of accounting for its investment. The equity method of accounting for a subsidiary has exactly the same effect on the parent's net income as if the subsidiary were consolidated: the parent shows as income its proportional share of the subsidiary's periodic income. The amount of net income is unaffected by the decision to consolidate. Amounts for individual balance sheet accounts, however, differ significantly depending on whether the subsidiary is consolidated or whether the equity method is used. The subsidiary's monetary items do not appear in consolidated balance sheets when the equity method is used. The monetary gains on these items may have a significant effect on the parent's GPLA net income.

General Electric Credit Corporation. GE owns 100 percent of the stock of GE Credit Corporation. GE does not consolidate the Credit Corporation because the assets, equities, and operations of the Credit Corporation are significantly different from those of the other companies in the GE consolidated statements. Most (about 95 percent) of the Credit Corporation's assets are receivables and most (about 90 percent) of its financing is debt. Thus the net monetary item position of the Credit Corporation is different from that of GE. The Credit Corporation has a significant excess of monetary assets over monetary liabilities and thus experiences purchasing power losses during inflation. GE, the parent company, has purchasing power gains because it is a net debtor.

GE's 1974 conventional income statement shows as revenues its 100-percent share of the Credit Company's conventional income of $42.7 million. If this equity in earnings is merely adjusted along with other revenues, as in (1), for one-half year of price change, then the GPLA equity method revenues would be about $45 million. If, however, the financial statements of the Credit Corporation are subjected to the adjustments (1)–(4) above, as shown in Exhibit 7.2, its GPLA income statement

---

[3] If 20 percent or more, but not greater than 50 percent, of the investee company is owned, the equity method must be used; consolidation is not permitted.

EXHIBIT 7.2

GENERAL ELECTRIC CREDIT CORPORATION

Income Statement for 1974

(Dollar Amounts Shown in Millions)

Adjustment numbers[a]		Historical dollars (shown in annual report)	In 12/31/74 dollars (as estimated)	Percentage change
(1)	Earned income	$561.3	$593.3	+5.7%
	Expenses[b]			
(3)	Depreciation[c]	$ 2.2	$ 2.9	+32.2
(1)	All other expenses	516.4	545.8	+5.7
	Total	$518.6	$548.7	+5.8
	Income before loss on monetary items	$ 42.7	$ 44.6	+4.4
(4)	(Loss) on net monetary items	—	(68.5)	—
	Net income (loss)	$ 42.7	$(23.9)	−156.0
(7)	Less preferred stock dividends	(6.8)	(7.2)	+5.7
(7)	Gain on preferred stock items	—	10.6	—
	Income (loss) to common stock	$ 35.9	$(20.5)	−157.0

[a] Keyed to description in Chapter Seven.

[b] As a finance company, GE Credit has no "cost of goods sold."

[c] Straight-line. Average life of depreciable assets is estimated to be 4.5 years; price index increased by 32.2 percent during the 4.5 years preceding December 31, 1974.

shows a *loss* of about $24 million before preferred stock items. This difference between the $45 million net income using the one-half year adjustment and the $24 million loss from applying the GPLA procedure to the individual assets and equities of the unconsolidated subsidiary is, then, about $69 million—more than 10 percent of the parent's conventionally reported net income.

The adjustments for preferred stock items are explained in (7), below. Because GE owns all of both the common and preferred stock of GE Credit, the general price level adjustments for preferred stock on the GE

Credit's GPLA income statement are exactly offset by corresponding adjustments on GE's GPLA income statement. For simplicity, then, we ignore the preferred stock in carrying over the historical and GPLA net income from the Credit Company (Exhibit 7.2) to GE (Exhibit 7.1). (GE's statements do not differentiate between the common and preferred stock investment in the Credit Corporation nor between common and preferred dividends received.)

When a parent company, such as GE, owns subsidiaries with a net monetary item position that is significant, whether a net creditor position, such as for GE Credit, or a net debtor position, such as for some of the unconsolidated subsidiaries of Alcoa (see Exhibit 9.1), then the subsidiary's financial statements should first be subjected to the GPLA analysis and the results "plugged into" the GPLA analysis for the parent. Thus Exhibit 7.2 shows adjustments (1)–(4) for GE Credit. The net income as conventionally reported and as adjusted are shown as Adjustment (5) in Exhibit 7.1 for the parent.

The five adjustments to conventional income statements just described will usually give an adequate picture of what GPLA adjusted income statements will look like. (Exhibit 8.7 shows the accuracy of these estimated adjustments for several companies.) Two other adjustments can be used to refine the estimated GPLA income still further.

(6) Gain or Loss on Foreign Net Monetary Items

A company may have monetary assets and liabilities denominated in foreign currencies. For the purposes of computing gain or loss on monetary items, Adjustment (4), foreign currency amounts are considered to be nonmonetary. The FASB requires that foreign monetary items be shown in the GPLA adjusted balance sheet in the same way that inventory and plant are shown. That is, the historical dollar amount of the item (as translated from local currency into dollars in accord with generally accepted accounting principles) reported in the conventional balance sheet must be adjusted for the change in general prices since the item was recorded in the accounts. However, the FASB requires that any GPLA adjusted liability that can actually be discharged in dollars for a smaller amount than is derived from the adjustment procedure should be written down to that amount. That is, a form of "lower-of-cost-or-market" treatment is used.

To take an example, suppose that a U.S. firm has borrowed francs and, because the exchange rate between francs and dollars has not changed during the year, that the loan could be repaid for $100 at both January 1 and December 31. That is, if $100 were converted into francs at the beginning or at the end of the year, then the loan could be fully paid off.

Then the GPLA balance sheet at January 1 would show a liability for $100 of January 1 purchasing power. The GPLA balance sheet at December 31 would show a liability for $100 of December 31 purchasing power. Assume 10 percent inflation in dollars during the year and observe what the *comparative* balance sheets issued at December 31 would look like:

	Dollars of December 31 Purchasing Power	
	January 1, 19XX	December 31, 19XX
Liability in francs ..	$110	$100

That is, in terms of December 31 purchasing power, the liability as of January 1 was for $110. During the year, the purchasing power borrowed, as measured in December 31 dollars, declined by $10. The GPLA amount of the liability would be "written down" to, and shown as, $100. The amount of the write-down, $10, is conceptually analogous to a monetary gain, but will not be classified as a monetary gain according to the FASB Exposure Draft. The gain will be included in GPLA "operating" revenues, perhaps with the other items of foreign exchange gain or loss. The effect of this accounting "write-down," which is explained in Chapter Six, is to treat foreign debt much like U.S. debt whenever exchange rates between currencies do not change radically over time.[4]

The amount of "gain" on foreign debt calculated in the example above is exactly the same as if the item were treated as monetary. Only its classification on the GPLA income statement changes. But the equality between the amounts of gain results from our assuming that exchange rates between the franc and the dollar did not change during the year. More likely, the exchange rate would change so that as of December 31, some amount other than $100 would be required to pay off the loan. Suppose that the loan could be paid off on December 31 with $102 (or $97). Then the comparative balance sheets stated in December 31 dollars would still show an opening balance for the loan of $110, but a December 31 balance of $102 (or $97). The "gain" on foreign debt would then total $110 − $102 = $8 (or $110 − $97 = $13). This amount consists of a gain of $10 on the debt minus (or plus) a foreign exchange loss (or gain) of $2 (or $3). In our estimates of GPLA income, we show as "gain" on foreign

<hr>

[4]In theory, exchange rates should change in direct proportion to the difference in rates of inflation in two countries. Empirical research tends to show that this hypothesized relation between exchange rates and rates of inflation is not always valid, particularly for developing countries. See Robert Z. Aliber and Clyde P. Stickney, "Accounting Measures of Foreign Exchange Exposure: The Long and Short of It," *The Accounting Review,* January 1975, pp. 44–57.

debt, the amount ($10 in the example) that results if exchange rates have not changed. This is proper even when exchange rates have changed, because that part of the gain or loss caused by the change in exchange rates is included in the historical income statement as other expense or as foreign exchange gain or loss, if it is separately disclosed.

For many companies, the splitting out of purchasing-power gain or loss on foreign items from Adjustment (4) and showing it as a separate item, (6), in GPLA operating income leads to an insignificant difference. GE is such a company; its gain on foreign debt is $1 million, whereas its gain on domestic debt is $177 million. The next several chapters show GPLA income statement results for over 100 companies. For some of these companies, the splitting out of gain on foreign debt and including the amount in GPLA operating income has a significant effect. For example, Abbott Laboratories had a gain on foreign debt during 1974 equal to 25 percent of estimated GPLA operating income before the gain on foreign debt. General Motor's gain on foreign debt of about $80 million during 1974 caused the estimated GPLA operating *loss* to be $240 million rather than a loss of about $320 million. Coca-Cola Company's gain on foreign debt during 1974 was about 5 percent of estimated GPLA operating income, but it was sufficient to give Coca-Cola a larger GPLA operating income than conventionally reported operating income. This helped to make Coca-Cola a rare exception; almost all other companies show GPLA operating income (that is, GPLA income before gain or loss on monetary items) that is smaller than conventionally reported net income.

(7) Purchasing Power Gains and Losses on Preferred Stock Items

Net income to common stock is the starting point in computing earnings per common share. Net income to common conventionally reported is net income less preferred stock dividends. In computing GPLA earnings per common share, preferred stock dividends are adjusted, assuming that they are declared evenly throughout the year, for one-half year of price change, as in Adjustment (1). The balance sheet amount of preferred stock is adjusted for general price level changes since the stock was recorded in the accounts. During periods of inflation, the GPLA amount of preferred stock will be increased much the same as inventory or plant is increased. When, however, the GPLA balance sheet amount of preferred stock is larger than the stated redemption value of that stock, as it usually is, then the amount is written down to stated redemption value. That is, if the GPLA amount of the preferred stock is larger than the redemption value of the preferred stock, then the GPLA balance sheet presents the preferred stock amount at redemption value. The amount of the preferred stock shown at redemption value is then treated in the accounts as a monetary item because its amount does not change when prices increase. The purchasing-power gain on this monetary item does not, however, affect net income. It is merely a redistribution among equity holders and does affect net income to common and, hence, earnings per common share.

GE Credit Corporation has preferred stock outstanding as well as common stock. Exhibit 7.2, for GE Credit, shows the effect of this adjustment for preferred stock. The preferred dividends, which are subtracted from net income, are adjusted for one-half year of price change and a gain on preferred stock is added to determine net income to common. General Electric owns 100 percent of all the GE Credit Company stock, common and preferred, so this added refinement does not change the GPLA income of GE. As mentioned earlier, we ignore the preferred stock adjustment in carrying results from Exhibit 7.2 to Exhibit 7.1. The preferred stock items are shown in Exhibit 7.2 so that we can illustrate all seven adjustments. GE Credit's monetary gain on "debt" in the form of preferred stock would just offset GE's monetary loss on the monetary asset, preferred stock. (Symmetry suggests that if GE Credit records a gain on preferred stock issued, then GE should record a loss on the preferred stock held.) For many companies, particularly some of the public utilities reported on in Chapter Nine, the gain on preferred stock items makes the comparison between GPLA and conventional earnings per common share much different from the comparison between GPLA and conventional net income.

SUMMARY

GPLA income statements differ in seven respects from conventional income statements. The one-half year adjustment for most revenues as well as most expenses except cost of goods sold and depreciation results in large dollar amounts of changes in these items. The adjustment for cost of goods sold tends to be a large absolute amount of dollars. This adjustment is meaningful to the degree that costs of inventory increase in proportion to general prices. Small differences in rates of price change make large dollar amounts of difference in GPLA net income because cost of goods sold is typically the major expense of an industrial company. The analyst wants to be wary of the GPLA cost of goods sold whenever there is evidence that inventory costs for a particular company change at rates much different from general price level changes. GPLA depreciation is usually much larger than conventional depreciation, at least on a percentage basis. This increased depreciation amount does not reflect increases in costs relevant to the firm unless its depreciable assets increase in price as general prices increase. Gain on net monetary items is usually large for industrial companies, which are net debtors, and reflects a real gain in purchasing power. Financial companies tend to be net lenders and experience purchasing-power losses during inflation. Thus statements for unconsolidated subsidiaries that are accounted for on the equity method should be separately adjusted for general price level changes. For some firms, foreign items and preferred stock lead to purchasing-power gains or losses that ought to be separately analyzed.

Chapter Eight

ESTIMATING GENERAL PRICE LEVEL ADJUSTED INCOME STATEMENTS

C HAPTER SEVEN EXPLAINS seven kinds of adjustments that make general price level adjusted income statements different from conventional ones. Analysts and auditors can prepare their own estimates of GPLA income statements. This chapter explains how and illustrates the procedures using the financial statements of the General Electric Company and the General Electric Credit Corporation. The final section of this chapter gives some indication of the accuracy of the estimating procedures. Chapter Nine illustrates the results of estimating GPLA income statements for a large sample of companies. Chapter Ten explains how to estimate the GPLA balance sheet and statement of changes in financial position from the conventional statements.

THE ESTIMATING PROCEDURE

This first section describes the procedure used in estimating the general price level adjustments described in the previous chapter. To use the estimating procedure for a particular company requires a copy of the financial statements, including the footnotes, as published in the company's annual report. An analyst who has separate financial statements for several prior years and for any unconsolidated subsidiaries may be able to refine the calculations somewhat, as is made clear below.

Price Index and Computing Rates of Changes in Prices over Time

To compute general price level adjusted income, you must have data for the GNP Deflator for each of the five quarters preceding the balance sheet date plus quarterly or annual data for certain earlier periods. The simplest thing to do is to get a table of the GNP Deflator by quarters for the past 10 or 15 years. (An abbreviated table is shown in a later section.

Official figures are published monthly in the *Survey of Current Business* by the U.S. Department of Commerce.)

Assume, for the purpose of exposition, that you are analyzing a company whose reporting year ends on December 31, 1975. Assume that the GNP Deflator for the fourth quarter of 1975 is 191 and the GNP Deflator for the fourth quarter of 1974 is 177.[1] Then the rate of price change for the year 1975 is computed as

$$\frac{191}{177} - 1 = 1.08 - 1 = 8 \text{ percent}$$

In the instructions that follow there are statements such as "adjust (a given financial statement item) for one-half year (or some other fraction of a year)." For example, most revenues for the year are to be adjusted for one-half year of price change. The procedure would be to adjust these revenues for 4 percent (equal to one-half of 8 percent).[2]

In general, if you are required to adjust prices for a fraction of a year, say 62 percent, then the rate of price change for that fraction of a year is, in our example, 4.96 percent (= 62 percent of 8 percent).[3]

(1) Adjusting Most Revenues and Some Expenses[4]

Revenues and other income are, for the most part, spread fairly evenly throughout the year. Therefore, adjusting the historically reported

[1]These numbers only approximate the actual GNP Deflator for those two quarters.

[2]A more accurate computation is to use

$$\sqrt{1.08} - 1 = (1.08)^{1/2} - 1 = 1.0392 - 1 = 3.92 \text{ percent}$$

as the average of price change for a half-year when prices went up by 8 percent for the whole year. This more exact computation, and the analogous ones for other fractions of a year, can be done if you have a computer or a calculator that raises numbers to fractional powers. We sometimes use the simpler, but less exact, procedure explained in the text (one-half year of price change is 4 percent) for hand calculations, but our computer program and all illustrations in Chapters Seven through Ten use the more accurate method described in this footnote and the next.

The FASB Exposure Draft on GPLA accounting recommends a different procedure, explained in Chapter Six. It is so clearly inferior to both the methods described here that we do not use it. This issue, including some discussion of whether it is dollars or units that are spread evenly throughout the year, is described at greater length in Chapter Six.

[3]The more accurate computation, analogous to the one described in the preceding footnote, is to use

$$(1.08)^{.62} - 1 = 4.89 \text{ percent}$$

as the rate of change in prices for 62 percent of a year during which prices increased by 8 percent.

[4]The adjustment numbers used in section headings correspond to those used in the preceding chapter's descriptions and exhibits.

amounts for one-half year of price change is usually satisfactory. If the annual report or other information indicates that a significant amount of revenue or other income occurred other than evenly throughout the year, then you may want to adjust that portion of revenues separately, for a different fraction of the year. Income derived from unconsolidated subsidiaries is adjusted separately; see Adjustment (5).

All expenses except cost of goods sold and depreciation (and other amortization) are assumed to be spread fairly evenly throughout the year and are adjusted for one-half year of price change.

(2) Adjusting Cost of Goods Sold

The adjustment to be used for cost of goods sold depends on whether the company uses a first-in, first-out (FIFO), last-in, first-out (LIFO), or weighted-average cost flow assumption. Some companies use both FIFO and LIFO—one for a part of inventories and the other for the remainder. For those companies we separate FIFO from LIFO cost of goods sold and sum the results of two separate adjustments. (GE's adjustments, discussed later, involve this complication.) Companies that do not report a specific cost flow assumption, but report that they use the "lower-of-cost-or-market inventory valuation" basis are assumed to use FIFO, unless the notes give contrary information.

The adjustment for cost of goods sold requires data from the income statement on cost of goods sold and data on beginning and ending inventories from the balance sheet. If the income statement does not disclose the cost of goods sold, then the notes to the financial statements must show cost of goods sold as reported to the SEC. (GE's annual report, for example, discloses cost of goods sold in the notes to the income statement.) Understanding the GPLA inventory adjustment may be easier if the reader uses Figures 8.1 and 8.2 in following the descriptions.

FIFO Adjustment. Under FIFO, cost of goods sold consists of the beginning inventory plus as much of the earliest purchases for the year as is necessary to equal cost of goods sold. The beginning inventory is adjusted for slightly more than one year's price change. The purchases that enter cost of goods sold are, on average, adjusted for somewhat more than one-half year's price change.

We assume that purchases occur fairly evenly throughout the year. Purchases for the year can be computed from the relation

> Purchases = ending inventory + cost of goods sold − beginning
> inventory

The average purchase which entered cost of goods sold was made

$$\frac{1}{2} \times \frac{\text{cost of goods sold} - \text{beginning inventory}}{\text{purchases}} \times 12$$

months after January 1. Purchases in FIFO cost of goods sold are adjusted for the price change during a fraction of this year labeled t_1 in Figure 8.1.

The beginning FIFO inventory is adjusted for this year's entire price change plus a fraction of last year's price change which we label t_2 in Figure 8.1. This fraction is

t_2 = fraction of last year's price change for adjusting beginning inventory

$$= .5 \times \left[1 - \frac{\begin{array}{c}\text{cost of goods} \quad \text{beginning inventory} \\ \text{sold last year} - \text{this year (= ending} \\ \text{inventory last year)}\end{array}}{\text{purchases last year}} \right]$$

General price level adjusted cost of goods sold for FIFO companies is, then,

Beginning inventory adjusted for a full year + the fraction of last year's price change equal to

$$\frac{1}{2} \times \frac{\text{cost of goods sold last year} - \text{beginning inventory this year}}{\text{purchases last year}}$$

$$+$$

(cost of goods sold − beginning inventory) adjusted for the fraction of a year equal to

$$1 - \left[\frac{\text{cost of goods} - \text{beginning inventory}}{\text{purchases}} \times \frac{1}{2} \right]$$

In practice, we adjust beginning inventory for price change occurring during one year plus

$$\frac{1}{2} \times \frac{\text{cost of goods sold this year} - \text{beginning inventory this year}}{\text{purchases this year}}$$

See Figure 8.1 for a graphical illustration of the price level adjustment procedure for cost of goods sold based on a FIFO cost flow assumption. The fraction of this year's price change used to adjust purchases that entered cost of goods sold is labeled t_1 in Figure 8.1. The fraction of last year's price change used to adjust beginning inventory (in addition to all of this year's price change) is labeled t_2 in Figure 8.1.

LIFO Adjustment (Inventory Increase—Normal Case). The adjustment for LIFO cost of goods sold in estimating general price level income depends on whether inventory increased or decreased during the

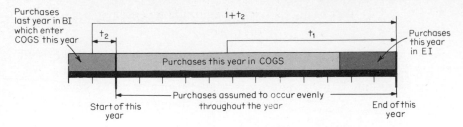

t_1 = fraction of year's price change used for adjusting purchases during the year that entered cost of goods sold

$$= 1 - \left(.5 \times \frac{\text{COGS} - \text{BI}}{\text{purchases}}\right)$$

t_2 = fraction of last year's price change used for adjusting beginning inventory (in addition to a full year of price change)

$$= .5 \times \left(1 - \frac{\text{COGS} - \text{BI}}{\text{purchases}}\right)$$

FIGURE 8.1. Illustration of fraction of year's price change used in price level adjustments of cost of goods sold assuming FIFO cost flow.

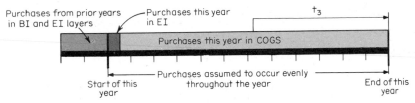

t_3 = fraction of year used for adjusting purchases during year which entered cost of goods sold

$$= .5 \times \frac{\text{COGS}}{\text{purchases}}$$

FIGURE 8.2. Illustration of fraction of year's price change used in price level adjustments of cost of goods sold assuming LIFO cost flow.

year. For most companies, most of the time, inventory amounts increase. The items that enter cost of goods sold under normal conditions are, then, the later purchases during the year. See Figure 8.2. When inventories are not declining, the average dollar of cost of goods sold was acquired

$$\frac{1}{2} \times \frac{\text{cost of goods sold}}{\text{purchases}} \times 12$$

months before the end of the year. Thus LIFO adjusted cost of goods sold is computed as cost of goods sold adjusted for a fraction of the year equal to

$$t_3 = \frac{1}{2} \times \frac{\text{cost of goods sold}}{\text{purchases}}$$

$$= \frac{1}{2} \times \frac{\text{cost of goods sold}}{\text{cost of goods sold} + \text{ending inventory} - \text{beginning inventory}}$$

LIFO Adjustment (Inventory Decrease). When inventory amounts decline during a year, part of cost of goods sold comes from beginning inventory. Under LIFO, the beginning inventory for a year reported on comparative balance sheets will usually be several years old as of the current balance sheet date. In our procedures we adjust the "dip into old LIFO layers" for 2 years, but information in a given annual report may indicate that even more adjustment is necessary. The dip into old LIFO layers is equal to

Beginning inventory − ending inventory

and this amount of cost of goods sold is adjusted for 2 years of price change, at a minimum.[5] The rest of cost of goods sold (cost of goods sold − beginning inventory + ending inventory) is adjusted for one-half year of price change.

Weighted-Average Adjustment. Under a weighted-average cost flow assumption, a firm assumes it uses equal portions of all goods available for sale. The total of goods available for sale is beginning inventory plus all purchases, which is also equal to cost of goods sold plus ending inventory. Purchases are assumed to be spread evenly throughout the year.

At the end of any year, the units in a weighted-average ending inventory are typically at least one-half year old. The exact age depends on the rate of growth in purchases and the inventory turnover. If purchases have been growing at the rate g per year, and s is the fraction of purchases remaining in ending inventory, defined as

$$1 - \frac{\text{cost of goods sold}}{\text{purchases}}$$

[5]The dip into old LIFO layers can be exactly dated (and correspondingly adjusted) if the analyst or auditor has annual reports for the last several years. For example, suppose that the dip into LIFO layers is 10 and the annual reports disclose the following year-end inventory amounts (starting with this year and going backward through time): 90, 100, 95, 91, 88. We can see that the dip of 10 into LIFO layers consists of 5 purchased almost 2 years ago, 4 purchased almost 3 years ago, and 1 purchased almost 4 years ago.

then the average dollar in a weighted-average ending inventory is approximately t_w years old, where[6]

$$t_w = \frac{1 + g + s}{2(1 + g - s)}$$

Under most normal circumstances, the average dollar in a weighted-average ending inventory is about three-quarters of a year old ($t_w = .75$). Exhibit 6.1 displays values of t_w for various combinations of growth rates g and fractions of purchases remaining in ending inventory, s.

Since goods available for sale are

Beginning inventory + purchases

the goods available for sale during a year expressed in end-of-year dollars are

Beginning inventory adjusted for (one year plus t_w years)
plus
Purchases adjusted for one-half year

The fraction

$$\frac{\text{Cost of goods sold}}{\text{Cost of goods available for sale}}$$

of all goods available for sale were actually sold. Thus the weighted-average cost of goods sold restated in December 31 dollars is

$$\frac{\text{Cost of goods sold}}{\text{Cost of goods available for sale}} \times \begin{array}{l}\text{goods available} \\ \text{for sale stated} \\ \text{in end-of-year} \\ \text{dollars}\end{array}$$

and can be computed as

$$\frac{\text{Cost of goods sold}}{\text{Cost of goods sold + ending inventory}} \times \left[\begin{array}{ll}\text{beginning} & \text{cost of goods sold} \\ \text{inventory} & \text{plus ending} \\ \text{adjusted} & + \text{inventory minus} \\ \text{for (one} & \text{beginning inventory} \\ \text{year +} & \text{all adjusted for} \\ t_w \text{ years)} & \text{one-half year}\end{array}\right]$$

---

[6]We omit the details of the derivation of this formula. It is based on the following relations. Let P_n represent purchases in year n, let EI_n represent ending inventory as of year n. Then,

$$EI_n = sP_n + sEI_{n-1}$$

and

$$P_n = (1 + g)P_{n-1}$$

When Both FIFO and LIFO Are Used. Many companies use FIFO for part of their inventories and LIFO for the rest. Typically the footnotes disclose the percentages, or numbers sufficient to calculate them, of ending inventory valued separately with LIFO and FIFO flow assumptions. Furthermore, for those inventories valued with LIFO the notes disclose (by SEC requirement) the amount, if it is material, by which ending inventory amounts would be increased if FIFO, or current costs, were used for these inventories. From this information, we can estimate the portion of cost of goods sold based on FIFO and the portion based on LIFO. We can use the inventory equation

Beginning inventory + purchases − ending inventory = cost of goods sold

to find any one of the four quantities if the other three are known. We use the percentage disclosed in the footnotes to find the portions of beginning and ending inventories valued at LIFO or FIFO. To find cost of LIFO (or FIFO) goods sold then requires that we know the purchases of the LIFO (or FIFO) goods. We estimate proportions of total purchases with the following equations:

$$\text{FIFO fraction of total purchases} = \frac{\begin{array}{l}\text{fraction of ending} \\ \text{inventories valued} \times \text{ending inventory} \\ \text{at FIFO}\end{array}}{\text{ending} \quad \text{inventory} + \begin{array}{l}\text{excess of FIFO valuation} \\ \text{over book value of LIFO} \\ \text{ending inventory}\end{array}}$$

$$\text{LIFO fraction of total purchases} = \frac{\left(\begin{array}{l}\text{fraction of ending} \\ \text{inventories valued} \times \begin{array}{l}\text{ending} \\ \text{inventory}\end{array} \\ \text{at LIFO}\end{array}\right) + \begin{array}{l}\text{excess of FIFO valuation} \\ \text{over book value of} \\ \text{LIFO ending inventory}\end{array}}{\text{ending} \quad \text{inventory} + \begin{array}{l}\text{excess of FIFO} \\ \text{valuation over book} \\ \text{value of LIFO ending} \\ \text{inventory}\end{array}}$$

In using these fractions, we assume that the portion of total purchases allocated to LIFO goods is the same as the proportion that LIFO goods would be of total inventories if all inventories were valued with FIFO. (This assumption is accurate to the degree that turnover rates for the two kinds of inventories are alike.)

We multiply the FIFO fraction of purchases by total purchases to get an assumed amount of purchases for FIFO goods. That amount plus the amount of FIFO ending inventories less the amount of FIFO beginning inventories is the assumed cost of FIFO goods sold. We apply the FIFO adjustment, described earlier, for the cost of FIFO goods sold using in the calculation only the FIFO portions of beginning and ending inventories.

The remainder of cost of goods sold, beginning inventory, and ending inventory is assumed to be valued at LIFO and we apply the LIFO adjustment, described above. The total adjusted cost of goods sold is the sum of the two separate adjustments.

(3) Adjusting Depreciation

To compute price level adjusted depreciation, ascertain the depreciation charges for the year and the accumulated depreciation as of the end of the year. Often, as for example in the annual reports of American Brands (1974) and Dow Chemical (1974), the amount of depreciation is not shown separately in the income statement, but is included in the cost of goods sold. In that case, the amount of depreciation charges can be estimated with reasonable accuracy from the amount of depreciation shown in the statement of changes in financial position.[7] [If depreciation is included in cost of goods sold, or not otherwise explicitly shown on the income statement, then subtract the depreciation from cost of goods sold before adjusting cost of goods sold with the method described in (2).] The amount of accumulated depreciation is shown either directly on the balance sheet or in notes.

If a company uses straight-line depreciation, then the average age of its depreciable assets in years is computed from[8]

$$
\begin{aligned}
\text{Average age of depreciable assets in years} &= \text{average life of depreciable assets} \times \text{fraction of life that has expired} \\
&= \frac{\text{total cost of depreciable assets}}{\text{depreciation charges for year}} \times \frac{\text{accumulated depreciation}}{\text{total cost of depreciable assets}} \\
&= \frac{\text{accumulated depreciation}}{\text{depreciation charges for year}}
\end{aligned}
$$

[7]Some of these depreciation charges are product costs, which will be included in ending inventory under a FIFO cost flow assumption. The needed refinements to correct for this are more trouble than they are worth in terms of effects on the amount of GPLA depreciation.

[8]To see how this computation works, consider an asset costing $10,000 on which accumulated depreciation is $3,000 at year end and for which annual straight-line depreciation charges are $1,000. We know that the asset has a 10-year life ($10,000/$1,000 per year) and that the asset is 30 percent gone as of the end of the year ($3,000/$10,000). Thus the asset is 30 percent of 10 years, or 3 years, old at the end of the year.

This assumes that there is not a material amount of fully depreciated assets still in use. If a company carries fully depreciated assets on its books, then the figure "accumulated depreciation/depreciation charges for year" will overstate the average life of depreciable assets. The analyst will not typically know that this phenomenon has occurred and, like us, can do nothing about it. The auditor, in checking client-prepared statements, can make the required change in the estimating procedure by subtracting accumulated depreciation on fully depreciated assets from "accumulated depreciation" before dividing by "depreciation charges for year."

If the company uses straight-line depreciation, then adjust the depreciation charges for a number of years equal to the average age of the depreciable assets.

If the company uses an accelerated depreciation method, then the procedure outlined above for the straight-line methods results in an overestimate of the actual average age. How much of an overestimate it is depends on this calculated average age, the growth rate over time of depreciable assets for that company, and the particular accelerated method used.

We have solved a series of linear difference equations to provide age-reducing factors to compute the average age of assets depreciated on the sum-of-the-years'-digits and double-declining-balance accelerated depreciation methods. These age-reducing factors are shown in Exhibits 8.1 and 8.2.

To use the tables to estimate the average age of assets depreciated on an accelerated basis requires an estimate of the growth rate in depreciable assets. The information for estimating growth rates is typically found in the historical summary of the annual report. Ideally, we want to find the growth rate in depreciable assets. Most published historical summaries do not provide this information, and some surrogate will be necessary. A good surrogate is the growth in the annual depreciation charge. Another substitute, but one not so good, is the growth in the total of noncurrent assets. If the average age of depreciable assets is computed under the straight-line procedure to be n, then the growth rate to use in entering the age-reducing tables is

$$\sqrt[n]{\frac{\text{Depreciable assets (or surrogate) as of balance sheet date}}{\text{Depreciable assets (or surrogate) as of } n \text{ years ago}}} - 1$$

Enter the appropriate table (Exhibit 8.1 or 8.2) of age-reducing factors with the average age assuming straight-line depreciation and the growth rate in depreciable assets. Typically, the implicit age and the implied growth rate will make you want to read a number within a block of four

EXHIBIT 8.1

AGE-REDUCING FACTORS FOR DEPRECIABLE ASSETS

Sum-of-the-Years'-Digits (SYD) Method

Unadjusted life in years*	Annual rate of growth (or decline) in depreciable assets (or surrogate)						
	−5%	0%	5%	10%	15%	20%	30%
3	.8476	.8571	.8660	.8742	.8818	.8889	.9016
4	.8189	.8333	.8467	.8589	.8702	.8805	.8986
5	.7988	.8182	.8360	.8522	.8669	.8802	.9030
6	.7833	.8077	.8299	.8499	.8679	.8838	.9105
7	.7706	.8000	.8266	.8503	.8712	.8896	.9193
8	.7597	.7941	.8250	.8523	.8760	.8964	.9283
9	.7500	.7895	.8247	.8554	.8817	.9038	.9372
10	.7412	.7857	.8252	.8592	.8878	.9113	.9455
11	.7330	.7826	.8263	.8634	.8941	.9187	.9531
12	.7254	.7800	.8278	.8680	.9004	.9259	.9600
13	.7180	.7778	.8298	.8727	.9068	.9328	.9661
14	.7110	.7759	.8319	.8776	.9130	.9393	.9714
15	.7043	.7742	.8343	.8825	.9190	.9453	.9760
20	.6728	.7683	.8479	.9065	.9454	.9692	.9907
25	.6436	.7647	.8626	.9278	.9649	.9837	.9967
30	.6159	.7623	.8772	.9455	.9782	.9918	.9989

*Accumulated depreciation/depreciation charges for year.

numbers in the table. The simplest procedure is to "eyeball" an interpolation, but our computer program uses an exact linear interpolation.

Once you have the age-reducing factor from the table, multiply the age found assuming straight-line depreciation by that factor and adjust the reported depreciation charges for the resulting number of years.

(4) Computing Gain or Loss on Monetary Items

To compute gain or loss on monetary items, first compute the average net monetary item position for the year. We use the average of the beginning and ending balances of monetary items. Monetary assets include cash, accounts receivable, bonds and notes held, and any other item that represents a claim to a definite amount of cash. [Foreign "monetary"

EXHIBIT 8.2

AGE-REDUCING FACTORS FOR DEPRECIABLE ASSETS

Double-Declining Balance (DDB) Method

Unadjusted life in years*	Annual rate of growth (or decline) in depreciable assets (or surrogate)						
	−5%	0%	5%	10%	15%	20%	30%
3	.7488	.7647	.7794	.7931	.8058	.8176	.8387
4	.7454	.7653	.7838	.8008	.8165	.8310	.8564
5	.7408	.7650	.7873	.8078	.8265	.8434	.8727
6	.7362	.7646	.7908	.8146	.8362	.8555	.8880
7	.7315	.7643	.7943	.8215	.8457	.8671	.9021
8	.7269	.7640	.7979	.8283	.8550	.8782	.9150
9	.7223	.7638	.8015	.8350	.8640	.8888	.9267
10	.7178	.7636	.8051	.8416	.8727	.8987	.9371
11	.7133	.7634	.8087	.8481	.8812	.9081	.9464
12	.7088	.7633	.8124	.8545	.8892	.9169	.9545
13	.7043	.7632	.8160	.8608	.8969	.9250	.9616
14	.6998	.7631	.8196	.8669	.9043	.9326	.9678
15	.6954	.7630	.8231	.8728	.9113	.9395	.9731
20	.6735	.7626	.8406	.9002	.9408	.9662	.9897
25	.6521	.7624	.8573	.9233	.9621	.9822	.9963
30	.6314	.7623	.8730	.9422	.9765	.9910	.9988

*Accumulated depreciation/depreciation charges for year.

items are not counted here. See Adjustment (6).] Monetary liabilities are generally all liabilities. The exceptions are foreign debt, the estimated liabilities for future expenditures under warranties, and the liability shown when the company has received cash in advance of delivering goods or services. This latter liability is often called "Advances from Customers" or "Rental Payments Received in Advance" or "Prepaid Subscriptions" or "Deferred Income." (Such items are often so small in proportion to total liabilities that they can safely be ignored for many companies. We have not ignored these items in our calculations.) Deferred taxes, deferred investment tax credits, and various "reserves" are also excluded from monetary items.

The major difficulty in determining monetary items is deciding whether or not the asset "Marketable Securities" is a monetary asset. If the marketable securities are commercial paper or government notes, then they are monetary. If the marketable securities are equity securities, or bonds held temporarily, then they are not monetary. Most firms do not disclose exactly what their marketable securities are, but other captions and footnotes often contain clues. The conservative treatment, when in doubt, is to treat marketable securities as monetary assets. (This increases the amount of the reported loss, or reduces the amount of reported gain on monetary items.)

To compute the average net monetary liability position for the year, add together the monetary liabilities at the beginning of the year and at the end of the year; then subtract the sum of monetary assets at the beginning and the end of the year. Divide the result by two. The result shows the average net debtor position of the company during the year, if the result is positive (as it usually is for industrials), and the average net creditor position if the result is negative. The monetary gain for the year is the average net debtor position multiplied by the rate of price change for the year. If the company was a net lender during a year of rising prices, it will have a loss on holdings of monetary items.[9]

If the company swapped nonmonetary items for monetary items, or vice versa, in large amounts at some time other than near mid-year, then you may want to adjust separately for that item of monetary gain or loss. If, for example, a company sold a large plant near the end of the year, and the proceeds of the sale are still held in monetary assets at year end, then our averaging process will overstate average monetary assets for the year and understate the gain (or overstate the loss) on holding monetary items.

(5) Adjusting Equity Method Revenues

When a parent uses the equity method, rather than consolidation, for its investment in a subsidiary with a substantial net position in monetary items, either as a lender or borrower, then the income statements of the unconsolidated subsidiary should be separately adjusted. In preparing GPLA financial statements for publication, the accountant should always prepare separate GPLA statements for the unconsolidated subsidiary. Analysts, in their work, should make estimated adjustments when an unconsolidated subsidiary has significant net monetary items.

Apply Steps (1)–(4), above [and perhaps (6) and (7), below], to the statements of the subsidiary company and pick up the parent's share of the subsidiary's adjusted income for the parent's adjusted income statement. In our experience sufficient information about the subsidiary is

---

[9]When there is an obvious excess of monetary assets over monetary liabilities, such as in the GE Credit Corporation illustration below, it is convenient to compute the average net monetary asset position by subtracting liabilities from assets.

typically given in the parent's annual report so that it is not necessary to get separate, detailed financial statements for the subsidiary, although these are usually available. Working with the subsidiary's summarized statements as shown in the parent's report will, however, usually preclude making the depreciation adjustment (3). Most major unconsolidated subsidiaries of industrial companies are finance or insurance companies, so they tend not to have any cost of goods sold expense and their depreciation expense is insignificant. Hence, Adjustment (2) is not essential and Adjustment (3) is not important. Adjustment (4), gain or loss on monetary items, is the major reason for separately analyzing the unconsolidated subsidiary. Once the adjusted income of the unconsolidated subsidiary is determined, the parent recognizes as revenue its share (frequently 100 percent) of that adjusted net income.

(6) Gain or Loss on Foreign Items

When the notes to the financial statements provide information on financial position of foreign branches and consolidated foreign subsidiaries, separate those monetary items, which are denominated in foreign currency, from the computations in (4). (Sometimes these amounts will have to be estimated from data on foreign working capital or total foreign assets.) Calculate a monetary gain or loss on these items just as in Adjustment (4). Include the resulting gain or loss as part of operating income, that is, as part of income before gain or loss on (domestic) monetary items. The rationale for this treatment is given in Chapters Six and Seven.

(7) Preferred Stock Items

The preceding adjustments lead to GPLA net income. If a company has preferred stock outstanding, then GPLA income to common stock is often of greater concern to analysts than is GPLA net income. To obtain GPLA income to common stock usually involves two steps. First, adjust preferred stock dividends for one-half year of price change. Subtract this amount from adjusted net income. Second, in many cases, there will be a gain, much like monetary gain, on preferred stock items. If the amount for preferred stock in the conventional balance sheet is approximately the same as, or greater than, the redemption or liquidation value of that preferred stock, then treat the preferred stock as a monetary item and apply Adjustment (4). Add this amount to net income less adjusted preferred dividends to derive GPLA net income to common.

The rationale for applying a treatment similar to that for monetary items to the preferred stock in some cases but not in others is explained in Chapter Four. If the balance sheet amount of preferred stock after adjustment is greater than redemption value, then the balance sheet amount is written down to redemption value and a gain to common stockholders is recognized. (This write-down is similar to the write-down of inventories to current replacement cost under the lower-of-cost-or-market procedure of conventional accounting.) The published financial statements are often vague about the relation between redemption value and the balance sheet amount. Preferred stock with $100 par value should normally be treated as monetary for these purposes. When in doubt, we include a "monetary gain" from preferred stock in GPLA income to common.

Preparing the Adjusted Income Statement

The information derived with Adjustments (1)–(7) can be summarized as shown in Exhibit 7.1 for the General Electric Company and in Exhibit 7.2 for the General Electric Credit Corporation. Chapters Nine and Ten discuss the implications of these adjustments.

ILLUSTRATION OF THE ESTIMATING PROCEDURE

To make the estimating procedure clearer and to provide a guide for analysts to follow in preparing their own estimates, we illustrate the procedure in this section. We start with the adjustments of 1974 income for General Electric Credit Corporation, a 100-percent owned unconsolidated subsidiary of the General Electric Company. We have referred to the adjustment of equity method revenue as Adjustment (5). Nevertheless, we start with GE Credit because adjusting its statements is somewhat easier than adjusting the GE statements and it provides a good "warm-up."

Price Index and Rate of Price Change During 1974

Exhibit 8.3 shows various values of the GNP Deflator price index for dates important to the estimating procedure. The rate of price increase for the year 1974 is $177.68/158.93 - 1 = 1.118 - 1 = 11.8$ percent. If prices are assumed to have increased uniformly throughout the year, price change during one-half year is equal to[10]

$$\text{Price change for one-half 1974} = \sqrt{1.118} - 1 = 5.7 \text{ percent}$$

---

[10]A simpler computation of the price change during one-half year is $\frac{1}{2} \times 11.8$ percent $= 5.9$ percent. $(1.059)^2$ is, however, greater than 1.118. Using one-half the year's price change (5.9 percent) rather than the price change for one-half year (5.7 percent) will bias the computations by assuming, in effect, that prices increased more rapidly in the second half of the year than in the first half. Such a bias results in slight *over*adjustments. See Chapter Six.

EXHIBIT 8.3

PRICE INDEX DATA FOR ILLUSTRATIONS

Quarter[a]	GNP Deflator (1958 = 100)[b]
4th, 1974	177.68
3rd, 1974	172.07
2nd, 1974	167.31
1st, 1974	163.61
4th, 1973	158.93
3rd, 1973[c]	155.67
4th, 1972[c]	146.50
3rd, 1968[d]	122.9
2nd, 1968[d]	121.7
Annual Averages	
1970[d]	135.2
1968[e]	122.3

[a]The GNP Deflator is an average for the quarter.

[b]The published number is periodically revised. These 1974 and 1973 numbers were taken from the *Economic Report of the President,* February 1975. By April 1975, the *Survey of Current Business* data on the GNP Deflator indicated a price increase for 1974 of almost 12 percent. (The data shown here indicate a price change for 1974 of 11.8 percent.) The changes in the published Deflator do not significantly alter our results. See, however, the discussion in Chapter Six at Exhibit 6.8.

[c]These are required for computations involving FIFO and weighted average cost flow assumptions for inventories.

[d]These are required for the depreciation calculations.

[e]This is required for the alternative depreciation calculations for GE.

Adjusting the Income Statement for GE Credit Corporation (Exhibit 8.4)

(1) Adjusting Revenues and Expenses Except Depreciation. GE Credit's revenues for the year 1974 were $561.3 million. Revenues are to be adjusted for one-half year. GE Credit's GPLA revenues are, then,

$1.057 \times \$561.3$ million = $593.3 million measured in 12/31/74 dollars

GE Credit's expenses for the year were $518.6 million, but these included $2.2 million of depreciation expense. Depreciation expense is adjusted separately. The remaining expenses of $516.4 million are assumed to occur evenly throughout the year and are adjusted for one-half year of price change. GE Credit's GPLA expenses, except depreciation are, then,

$$1.057 \times \$516.4 \text{ million} = \$545.8 \text{ million measured in } 12/31/74 \text{ dollars}$$

(3) Adjusting Depreciation. GE Credit has no cost of goods sold, so there is no Adjustment (2). GE Credit's conventional depreciation charge for 1974 was $2.2 million. This information, the fact that the straight-line method is used, and the amount of accumulated depreciation, which is required for this adjustment, are not given in GE's annual report. We found the information in the separate annual report of GE Credit. The separate adjustment of depreciation does not significantly affect GE Credit's GPLA income. We show the adjustment for illustrative purposes.

GE Credit's accumulated depreciation as of December 31, 1974, was about $9.8 million. Thus the average dollar's worth of depreciable assets was acquired about

$$\frac{\$9.8 \text{ million}}{\$2.2 \text{ million per year}} = 4.45 \text{ years}$$

before December 31, 1974. Therefore depreciation expense must be adjusted for about 4.5 years of price change. Four and one-half years before December 31, 1974, occurred at midyear 1970. Exhibit 8.3 shows that the GNP Deflator for mid-1970 (annual average) is 135.23. The GNP Deflator was about 178 as of the fourth quarter of 1974, so general prices increased by about

$$\frac{178}{135} - 1 = 32 \text{ percent}$$

during the 4.5 years preceding December 31, 1974. GE Credit's adjusted depreciation expense for 1974 is, then

$$1.32 \times \$2.2 \text{ million} = \$2.9 \text{ million.}[11]$$

(4) Gain or Loss on Monetary Items. GE Credit held the following balances of monetary items:

---

[11]If depreciation had been included in Adjustment (1), GPLA depreciation would have been computed as $1.057 \times \$2.2$ million = $2.33 million. The difference, about $.6 million, is less than 3 percent of GE Credit's GPLA net loss.

	($ in Millions)	
	12/31/74	12/31/73
Monetary assets (cash, marketable securities, and receivables)	$4,211.9	$3,503.0
Monetary liabilities (all liabilities excluding deferred credits)	3,561.8	2,992.4
Net monetary assets	$650.1	$510.6

GE Credit was a net lender during 1974. The average net monetary asset position was $580.35 [= .5 × ($650.1 + $510.6)] million. Thus GE Credit's loss from being a net lender during 1974 when prices increased by 11.8 percent was

$$.118 \times \$580.35 \text{ million} = \$68.5 \text{ million}$$

This loss alone is about 1.5 times as large as GE Credit's reported income.

(7) Preferred Stock Items. GE owns all of both the common and preferred stock of GE Credit, so the following adjustment is not required in assessing the effects of inflation on GE. (The Credit Corporation's "monetary" gain on preferred stock is just offset by GE's loss on the same stock held as an investment.) Nevertheless, we illustrate the adjustment of preferred stock items for completeness.

GE Credit had $90 million of preferred stock outstanding during all of 1974 and declared $6.8 million of dividends on preferred stock. The GPLA amount of preferred dividends, assuming they accrue evenly throughout the year, is

$$1.057 \times \$6.8 \text{ million} = \$7.2 \text{ million}$$

Assuming the preferred stock had aggregate redemption value of about $90 million, the "monetary gain" from the preferred stock during the year when prices increased by 11.8 percent is

$$.118 \times \$90 \text{ million} = \$10.6 \text{ million}$$

All of the adjustments for GE Credit are summarized in Exhibit 8.4, which is identical to Exhibit 7.2. Instead of the reported net income of $42.7 million, GE Credit had a GPLA net loss of $23.9 million. Thus we see the importance of treating unconsolidated subsidiaries separately.

EXHIBIT 8.4

GENERAL ELECTRIC CREDIT CORPORATION

Income Statement for 1974

(Dollar Amounts Shown in Millions)

Adjustment numbers[a]		Historical dollars (shown in annual report)	In 12/31/74 dollars (as estimated)	Percentage change
(1)	Earned income	$561.3	$593.3	+5.7%
	Expenses[b]			
(3)	Depreciation[c]	$ 2.2	$ 2.9	+32.2
(1)	All other expenses	516.4	545.8	+5.7
	Total	$518.6	$548.7	+5.8
	Income before loss on monetary items	$ 42.7	$ 44.6	+4.4
(4)	(Loss) on net monetary items	—	(68.5)	—
	Net income (loss)	$ 42.7	$(23.9)	−156.0
(7)	Less preferred stock dividends	(6.8)	(7.2)	+5.7
(7)	Gain on preferred stock items	—	10.6	—
	Income (loss) to common stock	$ 35.9	$(20.5)	−157.0

[a] Keyed to description in Chapter Seven.

[b] As a finance company, GE Credit has no "cost of goods sold."

[c] Straight-line. Average life of depreciable assets is estimated to be 4.5 years; price index increased by 32.2 percent during the 4.5 years preceding December 31, 1974.

Adjusting the Income Statement for the General Electric Company (Exhibit 8.6)

All of the information for making the following calculations is contained in the 1974 annual report of the General Electric Company.[12]

[12] An annotated version of this annual report, including identification of all monetary items, appears in Sidney Davidson, James S. Schindler, Clyde P. Stickney, and Roman L. Weil, *Accounting: The Language of Business,* 2nd ed., Thomas Horton & Daughters, Inc., Glen Ridge, N.J., 1975.

(1) Adjusting Most Revenues and Expenses Except Cost of Goods Sold and Depreciation. GE's revenues for the year 1974, except those revenues recognized under the equity method from GE Credit, were $13,556 million. Revenues are adjusted for one-half year; GE's GPLA revenues are, then,

$$1.057 \times \$13,556 \text{ million} = \$14,334 \text{ million}$$

GE's expenses except cost of goods sold and depreciation were $2,853 million. These are to be adjusted for one-half year and become

$$1.057 \times \$2,853 \text{ million} = \$3,017 \text{ million}$$

(2) Adjusting Cost of Goods Sold. GE uses LIFO for about 80 percent of its inventories and FIFO for about 20 percent. Historical cost of goods sold was $10,137.6 million, but this amount includes $376.2 million of depreciation, which is adjusted separately. Cost of goods sold to be adjusted here is $9,761.4 (= $10,137.6 − $376.2) million. In this section we occasionally use some standard abbreviations: *COGS* means cost of goods sold, *BI* means beginning inventory, and *EI* means ending inventory.

DETERMINING PURCHASES. Ending inventory was $2,257.0 million and beginning inventory was $1,986.2 million. We calculate from the inventory equation that total purchases (in millions) during the year must have been

$$
\begin{aligned}
\text{Purchases} &= \text{COGS} + \text{EI} - \text{BI} \\
&= \$9,761.4 + \$2,257.0 - \$1,986.2 \\
&= \$10,032.2
\end{aligned}
$$

SEPARATING LIFO AND FIFO COMPONENTS. GE's footnotes disclose that the 80 percent of ending inventories valued with a LIFO cost flow assumption would have a book value $783.7 million larger if a FIFO assumption had been used.[13] The LIFO portion of ending inventory is $1,805.6 (= .80 × $2,257.0) million. This LIFO inventory would have been shown at $2,589.3 (= $1,805.6 + $783.7) million if FIFO had been

---

[13]The book value at the beginning of the year of LIFO inventory would have been $429.7 million larger if FIFO had been used. Hence, we know that in the time since GE adopted LIFO, cumulative pretax earnings have been $783.7 million less than if FIFO had been used and 1974's pretax earnings were $354.0 (= $783.7 − $429.7) million less. No other choice between generally accepted accounting principles usually has a greater effect on conventionally reported income than the choice between LIFO and FIFO. If a firm's cost of inventory increases at the same rate as the GNP Deflator and inventory dollar amounts do not decrease over time, then GPLA cost of goods sold will be the same, regardless of the cost flow assumption.

used. Total ending inventory would have been shown at $3,040.7 (= $783.7 + $2,257.0) million if FIFO had been used. Hence we know that 85.2 percent (= $2,589.3/$3,040.7) of total inventories are valued with LIFO and we assume that 85.2 percent of purchases are for LIFO items. Thus, we can disaggregate beginning inventory, ending inventory, and cost of goods sold as shown in Exhibit 8.5. (If goods valued with LIFO constitute a given percentage of ending inventories and prices are rising, then the cost of LIFO-valued goods sold will be a higher percentage of total cost of goods sold.)

LIFO ADJUSTMENT. Under a LIFO cost flow assumption for inventories, the purchases that enter cost of goods sold are the last purchases of the year. Purchases of LIFO items are $8,457.4 million (Exhibit 8.5). For LIFO goods, an amount of purchases equal to LIFO COGS/LIFO purchases = $8,331/$8,457 = 98.5 percent of LIFO purchases during the year entered cost of goods sold. These purchases on average occurred 5.9 (= $12 \times .985/2$) months before the end of the year. Thus, the average dollar of cost of goods sold was dated about July 5. (December 31 less 5.9 months is about July 5.)

EXHIBIT 8.5

SEPARATING LIFO FROM FIFO AMOUNTS OF BEGINNING INVENTORY, ENDING INVENTORY, AND COST OF GOODS SOLD

General Electric Company, Year of 1974

	Percentages		Dollar Amounts in Millions				
	LIFO	FIFO	Total	=	LIFO	+	FIFO
Beginning inventory ...	80.0%[a]	20.0%	$ 1,986.2		$ 1,589.9		$ 397.2
Purchases	85.2[b]	14.8	10,032.2		8,547.4		1,484.8
Goods available for sale	...	....	$12,018.4		$10,136.4		$1,882.0
Less ending inventory ..	80.0[c]	20.0	2,257.0		1,805.6		451.4
Cost of goods sold	...	....	$ 9,761.4		$ 8,330.8		$1,430.6

[a] Assumed same as for ending inventory; previous year's annual report shows 84 percent, which can be used for greater accuracy. We use the 80 percent figure because that is the only information disclosed in the 1974 annual report.

[b] Excess of FIFO cost over LIFO cost of LIFO inventories was $783.7 million as of December 31,1974. If LIFO inventories were valued with FIFO, then those inventories would represent 85.2 of ending inventory: 85.2 percent = ($783.7 + .80 × $2,257.0)/($783.7 + $2,257.0).

[c] From annual report.

The rate of price change in the last 5.9 months of 1974 (.488 of a year) was 5.6 percent. Thus, the cost of LIFO goods sold adjusted for a 5.6-percent increase in prices is

LIFO COGS
adjusted   = $8,331 × 1.056 = $8,798
in millions

FIFO ADJUSTMENT. Under a FIFO cost flow assumption for inventories, the cost of goods sold consists of beginning inventory plus the purchases from the earlier part of the year.

The beginning FIFO inventory (see Exhibit 8.5) must be adjusted for somewhat more than a full year. To use the notation introduced in Figure 8.1, the beginning FIFO inventory must be adjusted for $1 + t_2$ years, where (all dollar amounts in millions)

$$t_2 = .5 \times \left(1 - \frac{COGS - BI}{purchases}\right)$$

$$= .5 \times \left(1 - \frac{\$1,431 - \$397}{\$1,485}\right)$$

$$= 15 \text{ percent of 1973's price change}$$

The FIFO beginning inventory in cost of goods sold is adjusted for 1.15 years of price change. The price change during the last 15 percent of 1973 (the last 60 percent of the fourth quarter of 1973) is calculated to be (see Exhibit 8.3)

$$\left(\frac{\text{Fourth quarter, 1973}}{\text{Third quarter, 1973}}\right)^{.60} - 1 = \left(\frac{158.93}{155.67}\right)^{.60} - 1 = 1.25 \text{ percent}$$

Beginning 1974 FIFO inventory in year-end 1974 dollars is thus equal to

$$1.1180 \times 1.0125 \times \$397 \text{ million} = \$449 \text{ million}$$

The purchases that enter cost of FIFO goods sold for GE in 1974 are the first $1,034 (= $1,431 − $397 = COGS − BI) million of purchases of FIFO goods (Exhibit 8.5). Thus, the average dollar of purchases of FIFO goods that entered cost of FIFO goods sold for GE in 1974 occurred ½ × $1,034/$1,431 × 12 months = 4.34 months after January 1, 1974, or on about May 12. The cost of FIFO goods sold minus FIFO beginning inventory must be adjusted for 7.66 (= 12.0 − 4.34) months—64 percent of a year. Prices increased by about 7.4 percent in the last 64 percent of 1974.

FIFO COGS = beginning FIFO inventory × price change for last 1.15 years
           + [(cost of FIFO goods sold − beginning FIFO inventory)
           × price change for .64 of one year]

FIFO COGS
adjusted   = ($397 × 1.118 × 1.013) + ($1,034 × 1.074)
in millions

           = $449 + $1,111

           = $1,560

COMBINING LIFO AND FIFO ADJUSTMENTS. The GPLA cost of LIFO goods sold was computed to be $8,798 million and the GPLA cost of FIFO goods sold was computed to be $1,560 million. Thus, GE's total adjusted cost of goods sold is $10,358 million,[14] an increase of 6.1 percent over conventional cost of goods sold.

WEIGHTED-AVERAGE ADJUSTMENT. The cost of goods sold under the weighted-average cost flow assumption is not needed for GE. For the sake of completeness, we illustrate the weighted-average adjustment. Here we assume that the $9,761 million cost of goods sold figure (which is taken from information in the annual report) is determined with a weighted-average assumption. The adjusted cost of goods sold would be calculated in steps as follows (all dollar amounts shown in millions):

(a) The fraction of purchases in ending inventory, s,

$$s = 1 - \frac{\text{COGS}}{\text{purchases}}$$

$$= 1 - \frac{\$9,761}{\$9,761 + \$2,257 - \$1,986}$$

$$= 1 - .973 = .027$$

(b) The ending inventory for 1974 was $2,257 and for 1973 was $1,986. Thus the growth rate, g, in inventories is[15]

---

[14]Because of rounding error at various stages of these "by-hand" computations, this answer is slightly different from that found with our computer program. Exhibits 7.1 and 8.6 report GE's GPLA cost of goods sold as $10,357 million.

[15]In general, if the historical summary discloses ending inventory for n years ago where n is as large as possible, then calculate the growth rate in inventories as

$$\sqrt[n]{\frac{\text{Ending inventory this year}}{\text{Ending inventory } n \text{ years ago}}} - 1$$

$$g = \frac{\$2,257}{\$1,986} - 1 = .136$$

(c) The average dollar in the weighted-average ending inventory is t_w years old where

$$t_w = \frac{1 + g + s}{2(1 + g - s)} = \frac{1 + .136 + .027}{2(1 + .136 - .027)}$$

$$= \frac{1.163}{2.218} = .524 \text{ years}$$

We assume that the average dollar in beginning inventory was also .524 years old as of January 1, 1974.

Thus, as of the end of 1974, the beginning inventory of $1,986 should be adjusted for 1.524 years of price change which requires an adjustment factor of

$$\frac{177.68}{158.93} \left(\frac{158.93}{146.50}\right)^{.524} = 1.167$$

(d) The GPLA weighted-average cost of goods sold would be

$$\frac{\text{COGS}}{\text{COGS} + \text{EI}} \times \left[\begin{array}{l} \text{BI adjusted for} \\ \text{1.524 years} \end{array} + \begin{array}{l} \text{COGS} + \text{EI} - \text{BI adjusted} \\ \text{for one-half year} \end{array}\right]$$

$$= \frac{\$9,761}{\$9,761 + \$2,257} \times [\$1,986 \times 1.167 + (\$9,761 + \$2,257 - \$1,984) \times 1.057]$$

$$= .812 \times (\$2,317 + \$10,604) = .812 \times \$12,921$$

$$= \$10,491$$

(3) Depreciation. GE's depreciation charge for the year 1974 was $376.2 million. The accumulated depreciation at December 31, 1974, was $2,831.5 million. Thus, if straight-line depreciation were used, the depreciable assets would have been acquired, on the average,

$$\frac{\$2,831.5}{\$376.2 \text{ per year}} = 7.53 \text{ years}$$

before December 31, 1974. GE, however, uses sum-of-the-years'-digits (SYD) depreciation, so that estimate must be reduced somewhat.

To use the SYD adjustment table requires an estimate of GE's annual growth rate in depreciable assets. GE presents the depreciation charges for several past years in its historical summary. The growth rate in depreciation charges provides a surrogate for the growth rate in depreciable assets. Depreciation charges for 1966 (8 years—the closest one shown to 7.53 years—prior to balance sheet date) was $233.6 million. Thus, the depreciation charges increased, on average, at a rate of 6.1 percent (= $\sqrt[8]{376.2/233.6}$ − 1) per year in the 8 years preceding December 31, 1974.

Entering the SYD adjustment table (Exhibit 8.1) for age 7.53 years and growth rate 6.1 percent and interpolating as necessary yields an adjustment factor of about .84. Thus GE's depreciable assets, according to our formula, are on average .84 × 7.53 years = 6.3 years old.

Therefore, depreciation charges must be adjusted for 6.3 years of price change. 6.3 years before December 31, 1974, occurred during the third quarter of 1968. We compute that prices increased by 44.9 percent during the 6.3 years before December 31, 1974.[16] The adjusted depreciation charge for GE in 1974, is, then, 1.449 × $376.2 million = $545 million.

(4) Gain or Loss on Net Monetary Items. The composition of GE's monetary items during 1974 is given in Exhibit 7.1. GE's average net monetary liabilities during 1974, when prices increased by 11.8 percent, was $1,503.7 million. Thus GE's purchasing power gain during 1974 was

$$.118 \times \$1,503.7 \text{ million} = \$177 \text{ million}$$

(5) Equity Method Revenues. We have already illustrated the adjustments for GE Credit Corporation. GE reported equity method revenues of $42.7 million from GE Credit. Exhibit 8.4 shows that GE Credit's GPLA net *loss* was $23.9 million. Since GE owns all the preferred stock of GE Credit, we can ignore the preferred stock of GE Credit in

---

[16]Refer to Exhibit 8.3 for information about the GNP Deflator. The exact computation of the rate of price increase is

$$\left(\frac{177.68}{122.9}\right) \times \left(\frac{122.9}{121.7}\right)^{\frac{(.30 - .25)}{.25}} - 1 = 44.9 \text{ percent}$$

A simpler, and relatively satisfactory, approach would view all plant acquisitions occurring during a given year as being made at the average price level of the year. In this case, the adjustment would be

$$\frac{177.68}{122.3} - 1 = 45.3 \text{ percent}$$

This method will, in some cases, yield slightly higher adjusted depreciation charges (if the decimal portion of the age in years of depreciable assets is less than .5) and in other cases, slightly lower adjusted depreciation charges (if the decimal portion of the age in years is greater than .5) than the method used in the body of the text. For GE, depreciation charges adjusted with this simpler alternative would be 1.453 × $376.2 million, or $547 million, which is $2 million (or 0.4 percent) greater than the amount calculated in the text.

making GPLA estimates for GE. Any adjustments for those items in GE Credit's income statement are exactly offset in GE's income statement. The primary purpose of applying a separate adjustment to finance companies is to pick up the monetary gain or loss from their net monetary items.

(6) Gain or Loss on Foreign Monetary Items. The notes of GE's annual report indicate that $8.4 million of GE's debt at the end of 1974, and $8.3 million at the end of 1973, is denominated in foreign currency. This debt is not counted in Adjustment (4), but is separately treated here. The average foreign debt position during the year was $8.35 million. The gain on foreign debt was, then, about

$$.118 \times \$8.35 = \$1 \text{ million}$$

This $1 million gain is insignificant for GE, but we show it separately to illustrate the procedure and its treatment in the GPLA income statement.

The estimated GPLA income statement is shown in Exhibit 8.6, which is identical to Exhibit 7.1.

HOW ACCURATE IS THE ESTIMATING PROCEDURE?

The previous sections have presented procedures for estimating general price level adjustments to reported income. The next chapter reports the results of applying these procedures to the financial statements of more than 100 major companies. We suggest that analysts can use these procedures for estimating general price level adjustments for companies of interest to them. How similar are the results using these procedures likely to be to the results that will be reported by major companies if general price level adjusted statements are required?[17] We attempt to answer that question, insofar as we can, in this section. Some of the instances where our estimates are poor provide guidance for refining the estimating procedure when certain symptoms are present.

We have partial, reported ("actual") general price level adjusted accounting figures for three named companies—Gulf Oil Corporation (1973), Shell Oil Company (1973 and 1974), and Indiana Telephone Corporation (1973 and 1974). A fourth company, called Company R (1973), helped us assess the accuracy of our procedures on a confidential basis. In addition, the AICPA commissioned a study of general price

---

[17]Others have devised estimating procedures for the same purpose. See *Business Week*, September 14, 1974, p. 96, and Russell J. Petersen, "An Examination of the Effects of Changes in the General Price Level on Published Financial Statements," Doctoral Dissertation, University of Washington, June 1971.

EXHIBIT 8.6

GENERAL ELECTRIC COMPANY

Income Statement for 1974

(Dollar Amounts Shown in Millions)

Adjustment numbers[a]		Historical dollars (shown in annual report)	In 12/31/74 dollars (as estimated)	Percentage change
	Revenues			
(1)	Sales and other income ...	$13,556	$14,334	+5.7%
(5)	Equity method revenue (loss)	43	(24)	−155.8
(6)	Gain on net foreign monetary items	—	1	—
	Total	$13,599	$14,311	+5.2
	Expenses and Deductions			
(2)	Cost of goods sold[b]	$ 9,761	$10,357	+6.1
(3)	Depreciation[c]	376	545	+44.9
(1)	All other expenses	2,853	3,017	+5.7
	Total	$12,990	$13,919	+7.1
	Income before gains on monetary items	$ 608	$ 392	−36.0
(4)	Gain on monetary items[d] ..	—	177	—
	Net income	$ 608	$ 569	−6.4

[a]Keyed to description in Chapter Seven. [b]Ending inventories are 80 percent LIFO, 20 percent FIFO.

[c]Sum-of-the-years'-digit method. Average life of depreciable assets is estimated to be 6.3 years; price index increased by 44.9 percent during the 6.3 years preceding December 31, 1974.

[d]The net monetary liabilities for GE are computed as follows:

	($ in Millions) 12/31/74	12/31/73
Monetary Liabilities		
Current liabilities and long-term (domestic) borrowings	$5,068.3	$4,401.3
Monetary Assets		
Cash, receivables (both long- and short-term), customer financing, recoverable costs, government securities, and advances to affiliates	3,430.5	3,031.7
Net Monetary Liabilities	$1,637.8	$1,369.6

The average of net domestic monetary liabilities for the year 1974 was $1,503.7 [= .5 × ($1,637.8 + $1,369.6)] million. The price change for the year was 11.8 percent. GE's gain from being a net debtor during 1974 when prices increased by 11.8 percent was, then, about .118 × $1,503.7 = $177 million. ($117.4 million of this gain is attributable to net current liabilities and the rest, $59.6 million, is attributable to net long-term monetary items. This information is required for the GPLA funds statement; see Exhibit 10.2.) Foreign debt is treated separately in Adjustment (6).

level accounting in 1968–1969.[18] The AICPA made available to us the financial statements for a dozen or so companies in that study. Those data contain three companies for which we can apply our estimating procedures. (The others cannot be tested because some vital information—such as the start-of-the-year balance sheet—was not available to us.) These are real companies, but their names were withheld. Next, the AICPA published results for a fictitious XYZ Company in APB Statement No. 3 which explains the general price level restatement procedure. Finally, one standard accounting reference book[19] contains a chapter on inflation accounting which shows a comprehensive example of general price level adjustments for another fictitious company, Demonstrator Corporation. Exhibit 8.7 presents partial comparisons of our results and reported figures for these ten companies. The results are partial in the sense that some of the real companies made available (published) only parts of their general price level adjusted financial statements. We compare our estimates with the published "actuals."

You can judge for yourself the results shown in Exhibit 8.7. Our estimated bottom lines—net income—for Gulf and Company R are within 6 percent of the companies' numbers. For Shell we are off by about 13 percent for 1973 and 10 percent for 1974. Indiana Telephone does not report gains on monetary items as suggested by the FASB, but our estimates of their net income before gain on monetary items is within 2 percent of the reported figures.

For some companies (such as Company P of the Rosenfield study) the estimates of GPLA income are in error by a substantially greater percentage than the components of income are in error. At first glance this may appear puzzling. Observe, however, that the denominator for each error calculation is the reported (that is, actual) GPLA income figure reported by the company and keep in mind that net incomes are typically less than 5 percent of revenues or cost of goods sold. Errors in estimates of the same absolute dollar amounts are, then, a much larger percentage of net income than they are of total revenues or of cost of goods sold.

For the fictitious AICPA example (XYZ Company), we do well for 1967, but poorly for 1968. The assumed 1968 operations of XYZ Company resulted in a drastic decline in income from 1967. Whereas revenues for 1968 were about 10 percent less than in 1967, income was about 75 percent less. When computing the deviation of our estimate of net income from the reported result, we divide by reported net income, which is small

---

[18]Paul Rosenfield, "Accounting for Inflation—A Field Test," *The Journal of Accountancy,* June 1969, pp. 45–50.

[19]Sidney Davidson, Ed., *Handbook of Modern Accounting,* McGraw-Hill Book Company, New York, 1970, chap. 30.

EXHIBIT 8.7

PERCENTAGES BY WHICH OUR ESTIMATES DEVIATE FROM THE REPORTED GENERAL PRICE LEVEL ADJUSTED AMOUNTS

[For each item, the number shown is our estimate divided by the general price level adjusted item as reported (by the Company or by the AICPA) minus one:

$$\text{Number shown} = \frac{\text{ours}}{\text{reported}} - 1$$

A positive number indicates an overestimate by us; a negative number, an underestimate.]

General price level adjusted financial statement item	Gulf Oil (1973)^a	Shell Oil (1973)^b	Shell Oil (1974)^b	Company R (1973)^c	Indiana Telephone (1973)^d	Indiana Telephone (1974)^d	AICPA—Rosenfield Study Co. H (1968)^e	Co. J (1968)^e	Co. P (1968)^e	AICPA XYZ Company (1967)^f	AICPA XYZ Company (1968)^f	Demonstrator Company (1960)^g
Revenues and other income	*	0.7%	1.28%	0.68%	0.90%	0.06%	0.72%	0.05%	0.25%	0.13%	1.38%	0.35%
Cost of goods sold	*	*	*	0.02	**	**	0.79	0.11	−1.78	0.07	0.75	0.18
Depreciation^h	5.93%	8.9	13.7	18.74	0.65	−1.77	6.33	2.99	3.45	2.62	−4.29	0.41
Other expenses and deductions	*	−10.1	1.11	0.62	0.81	1.07	0.94	−0.29	0.31	−0.23	6.30	0.03
Income before gain or loss on monetary items	*	−16.0	−11.9	−9.97	1.76	−4.05	10.77	−1.43	24.67	−3.41	60.8^i	5.01
Gain or loss on monetary items	*	−6.6	1.48	5.80	***	***	11.17^j	−6.08	−53.33	−1.00	−45.1^i	−4.21
Net income	5.23^k	−13.4	−9.47	−5.78	***	***	−3.03	−2.46	7.33	−3.38	30.5	4.62

*Not reported by the Company.

**Indiana Telephone Corporation has no cost of goods sold.

***Not computed by Indiana Telephone in accordance with APB Statement No. 3.

^{a}Gulf Oil Corporation, *The Orange Disc*, July–August 1974, p. 31.

[b]Shell Oil Company, *1974 Annual Report, Statistical Supplement*, p. 5.

[c]From the company itself on a confidential basis. The company reports that its depreciable assets are only about half as old as our computation (accumulated depreciation/depreciation for the year) indicates.

[d]Indiana Telephone Corporation, *Annual Reports for 1973 and 1974*. For 1974, Revenues and Other Expenses were adjusted by 4.5 percent [= (fourth-quarter 1974 GNP Deflator/1974 annual average) − 1] rather than for a half-year of price change, which was 5.7 percent. Thus, we have used the same one-half year adjuster as did Indiana Telephone.

[e]AICPA data compiled by Paul Rosenfield. See Paul Rosenfield, "Accounting for Inflation—A Field Test," *The Journal of Accountancy*, June 1969, pp. 45–50.

[f]American Institute of Certified Public Accountants, Accounting Principles Board Statement No. 3, "Financial Statements Restated for General-Price Changes," June 1969, Exhibit B.R.-3 (12/31/68).

[g]Robert T. Sprouse, "Adjustments for Changing Prices," in S. Davidson, Ed., *Handbook of Modern Accounting*, McGraw-Hill Book Company, New York, 1970, chap. 30, p. 26.

[h]Straight-line method is used by all companies.

[i]See text for explanation of these large deviations. Our estimates are off by only $95,000 for income items and less than $40,000 for gain on monetary items. Revenues for the year were $27 million.

[j]We overstate the amount of the *loss* on monetary items.

[k]We include marketable securities in monetary items; it is not clear what Gulf does.

145

for 1968. When the denominator is small, the resulting percentage difference can be large even when the absolute deviation is not.

The large difference between our estimate for gain on monetary items for XYZ in 1968 and the reported figure is caused by XYZ's selling a nonmonetary asset on December 31, 1968. The cash realized from that sale is larger than the total amount of net monetary liabilities. Our standard procedure assumes that all inflows of cash occur evenly throughout the year; that assumption substantially reduced both the estimated average net monetary liability and the gain on monetary items for the year from that reported by the XYZ Company. Because the nonmonetary asset sold was converted into the monetary asset cash on December 31, 1968, this transaction did not affect *reported* gain on monetary items at all. When we account separately for this one transaction, the error in reporting gain on monetary items for XYZ Company in 1968 is reduced from 45 percent to less than 20 percent.

The estimates for the Demonstrator Corporation are gratifyingly accurate. The primary cause of the overadjustments for ordinary income items is from our use of the more accurate "half-year adjuster" discussed in Chapter Six. Our adjustments for a half-year are always larger than those found by following the simpler procedures. We surmise, but cannot be sure, that the four real companies used in our comparisons with 1973 and 1974 data have used the method that adjusts for 4½ months on average, rather than the method we suggest, which adjusts for 6 months. We know that Demonstrator Corporation's adjustments for items spread evenly throughout the year were made using the 4½-month technique. In general, during times of increasing prices, the result of using only 4½, rather than 6, months for adjusting items spread fairly evenly throughout the year is to underestimate general price level adjusted profits. The items that are spread evenly throughout the year are (1) nearly all revenues and (2) many expenses. Because the sum of "nearly all revenues" exceeds the sum of "many expenses" for almost all companies, the excess—a partial gross margin—is understated.

All the companies for which we can assess the accuracy of our methods use straight-line depreciation. We cannot, therefore, test the accuracy of our methods for firms using accelerated depreciation until some such firms publish their general price level adjusted depreciation amounts.

Chapter Nine

ESTIMATES OF GENERAL PRICE LEVEL ADJUSTED INCOME

USING THE PROCEDURES DESCRIBED in Chapter Eight, we estimated GPLA income for over 100 major corporations. This chapter reports and comments on the resulting estimates.

COMPANIES REPORTED ON

We report GPLA income estimates for (1) the 30 companies in the Dow Jones Industrial Index, (2) 44 other large companies, and (3) a cross section of companies in several specific industries. The industries singled out for separate study are steel, pharmaceuticals, automobile and truck manufacturers, and public utilities. Steel and pharmaceutical companies were selected for comparison because of the striking differences in the structures of their assets and equities. Steel tends to have large amounts of plant assets and debt financing compared with pharmaceuticals. Pharmaceuticals' balance sheets do not report their major resources—knowledge and patents—and their financing is primarily from capital stock, rather than debt. The auto manufacturers all use a FIFO cost flow assumption for inventories, whereas almost all the steel companies use LIFO. The different effects on GPLA income statements of FIFO and LIFO cost flow assumptions are discussed for steels and autos. Public utilities have no cost of goods sold, but do have large amounts of relatively old plant, and their financing includes large amounts of debt and preferred stock. Moreover, public utility GPLA net incomes are uniformly much larger than income conventionally reported, which may pose problems for these companies and their regulators in the setting of utility rates.

REPORTING FORMAT

All of our estimated GPLA income results are reported in identical formats. Refer to Exhibit 9.1, which shows the conventional and estimated

EXHIBIT 9.1

ALUMINUM COMPANY OF AMERICA (ALCOA)

Income Statement for 1974

(Amounts Shown in Millions of Dollars)

Adjustment numbers[a]		Historical dollars (shown in annual report)	GPLA in 12/31/74 dollars (as estimated)	GPLA amount as percentage of historical dollar amount	Reference number for results exhibits[b]
	Revenues				
(1)	Sales and other income .	$2,762.6	$2,921.0		
(5)	Equity method revenue (loss)	(3.3)	24.7		
(6)	(Loss) on net foreign monetary items	—	(1.7)[c]		
	Total	$2,759.3	$2,944.0		
	Expenses and Deductions				
(2)	Cost of goods sold[d]	$2,013.9	$2,123.0		
(3)	Depreciation[e]	164.7	271.3		
(1)	All other expenses	407.6	431.0		
	Total	$2,586.2	$2,825.3		
	Income before gain on monetary items	$ 173.1	$ 118.7	69%	[A]
(4)	Gain on net monetary items	—	100.8[f]		
	Net income	$ 173.1	$ 219.5	127	[B]
(7)	Less preferred stock dividends	(2.5)	(2.6)		
(7)	Gain on preferred stock items	—	7.8		
	Income to common stock	$ 170.6	$ 224.7	132	[C]

[a] Keyed to description and procedures in Chapters Seven and Eight.

[b] Percentages shown on these lines are carried to Columns (A), (B), and (C), respectively, of Exhibits 9.2–9.7.

[c] Consists of $2.1 million gain on long-term foreign debt less a $3.8 million loss on current foreign monetary items.

[d] LIFO cost flow assumption used by Alcoa.

[e] Straight-line method used by Alcoa.

[f] Consists of $105.14 million gain on long-term domestic debt less $4.39 million loss on current domestic monetary items.

GPLA income statements for the Aluminum Company of America (Alcoa). The left-hand column shows adjustment numbers (1)–(7) keyed to the discussion in Chapters Seven and Eight. The letters [A], [B], and [C] in the right-hand column of Exhibit 9.1 refer to the three estimates of GPLA income shown as a percentage of reported net income. Item [A] in Exhibit 9.1 refers to the restated income before gain on monetary items as a percentage of conventionally reported net income (69 percent for Alcoa), and is shown in Column (A) of Exhibit 9.2. Item [B] in the right-hand column of Exhibit 9.1 refers to GPLA net income as a percentage of conventionally reported net income (127 percent for Alcoa) and is shown in Column (B) of Exhibit 9.2. Finally, Item [C] in Exhibit 9.1 refers to GPLA income to common as a percentage of conventionally reported net income to common (132 percent for Alcoa), and is shown in Column (C) of Exhibit 9.2. The results shown in Column (C) are essentially equal to GPLA earnings per common share as a percentage of conventionally reported earnings per share. Columns (A), (B), and (C) of Exhibits 9.2–9.7 show analogous information for the other companies.

RESULTS

We show the estimated GPLA results for the 30 companies in the Dow Jones Index, 44 other large companies, 12 steel companies, 12 pharmaceuticals, 6 auto or truck manufacturers, and 24 public utilities as follows:

Companies	Exhibit number
Dow Jones Industrials	9.2
Other 44	9.3
Steel companies	9.4
Pharmaceutical companies ..	9.5
Auto/truck companies	9.6
Public utilities	9.7

Caveat

The percentages shown in these exhibits are in no way a criterion of the firm's GPLA performance, but instead merely relate GPLA income to conventionally reported income. For a firm that reported a large net income on a conventional basis, a GPLA income percentage of 80 may still mean a substantially better performance after adjustment than does an adjustment percentage of 115 for a firm that reported unsatisfactory profits on a conventional basis. Eighty percent of very good may still be good, whereas 115 percent of terrible may still be poor.

Effects Differ Among Firms

The results demonstrate clearly the error of the frequently stated naive view that all firms are affected relatively equally by inflation, and that a

EXHIBIT 9.2

THE 30 COMPANIES IN THE DOW JONES INDUSTRIAL INDEX

Estimates of General Price Level Adjusted Income Statements

(Amounts for 1974)

Company	Adjusted income before gain on monetary items, as a percentage of reported net income (A)	Adjusted net income, including gain on monetary items, as a percentage of reported net income[a] (B)	Adjusted earnings per share as a percentage of reported earnings per share[b] (C)
Allied Chemical	60	90	90
Alcoa	69	127	132
American Brands	56	110	117
American Can	63	105	110
AT&T	76	189	208
Anaconda	94	110	110
Bethlehem Steel	64	83	83
Chrysler	602[c]	302[c]	302[c]
Du Pont	43	46	52
Eastman Kodak	85	74	74
Esmark	7	60	66
Exxon	85	88	88
General Electric	64	94	94
General Foods	20	67	67
General Motors	−34[d]	−43[d]	−42[d]
Goodyear	1	90	90
International Harvester	−45[d]	43	43
International Nickel	83	95	95
International Paper	64	81	81
Johns-Manville	84	105	105
Owens-Illinois	68	137	142
Procter & Gamble	83	98	98
Sears	3	−4[d]	−4[d]
Standard Oil of California	65	87	87
Texaco	96	104	104
Union Carbide	86	93	93
U.S. Steel	63	79	79
United Technologies (United Aircraft)	−4[d]	25	25

EXHIBIT 9.2 (*Continued*)

Company	Adjusted income before gain on monetary items, as a percentage of reported net income (A)	Adjusted net income, including gain on monetary items, as a percentage of reported net income[a] (B)	Adjusted earnings per share as a percentage of reported earnings per share[b] (C)
Westinghouse Electric	-334^d	-166^d	-165^d
Woolworth	-68^d	66	63
Median	63.5^e	87^e	87^e
Interquartile range	$83.0-5.0^e$	$104.5-63.0^e$	$104.5-64.5^e$

[a]Monetary items are those classified as monetary in FASB Exposure Draft dated December 31, 1974. Deferred taxes and deferred investment tax credits are not included, although we believe they should be.

[b]Strictly speaking, this column shows adjusted net income to common as a percentage of reported net income. For companies with dilutive securities outstanding, percentages below (above) 106 would be slightly increased (decreased) in comparing earnings per share amounts. (106 represents the adjustment factor for one-half year of price change—one plus .057.) A number in this column is equal to the corresponding number in Column (B) when the company has no preferred stock outstanding or when the purchasing power gain for the year on preferred stock outstanding just equals, and offsets, the price level adjusted amount of preferred dividends declared. A number in this column is less than the corresponding number in Column (B) when the price level adjusted amount of preferred dividends is greater than the purchasing-power gain on preferred stock.

[c]Estimated loss as a percentage of reported loss.

[d]Loss equal to indicated percentage of positive net income.

[e]See footnote *e* to Exhibit 9.6.

single overall adjustment factor applied to the reported profits of all firms will yield satisfactory results.[1] For the Dow 30, the range in Column (B) is from a GPLA loss of more than three times as large as conventionally reported net loss (Chrysler) to a GPLA adjusted income almost twice as large as reported income (AT&T). GPLA net income as a percentage of conventionally reported net income ranged from 24 percent (Merrill Lynch) to 256 percent (Fuqua) for the other 44. The range from top to bottom is extremely sensitive to the performance of outliers. Hence much of the discussion which follows is in terms of the interquartile range, the difference between the 75th percentile performance and the 25th percentile performance. For the Dow 30, the interquartile range of GPLA net income as a percentage of conventional net income is from 104.5 to 63.0, a spread of 41.5 percentage points. For the other 44, the interquartile range in Column (B) is from 116.5 to 81.5, a spread of 34.5 percentage points. The interquartile range for the other 44 is somewhat smaller than for the Dow 30. This indicates that, at least for these purposes, the other 44 are more

[1]We are not the first to challenge the validity of the naive view that a constant adjustment factor will suffice. See Russell J. Petersen, "Interindustry Estimation of General Price-Level Impact on Financial Information," *The Accounting Review*, 48, 1 (January 1973), pp. 34–43.

EXHIBIT 9.3

FORTY-FOUR MAJOR COMPANIES

Estimates of General Price Level Adjusted Income Statements

(Amounts for 1974)

Company	Adjusted income before gain on monetary items as a percentage of reported net income (A)	Adjusted net income, including gain on monetary items, as a percentage of reported net income[a] (B)	Adjusted earnings per share as a percentage of reported earnings per share[b] (C)
Anheuser-Busch	69	92	92
Ashland Oil	79	115	122
Avon	96	94	94
Baxter Labs	42	101	101
Brunswick	12	66	66
Caterpillar	85	122	122
Chemetron	70	91	91
Coca-Cola	95	83	83
Copperweld	97	107	107
Dart Industries	45	80	77
Dow Chemical	97	118	118
Dr Pepper	95	77	77
Fuqua Industries	73	256	266
Gould	40	78	80
Gulf Oil	78	83	83
Hilton Hotels	50	165	165
Holiday Inns	78	166	167
Homestake Mining Company	95	81	81
ITT	73	120	123
Jewel Companies	−9[c]	85	86
Kellogg	87	85	86
Koppers	84	108	112
Lehigh Portland Cement	27	29	29
Liggett & Myers	21	88	97
Martin Marietta	71	103	103
Merrill Lynch	106	24	25
Minnesota Mining and Manufacturing (3M)	67	74	74
Northwest Industries	84	102	110
Pabst Brewing Company	52	38	38
J. C. Penney	41	117	117
Philip Morris	39	110	111

EXHIBIT 9.3 (*Continued*)

Company	Adjusted income before gain on monetary items as a percentage of reported net income (A)	Adjusted net income, including gain on monetary items, as a percentage of reported net income[a] (B)	Adjusted earnings per share as a percentage of reported earnings per share[b] (C)
Revlon	76	73	73
Rockwell International	28	92	111
Safeway Stores	48	121	121
Joseph Schlitz Brewing	80	102	102
Shell Oil	86[d]	97[d]	97[d]
Texas Instruments	79	69	69
Time Inc.	70	79	79
Trans Union	20	207	207
UAL (United Air Lines)	25	106	106
Walgreen	66	225	225
Weyerhaeuser	85	118	118
Xerox	78	90	90
Zenith	53	86	86
Median	72	93	97
Interquartile range	84–45	116–81.5	117.5–80.5

[a]See footnote *a* to Exhibit 9.2.

[b]See footnote *b* to Exhibit 9.2.

[c]Loss equal to indicated percentage of positive net income.

[d]Shell published GPLA Statements in 1975. The numbers shown in this row are calculated from Shell's statements. Shell, however, includes deferred taxes among monetary liabilities. We approve of this treatment, but the FASB does not, at least in its exposure draft. Columns (B) and (C) show 100 percent when deferred taxes are included in monetary items, as was done by Shell in its annual report.

homogeneous than the Dow 30. (By this criterion, the steels, reported on below, are most homogeneous because the interquartile range of GPLA net income is 16 percentage points. The pharmaceutical companies are next most homogeneous, range 22 percentage points, and the public utilities next, 39 points.)

These results indicate several points worthy of note. Companies like AT&T, Fuqua, and Trans Union (and the public utilities discussed later), with relatively large amounts of debt, may report very much larger GPLA income in times of general price increases, because of monetary gains, than they report on conventional income statements. Companies such as Walgreen, with substantial declines in reported 1974 net income from previous levels, may get a large percentage boost to GPLA income from monetary gains. In 1974 Walgreen's GPLA income was 225 percent of net income, but in 1973 was only 64 percent of net income.[2] Walgreen's debt stayed relatively constant and the monetary gain on it is a much larger percentage of 1974's relatively low net income than of 1973's higher income.

Income Before Monetary Gain Reduced for Almost All Firms

The figures for adjusted income before monetary gains confirm the often-stated view that conventionally reported earnings have a substantial inflation component. In almost every case, this partially adjusted income figure is lower than the net income published in the financial statements. The reduction is caused by large adjustments of depreciation and, for FIFO companies, of cost of goods sold. The exception among the companies we illustrate is Merrill Lynch.

Merrill Lynch's increase is equal to exactly one half-year of price change. As a service company, it has no cost of goods sold and insignificant depreciation. All its revenues and expenses are adjusted for one-half year of price change. Although Chrysler shows a large positive number in Column (A), this indicates that the adjusted loss is much greater than the reported loss.

GPLA Net Income Surprisingly High in Relation to Reported Net Income

When monetary gains from net borrowings are included, the resulting GPLA net income was a surprisingly high percentage of conventional net income. For the Dow 30, GPLA net income for about half of the companies was 90 percent or more of reported net income and in eight cases exceeded reported net income. For the other 44 in Exhibit 9.3, GPLA net income in 20 cases was equal to or greater than reported net income. The significance of the monetary gains that causes these results is discussed in Chapters Seven and Ten.

Several companies, such as Eastman Kodak, GM, and Sears (Dow list), and Avon, Kellogg, Merrill Lynch, and Texas Instruments in Exhibit 9.3, are net lenders; that is, their monetary assets exceed their monetary liabilities. These companies consequently show losses on monetary liabili-

[2]Sidney Davidson and Roman L. Weil, "Inflation Accounting: What Will General Price Level Adjusted Income Statements Show?" *Financial Analysts Journal,* 31, 1 (January/February 1975), Table 2.

ties. The importance of gains or losses on net monetary items is nowhere more strongly indicated than in the case of Merrill Lynch. In Exhibit 9.3, Merrill Lynch shows the largest GPLA income before monetary items as a percentage of conventional net income, Column (A), but the smallest GPLA net income as a percentage of conventional net income, Column (B). Merrill Lynch rises to the top of Column (A)'s results because, as a service company, it has no cost of goods sold and insignificant depreciation expense. It falls to the bottom of Column (B)'s results because, as a financial company, it has a large excess of monetary assets (at least under our interpretation of FASB classifications) over monetary liabilities.

GPLA earnings per common share, as a percentage of conventional earnings per common share, Columns (C), are slightly larger, on average, than the numbers in Columns (B). Most of these companies do not have relatively large amounts of preferred stock financing.

INDUSTRY STUDIES[3]

In addition to the 74 companies reported on above, we have examined four separate industries—steel, pharmaceuticals, automobile/truck manufacturers, and public utilities.

Steel Manufacturers

Exhibit 9.4 shows GPLA results for the 12 largest (based on 1974 sales) steel manufacturers. These companies use a LIFO cost flow assumption for all, or nearly all, inventories and all have relatively old plants. In addition, their financing includes significant portions of long-term debt.

Pharmaceutical Manufacturers

Exhibit 9.5 shows GPLA results for the 12 largest (based on 1974 sales) drug manufacturers. The companies are characterized by their relatively small investments in plant and by relatively small amounts of debt financing. The major resource of these companies is knowledge represented by patents and other results of research and development. Under generally accepted accounting principles these resources, to the degree they were developed by the firm rather than purchased from others, do not appear

---

[3]The results in this section are based in part on work done by Day-Luan Yang (steels and pharmaceuticals), Christine Ciarfalia and James Skrydlak (public utilities); and Samy Sidky (all others).

EXHIBIT 9.4

TWELVE STEEL MANUFACTURERS (RANKED BY 1974 SALES)

Estimates of General Price Level Adjusted Income Statements

(Amounts for 1974)

Company	Adjusted income before gain on monetary items as a percentage of reported net income (A)	Adjusted net income including gain on monetary items, as a percentage of reported net income[a] (B)	Adjusted earnings per share as a percentage of reported earnings per share[b] (C)
U.S. Steel	63	79	79
Bethlehem Steel	64	83	83
Armco Steel (90% LIFO ending inventory)	80	113	113
Republic Steel	74	93	93
National Steel	67	94	94
Inland Steel (71% LIFO ending inventory)	68	96	96
Lykes-Youngstown	70	110	111
Wheeling-Pittsburgh	74	97	101
Allegheny Ludlum	87	134	139
Kaiser Steel	78	103	106
Cyclops	67	110	110
Interlake (82% LIFO ending inventory)	73	98	98
Median	71.5	97.5	99.5
Interquartile range	74–67	110–94	110–94

[a] See footnote *a* to Exhibit 9.2.

[b] See footnote *b* to Exhibit 9.2.

on the balance sheet. For stable, or slowly growing, firms this omission has little impact on the conventional income statement. That is, any one year's R & D expenses will approximate the amortization of past years' R & D costs if the firm is not growing. On a GPLA basis, however, if R & D costs had been capitalized, their subsequent amortization charge would be increased by the price level change since the costs were incurred. Thus the conservative policy of expensing all R & D costs results in a smaller increase in GPLA expenses, with the result that adjusted operating income as a percentage of reported operating income (Column A) is relatively high for pharmaceutical companies. The median is 79 as compared with 71.5 for the steel companies, −71 for the autos, and 63.5 for the Dow companies.

EXHIBIT 9.5

TWELVE PHARMACEUTICAL MANUFACTURERS (RANKED BY 1974 SALES)

Estimates of General Price Level Adjusted Income Statements

(Amounts for 1974)

Company	Adjusted income before gain on monetary items as a percentage of reported net income (A)	Adjusted net income, including gain on monetary items, as a percentage of reported net income[a] (B)	Adjusted earnings per share as a percentage of reported earnings per share[b] (C)
American Home Products ..	86	80	80
Johnson & Johnson	83	77	77
Warner Lambert	55	41	41
Bristol Myers	84	91	90
Pfizer (LIFO)	98	108	108
Merck	83	83	83
(Eli) Lilly	84	73	73
Squibb	70	77	77
American Hospital Supply ..	49	59	59
Sterling Drug	75	52	52
Upjohn	64	83	83
Abbott Laboratories	55	61	60
Median	79	77	78
Interquartile range	84–64	83–61	83–60

[a]See footnote *a* to Exhibit 9.2.

[b]See footnote *b* to Exhibit 9.2.

Automobile and Truck Manufacturers

Exhibit 9.6 shows GPLA results for six manufacturers of automobiles and trucks.[4] These companies are characterized by use of a FIFO cost flow assumption (except for Fruehauf) and relatively old plant.

[4]We modify our estimation procedures somewhat for these companies. Most of these companies report an expense item "amortization of special tools" in their income statements. Such expenses ought in principle to be adjusted in just the same manner as depreciation—for a number of years equal to accumulated depreciation divided by depreciation for the year. These companies do not report the accumulated amortization on special tools. We assume that these tools have an average life of 3 years and thus adjust their amortization expense for one and one-half years. A similar procedure is used for the steel company, Republic, which reports separate amortization charges, but not accumulated amortization, of blast furnace linings.

EXHIBIT 9.6

SIX AUTOMOBILE AND TRUCK MANUFACTURERS (RANKED BY 1974 SALES)

Estimates of General Price Level Adjusted Income Statements

(Amounts for 1974)

Company	Adjusted income before gain on monetary items as a percentage of reported net income (A)	Adjusted net income, including gain on monetary items, as a percentage of reported net income[a] (B)	Adjusted earnings per share as a percentage of reported earnings per share[b] (C)
General Motors	-34^d	-43^d	-42^d
Ford	-108^d	7	7
Chrysler	602^c	302^c	302^c
American Motors	-22	97	97
White Motor	-109^d	60	65
Fruehauf Corp (LIFO) ..	23	171	172
Median	-71^e	33.5^e	36^e

[a]See footnote *a* to Exhibit 9.2.

[b]See footnote *b* to Exhibit 9.2.

[c]Estimated loss as a percentage of reported loss.

[d]Loss equal to indicated percentage of positive net income.

[e]Because Chrysler showed a reported loss and the effect of GPLA adjustments was to increase that loss, the percentage shown for Chrysler in all three columns is positive. The GPLA adjustments reduce adjusted income, so we treat Chrysler as having a large negative percentage for the purpose of calculating the median (and interquartile range in Exhibit 9.2).

Importance of the Cost Flow Assumption. No other choice between generally accepted accounting principles usually has as large an impact on conventional net income as the choice of cost flow assumptions for inventory and cost of goods sold. In times of rising prices, the choice of LIFO, rather than FIFO or weighted-average, results in significantly larger reported cost of goods sold and significantly smaller reported income on conventional income statements.

The adjustment of cost of goods sold in price level accounting for LIFO companies is substantially smaller than for FIFO companies, because LIFO assumes that the latest purchases, for which the price level adjustment is relatively small, are the ones included in cost of goods sold. For FIFO companies the adjustment is larger, because it reflects the greater price level change since the earlier purchases were made. If the GNP

Deflator exactly measured the rate of price increase for a given firm's inventory items, adjusted cost of goods sold would be the same under a LIFO assumption as under a FIFO assumption.[5] The larger amount reported on conventional income statements for cost of goods sold under LIFO would have a smaller adjustment; the smaller FIFO cost of goods sold would have a larger adjustment. The adjusted amounts would be equal, again assuming that the GNP Deflator was a good measure of price increases for this firm's inventory items.

We have compared the cost of goods sold adjustments for the LIFO steel companies with the cost of goods sold adjustments for the FIFO auto/truck companies. For the LIFO steel companies, the median adjustment is 5.64 percent of reported cost of goods sold, with an interquartile range from 5.68 to 5.57 percent. The five FIFO auto/truck companies have a median adjustment of 8.16 percent, and the middle three range from 7.93 to 8.19 percent. The adjustment for the auto/truck companies is thus about 45 percent larger than for the LIFO steel companies. The difference in results of adjusting cost of goods sold is compounded by the fact that on the conventional income statements cost of goods sold is a greater percentage of total expenses for auto/truck companies than for steel companies. (This, despite the fact that auto/truck companies are on FIFO, which tends to minimize reported cost of goods sold.) The auto/truck companies thus get a larger percentage increase in a cost of goods sold figure that is already a larger percentage of reported total expenses than for steels. With this sharp difference in adjustments to cost of goods sold, GPLA operating income as a percentage of conventional net income is substantially smaller for the FIFO auto/truck companies than for the LIFO steel companies. The median GPLA operating income to reported net income percentage for auto/truck companies is −71.0, but for steels is +71.5.

An additional indication of this effect is given in Exhibit 9.5. There, only one of the pharmaceuticals, Pfizer, uses LIFO for most of its inventories. That Pfizer's percentage in Column (A) is the largest is explained primarily by the fact that its cost of goods sold is adjusted by less than 5 percent, whereas the FIFO companies' cost of goods sold are adjusted by from 8.9 percent (American Home Products) to over 12.5 percent (Lilly and Merck).

WEIGHTED-AVERAGE COST FLOW ASSUMPTION. Nine of the companies in our samples use a weighted-average cost flow assumption for

[5]See Sidney Davidson, Samy Sidky, and Roman L. Weil, "Inflation Accounting: How Well Do General Price Level Adjustments Reflect Current Costs of Inventory?" *Proceedings of the First Topical Research on Accounting Conference,* The Vincent C. Ross Institute of the College of Business and Public Administration, New York University, 1975.

inventories. The following list shows the nine and the percentage increase in GPLA cost of goods sold over conventional cost of goods sold:

Liggett & Myers	9.4%	Texas Instruments ..	7.2%
International Nickel ..	8.7	Kellogg	7.0
Bristol Myers	8.4	Pabst	6.5
American Brands	8.3	Procter & Gamble ...	5.8
General Foods	7.4		

The median of these adjustments is 7.4 percent, which is much more like the FIFO results than the LIFO results, although it does lie between the two.

Public Utilities[6]

Exhibit 9.7 shows GPLA results for 1973 and 1974 for the 24 public utilities in the Dow Jones and Standard & Poor's Utility Indexes. We show results for 2 years so that GPLA effects in years with significantly different rates of price change can be compared.

GPLA operating income, before gain on monetary items (Column A), was substantially less than the conventional net income for all firms, reflecting the sharply higher GPLA depreciation charges. When gain on monetary items is added to obtain GPLA net income (Column B), the GPLA net income amounts for all firms are well above the net incomes reported in the published financial statements. All but three in 1973 and all but one in 1974 show adjusted net income more than 50 percent higher than that conventionally reported. The 1974 exception (Northern Natural Gas) is one of the three 1973 exceptions, all of which were gas companies.

Earnings per share figures (Column C), reflecting the gains from having preferred stock outstanding, are even more sharply higher than those currently reported. In almost half the cases in 1973 and about 80 percent in 1974, adjusted earnings per share is more than double the figure conventionally reported. Observe that for 1974, the interquartile range for GPLA income before monetary gain is 9 percentage points but for GPLA net income is 39 points. We infer that the operations of the

---

[6]This section is based on, and updates, results reported by Sidney Davidson and Roman L. Weil, "Inflation Accounting: Public Utilities," *Financial Analysts Journal*, 31, 3 (May/June 1975), pp. 30–34, 62.

public utilities in our sample are more homogeneous than are their financing structures (debt-equity ratios).

GPLA Effects Under Varying Rates of Inflation.

It is easier to generalize about the effects of varying rates of inflation on GPLA income of public utilities than for most other industries because most public utilities have miniscule inventories and cost of goods sold. There are then only two major offsetting forces at work: higher depreciation expense and gain on the net monetary items making up the corporation's net debtor position. There is, however, no *a priori* basis for deciding which force will be greater. The answer depends primarily on three factors:

1. the rate of change in the price level this year relative to change in earlier years,

2. the estimated service life of plant assets, and

3. the capital structure of the utility.

The depreciation adjustment reflects a portion (equal to the depreciation rate) of the *cumulative change* in prices since the assets were acquired. The gain from debtor position depends on this year's change in prices and the portion of financing obtained from debt, rather than equity, sources.

The relationship between the two forces can be expressed using the following symbols:

$$A = \text{acquisition cost of total assets (most of which are plant)}$$

$$D = \text{debt ratio} = \text{debt/(debt plus equity)}$$

$$= \text{debt/(cost of total assets)}$$

$$P_i = \text{percentage price change during the year } i$$

$$s, s + 1, \ldots, t = \text{years from acquisition of assets to present}$$

$$n = \text{average service life of assets}$$

The depreciation adjustment is approximately[7] equal to the depreciation rate times the cumulative price change since the average asset was acquired times the cost of all assets on hand. Symbolically this can be expressed as

$$\frac{1}{n}\left(\sum_{i=s}^{t} P_i\right) A$$

[7]This approximation assumes that inventories of materials and supplies are not significant.

EXHIBIT 9.7

TWENTY-FOUR UTILITIES IN DOW JONES AND STANDARD & POOR'S INDEXES

Estimates of General Price Level Adjusted Income Statement Amounts

Company	For 1974			For 1973		
	Adjusted income before gain on monetary items as a percentage of reported net income[c] (A)	Adjusted net income, including gain on monetary items, as a percentage of reported net income[a,c] (B)	Adjusted earnings per share as a percentage of reported earnings per share[b] (C)	Adjusted income before gain on monetary items as a percentage of reported net income[c] (A)	Adjusted net income, including gain on monetary items, as a percentage of reported net income[a,c] (B)	Adjusted earnings per share as a percentage of reported earnings per share[b] (C)
Allegheny Power System[f]	57	227	309	74%	183%	222%
American Electric Power	66	277	350	80	176	202
Cincinnati Gas and Electric	64	214	288	77	157	188
Cleveland Electric Illuminating	74	208	261	75	159	188
Columbia Gas System	48	200	204	63	162	162
Commonwealth Edison	60	229	285	71	167	197
Consolidated Edison	71	239	328	78	176	229
Consolidated Natural Gas	56	183	183	64	151	151
Consumers Power	37	330	620	66	195	258
Dayton Power and Light	65	226	302	71	174	212
Detroit Edison	61	286	411	75	186	246
Houston Light and Power	78	214	239	85	157	172
Indianapolis Power and Light	57	236	310	75	160	184
Niagara Mohawk Power	67	225	286	62	196	256
Northern Natural Gas	69	138	145	48	144	158
Northern States Power	66	238	315	75	176	220

Pacific Gas and Electric	68	197	252	75	155	185
Panhandle Eastern Pipe Line	49	176	185	64	142	148
Peoples Gas Co. (9/30 year-end)[c] ...	64	176	196	66	149	162
Philadelphia Electric Co.	73	228	328	80	169	218
Public Service Electric and Gas Co. .	69	228	299	76	169	210
Southern California Edison	77	187	238	74	168	213
Southern Company[c]	61	299	411	74	205	250
United Gas Co. (Entex Inc. 5/30 year-end)	78	154	154	78	114	114
Median	65.5	225.5	287	74.5	167.5	198
Interquartile range	69–60	236–197	315–238	76–66	176–157	220–184

[a]See footnote *a* to Exhibit 9.2.

[b]See footnote *b* to Exhibit 9.2.

[c] "Reported net income" excludes dividends on preferred stock of consolidated subsidiaries. For the three companies that subtract dividends on preferred stock of consolidated subsidiaries in determining net income, we add these dividends back to reported net income. We treat these dividends, then, as though they were dividends of the consolidated entity, as we think they are.

The gain from being a debtor is approximately[8] equal to this year's price change times total net debt. Debt is, however, equal to the debt ratio times total assets, so the adjustment is equal to this year's price change times the debt ratio times the cost of all assets on hand. Symbolically this can be expressed as

$$DP_t A$$

For example, assume a firm whose assets have an estimated average service life of 15 years (= depreciation rate of 6⅔ percent) and are on the average 9 years old. Assume further that the cumulative price increase during the past 9 years has been 60 percent (averaging a little under 5.5 percent compounded annually), the rate of price increase this year is 12 percent, and the debt ratio is 50 percent. The depreciation adjustment equals

$$\frac{1}{15}(.60)A = .04A$$

The gain on debt equals

$$.50(.12)A = .06A$$

Thus the gain on debt exceeds the extra depreciation charges and adjusted income is higher than conventional income.

If the rate of price increase this year were lower than the previous annual average, say 5 percent, the gain on debt would fall to

$$.50(.05)A = .025A$$

and adjusted income would be less than conventional income. Similarly, a reduction in the debt ratio would reduce the gain from the net debtor position.

The substantial excess of gain on monetary debt over the depreciation adjustment in 1974 (1973) results primarily from the inflation rate during 1974 (1973) being 11.8 (7.4) percent, whereas the average rate of inflation over the 8 or 9 years (which represents the average age of assets for most utilities in the sample) preceding 1973 was less than 4 percent. Because the inflation during 1974 exceeds that during 1973, the excess of gain from monetary debt over the depreciation adjustment is higher in 1974 than in 1973, and monetary gains boost 1974 GPLA net income to even

---

[8]This approximation assumes that current liabilities are equal to monetary assets (= cash plus receivables). For all 24 utilities in the sample current liabilities exceed monetary assets, but the amount of the excess is relatively small compared with the amount of debt outstanding.

higher percentages of conventional net income than in 1973. Results for 1975 should be more like those in 1973 than in 1974. We show the 1973 and 1974 results side by side in Exhibit 9.7.

As expected from the analysis above, more rapid inflation decreases GPLA operating income, before monetary gains, but increases GPLA net income and GPLA earnings per share. The effect on GPLA operating income (Column A) is relatively modest; the median falls by 9 percent of conventional net income from 74.5 percent in 1973 to 65.5 percent in 1974. This relatively small decline is caused by the phenomenon referred to above: the higher inflation rate operates only on the portion of the plant account that represents depreciation for the current year.

The effect on GPLA net income is much more substantial. The median GPLA net income rises by 58 percentage points to 225.5 percent from 167.5 percent of conventionally reported income. Eighty percent of the companies report GPLA net income more than double conventional net income. The effect on GPLA earnings per share is even greater. The median increases by about 90 percentage points of reported net income and about half the companies show GPLA earnings per share more than three times as great as that conventionally reported.

The Effect of General Price Level Adjustments on Rate Regulation.

How, if at all, will general price level adjustments affect rate regulation? Will regulatory agencies accept GPLA depreciation expense figures without taking into account the reported gain on the net monetary debt position? This is the question that is almost certainly uppermost in the minds of utility management. Some analysts suggest that if regulators take gain on monetary items into account as well as the depreciation adjustment, "this could cause regulatory commissions to hold down rate increases or in extreme situations even cause rate reductions, thereby causing more problems for those already having financial difficulties."[9]

One offsetting factor that must be taken into account if price level adjustments are used for rate purposes is their effect on the rate base. If net income is stated in current dollars, logic suggests that the rate base must also be restated. In periods of price increase, the rate base will be restated upwards but will that increase be as great as the increase in profits including the monetary gain? As in the comparison of adjusted depreciation and monetary gains earlier, no general answer can be given. Again it is the rate of change in prices this year relative to price changes in earlier years that is the dominant factor.

[9]Philip J. Harmelink and Philip L. Kintzele, "Price Level Adjustments on Electric Utility Statements," *Public Utilities Fortnightly*, 95, 4 (February 13, 1975), p. 33.

For 1974, the median increase in depreciation charges from general price level adjustments for the 24 utilities in the sample was 59.4 percent, but it was only 45.5 percent for 1973. Presumably these numbers approximate the percentage by which the rate base would increase in GPLA original cost jurisdictions. The median increase in net income, including monetary gains from the price level adjustment, was 125.5 percent in 1974 but only 67.5 percent in 1973 (see Columns B of Exhibit 9.7). If rate regulation were based on price level adjusted data including monetary gains, both 1973 and 1974 would have been years of rate reductions.

The problem clearly arises from including monetary gains in GPLA net income. This is ironic, because in many ways the gain or loss from holding monetary items is the most meaningful of the general price level adjustments, as is discussed in Chapters Seven and Ten. The gain from being in a net monetary liability position, although real, does not produce a current flow of cash. If it and the other general price level adjustments are taken into account in rate regulation, there will be accentuated financial difficulties for utilities.

The utilities that will be hurt the most for rate-setting purposes are just the ones whose incomes are given the largest percentage boost by price level adjustments—those with new plants and substantial amounts of debt, relatively speaking.

Are All Public Utility Assets Monetary?[10] Suppose that a firm owned land that it had leased in perpetuity for $10,000 per year. Although land is generally a nonmonetary asset, the future benefits in specific dollar amounts from this particular piece of land are known today. The present value of the land depends only on the discount rate. If the discount rate for this stream of payments is 8 percent per year, then the present value of the land is $125,000 (= $10,000/.08). On GPLA financial statements we would want to show the historical cost of the land adjusted for changes in the general price level, so long as that amount is less than $125,000. That is, if the GPLA amount is less than the present value of the land, then the land is a nonmonetary asset in financial statements based on historical cost principles. If, however, the GPLA amount of the land is larger than $125,000, then we would want to show the land on GPLA balance sheets at $125,000 and treat it as a monetary asset in computing gain or loss on monetary items for GPLA income statements.

Now consider the plant assets of a public utility. In original-cost jurisdic-

---

[10]We acknowledge help from conversations with Myron J. Gordon and J. Leslie Livingstone in clarifying our thoughts on this subject. See Myron J. Gordon, *The Cost of Capital to a Public Utility*, The Institute of Public Utilities, Michigan State University, East Lansing, 1974.

tions, typical for most public utilities, the regulatory agency sets rates based on estimates of the cost of capital and on the historical cost to the enterprise *first* devoting the asset to public service. In such a regulatory environment, public utility assets have much the same characteristics as the land discussed in the preceding paragraph. For a public utility plant asset, once the depreciation schedule is determined (usually at the moment of purchase), the stream of depreciation charges and the contribution to the rate base of this asset is determined for each period of the asset's life. From these numbers, the cash flow the utility will be permitted to earn each period can be determined in advance just as in the earlier example of the leased land.

So long as the cost of capital used by the regulatory agency in setting rates takes into account the anticipated rate of inflation, then the owners of a public utility will be fairly compensated for their investments. In this case, nearly all the plant assets of the public utility should be treated as monetary items. Then, we would see that the public utilities would have an excess of monetary assets over monetary liabilities, not vice versa, and would show monetary losses in GPLA income statements. Under this view, the only major nonmonetary items in public utility balance sheets are stockholders' equity accounts (and the asset construction in process, which is not part of the rate base). The monetary loss during a year would be approximately equal to the average stockholders' equity multiplied by the rate of inflation for the year. This would be subtracted from other income (where revenues are based on a cost of capital which takes pure return, anticipated inflation, and risk into account). The result would be a net income figure that contained only elements of pure return and risk, which is what we want in the first place for the purpose of regulation.

The matter is, in general, much more complicated than we indicate here, because the behavior of regulatory agencies varies with respect to incorporating anticipated inflation into estimates of the cost of capital. Each jurisdiction presents its own problems. Overall, however, we are even more skeptical of the mandatory use of GPLA accounting by regulated industries than we are of its use in other industries. If regulated industries must report GPLA net income based on the same principles used for nonregulated industries, then there will be increased opportunity for misunderstanding in the regulatory process. On the other hand, managements of regulated industries complain as much or more about increased plant asset costs as do managements of nonregulated industries. So long as regulatory agencies allow an adequate cost of capital—including anticipated inflation—then the public utilities do not have the same problems in raising cash to replace plant assets as do nonregulated industries. That is, under proper regulation, where inflation is a component of the cost of capital, owners of regulated industries are shielded from the effects of anticipated inflation. (Owners are affected, however, by the differences between anticipated and actual inflation rates.)

We conclude by wondering if the public is not best served when regulated industries are exempt from inflation accounting. Exemption would be a mixed blessing for utility managements, who like the upward adjustments of depreciation and plant asset costs associated with GPLA accounting, but dislike being credited with gains on monetary items. See, for example, the 1974 financial reports of Indiana Telephone Corporation and Toledo Edison, both of which display GPLA financial statements that do not report most of the monetary gains on debt in GPLA net income.

Chapter Ten

IMPLICATIONS FOR ANALYSIS OF GENERAL PRICE LEVEL ADJUSTED FINANCIAL STATEMENTS

T HE PRECEDING CHAPTER reports our estimates of GPLA income statement amounts for over 100 major corporations. Our major results can be summarized as follows:

1. Effects of general price level adjustments differ substantially among firms.

2. GPLA income before recognizing gain (or loss) on net monetary items is less than conventional net income for nearly all firms and is substantially less for many.

3. GPLA net income, after recognizing gain or loss on net monetary items, is surprisingly (at least to us) high in relation to conventionally reported net income.

This chapter explores some more detailed implications of general price level adjustments for financial statement analysis and shows how to estimate the GPLA funds statement and GPLA balance sheet.

FORM OF PUBLISHED GPLA FINANCIAL STATEMENTS

The FASB does not propose to require complete, line-by-line, GPLA financial statements. Rather, it proposes to require excerpts from them as supplementary disclosures. Exhibit 10.1 reproduces Shell Oil's published GPLA financial statements for 1974. The amount of detail shown there is somewhat greater than that required by the FASB. As we discuss below, however, even this disclosure is not, in our opinion, completely adequate for the needs of analysis. The GPLA information is shown in the first three columns of Exhibit 10.1, labeled "Current Dollars."

EXHIBIT 10.1

FROM THE 1974 ANNUAL REPORT OF SHELL OIL COMPANY, STATISTICAL SUPPLEMENT

Supplementary Price Level Adjusted Financial Information

(Millions of dollars except per share amounts)	CURRENT DOLLARS*			HISTORICAL DOLLARS		
	1974	1973	1972	1974	1973	1972
Summary Statement of Income						
Revenues	$8,866.7	$6,614.4	$5,876.1	$8,493.0	$5,749.6	$4,849.8
Costs and expenses:						
Depreciation, depletion, etc.	654.2	626.5	585.4	502.9	441.7	396.8
Income, operating and consumer taxes	1,320.2	1,236.2	1,163.6	1,264.5	1,074.6	960.4
Interest & discount amortization on indebtedness	63.5	69.9	72.0	60.8	60.8	59.4
Other costs & expenses	6,317.3	4,426.2	3,866.1	6,044.3	3,839.8	3,172.7
Income before purchasing power gain or loss on monetary items	$ 511.5	$ 255.6	$ 189.0	$ 620.5	$ 332.7	$ 260.5
Purchasing power gain (loss) on:						
Long term debt	117.0	82.9	36.4	—	—	—
Other monetary items	(5.1)	(4.8)	2.2	—	—	—
Net income	$ 623.4	$ 333.7	$ 227.6	$ 620.5	$ 332.7	$ 260.5
Summary Balance Sheet						
Current assets	$2,161.7	$1,953.4	$1,925.2	$2,072.2	$1,713.1	$1,596.1
Investments & long term receivables	129.5	110.3	106.1	116.0	91.7	84.1
Properties, plant & equipment (net)	5,146.6	4,906.7	4,923.3	3,905.3	3,526.9	3,438.9
Deferred charges	42.3	61.4	67.5	35.4	49.5	52.5
Current liabilities	1,272.6	1,097.4	1,113.4	1,272.6	981.6	928.2
Long term debt	976.6	1,119.0	1,230.3	976.6	1,000.9	1,025.6
Deferred credits—federal income taxes	320.0	339.5	351.4	320.0	303.6	292.8
Shareholders' equity	$4,910.9	$4,475.9	$4,327.0	$3,559.7	$3,095.1	$2,925.0
Per Share Data†						
Net income	$ 9.25	$ 4.95	$ 3.38	$ 9.21	$ 4.94	$ 3.86
Cash dividends	$ 2.56	$ 2.76	$ 2.91	$ 2.45	$ 2.40	$ 2.40

Ratios (see definitions on page 36)

Return on shareholders' equity	13.9%	7.7%	5.3%	20.0%	11.4%	9.2%
Return on total capital	11.7%	6.6%	5.0%	16.0%	9.2%	8.0%
Net income: revenues**	7.7%	5.9%	4.6%	8.1%	6.7%	6.3%
Dividends: net income	27.7%	55.7%	86.1%	26.6%	48.6%	62.1%
Debt: total capital	16.6%	20.0%	22.1%	21.5%	24.4%	26.0%

*Based on purchasing power dollars at December 31, 1974.
†Per weighted average share outstanding each year.
**Excluding consumer excise and sales taxes.

REPORT OF INDEPENDENT ACCOUNTANTS

To the Board of Directors and Shareholders of Shell Oil Company:

We have examined the financial statements of Shell Oil Company appearing in the Annual Reports to Shareholders for the years 1974, 1973 and 1972, which are covered by our reports dated February 4, 1975 and February 4, 1974. Those financial statements do not reflect the changes in the general purchasing power of the U.S. dollar from the time transactions took place. We have also examined the supplementary information for the years 1974, 1973 and 1972 restated for effects of changes in the general price level as described in the Explanatory Note on page 4. In our opinion, the supplementary Summary Statement of Income, Summary Balance Sheet and Per Share Data shown above present fairly the historical financial information restated in terms of the general purchasing power of the U.S. dollar at December 31, 1974 in accordance with guidelines, consistently applied, recommended in Accounting Principles Board Statement No. 3 and a Proposed Statement of Financial Accounting Standards, except for the treatment, with which we concur, of deferred income taxes as monetary items.

Price Waterhouse & Co.

1200 Milam Street
Houston, Texas 77002
February 4, 1975

Authors' Note: We estimate that the "Purchasing power loss on other monetary items" of $5.1 million during 1974 consists of a $36.8 million gain on deferred tax items less a $41.9 million loss on current monetary items. Shell was a net lender of current monetary items during 1974. This information is required for the GPLA statements of changes in financial position, Exhibit 10.2.

REVENUES AND EXPENSES SPREAD FAIRLY EVENLY THROUGHOUT THE YEAR

As Chapters Seven through Nine point out, most revenues and all expenses except cost of goods sold and depreciation are assumed to occur fairly evenly throughout the year. These items are adjusted for one-half year of price change. An analyst will want to scrutinize the form of this adjustment. Chapter Six points out that there are several ways to calculate "one-half year of price change." In comparing companies the analyst will want to check that they all use the same one-half-year adjuster. The percentage increase of GPLA revenues (or other items spread evenly throughout the year) over the conventional amount can be compared with various measures of one-half year of price change to ascertain the method used.

We believe that the best measure of one-half year's price change is

$$\sqrt{\frac{\text{GNP Deflator for last quarter of this year}}{\text{GNP Deflator for last quarter of last year}}} - 1$$

A simpler and relatively satisfactory half-year adjuster is

$$\frac{1}{2} \times \left(\frac{\text{GNP Deflator for last quarter of this year}}{\text{GNP Deflator for last quarter of last year}} - 1 \right)$$

Some companies, including Shell, use the following measure of one-half year's price change (which is recommended in APB Statement No. 3 and in the FASB Exposure Draft):

$$\frac{\text{GNP Deflator for last quarter of this year}}{\text{Average GNP Deflator for this year}} - 1$$

For 1974, our "best" measure yields a measure of one-half year of price change of 5.73 percent (5.90 percent for the simpler method), whereas the method used by Shell yields a measure of 4.45 percent. The difference between these two measures increases as the rate of inflation increases.

Shell adjusted four items in its GPLA income statement, shown in Exhibit 10.1, for one-half year of price change. These are "Revenues," "Income, operating and consumer taxes," "Interest & discount amortization on indebtedness," and "Other costs and expenses." The algebraic sum of these items in the conventional income statement shows a contribution of $1,123.4 million to 1974 income. Each of these components is adjusted for 4.4 to 4.5 percent, depending on rounding error, and their adjusted total contributes $1,165.7 million to GPLA income. Now, $1,165.7 is only 3.75 percent larger than $1,123.4—the rounding error has accumulated so that the total of GPLA items to be adjusted for one-half year of price change is adjusted by about 2 percentage points less than the 5.73 percent we think best. If the $1,123.4 contribution to conventional income were adjusted for 5.73 percent, the total of these items would be $1,187.8 million, $22 million larger than Shell shows. This $22 million is more than 4 percent of GPLA income before monetary gains as reported by Shell and more than 3.5 percent of Shell's reported GPLA net income.

The half-year price adjuster used makes a difference when prices increase as rapidly as they did in 1974. (See Exhibit 6.10.) Many, perhaps most, firms will use, we assume, the procedure that Shell used. Be aware of the possibly significant impact on reported GPLA numbers of this technical choice. To "correct" the published numbers to secure uniformity is easy, as the above demonstration shows.

COST OF GOODS SOLD

We have seen that LIFO companies get a relatively smaller adjustment to cost of goods sold than do FIFO companies in times of rising prices and increasing inventories. Chapter Nine points out that this is not happenstance, but that one should expect this phenomenon.[1] The cost of goods sold adjustment for a LIFO company is generally just under one-half year of price change, whereas for a FIFO company it is usually two-thirds to three-fourths of a full year's price change, roughly 40 percent more. Thus we can predict that, other things being equal, GPLA income will be a smaller percentage of conventional income for a FIFO firm than for a LIFO firm. The firms that will be most affected by this difference are, of course, those for whom cost of goods sold is a large fraction of total expenses, such as retailers. Thus, we expect to see, other things than cost of goods sold being equal, a larger GPLA impact on Sears, a FIFO retailer, than on Coca-Cola or Eastman Kodak, both LIFO firms.

DEPRECIATION

The older the plant, the greater will be the excess of GPLA depreciation over conventional depreciation. The specific price changes of plant assets for a given firm are likely to depart more from general price level changes than any other item. This is true because plant assets are, on average, older than other assets and there is a longer period for the several price series to diverge. One implication of this phenomenon is discussed below under ratio analysis. The analyst may wish to use a more specific plant

---

[1]We repeat a statement from Chapter Nine: If a given firm's inventory increases in price at the same rate as the GNP Deflator, then its GPLA cost of goods sold is independent of the cost flow assumption. Because a LIFO firm has a larger cost of goods sold on a conventional basis in time of rising prices, its conversion to GPLA cost of goods sold is a smaller percentage increase.

asset price index to compute a different adjusted depreciation charge. Public utilities, steels, and auto/truck manufacturers, in our industry studies in Chapter Nine, have relatively large depreciation charges as a percentage of total expenses. For interindustry comparisons involving these industries, the analyst may find it especially important to substitute depreciation charges adjusted by a specific index for the GPLA adjustments.

UNCONSOLIDATED SUBSIDIARIES

Unconsolidated subsidiaries are not likely to have significant cost of goods sold or depreciation charges because most of them are finance companies or insurance companies. No special problems for analysts are likely to arise except, perhaps, for the half-year adjuster with regard to the GPLA income statements of such unconsolidated subsidiaries. Once the GPLA statement is prepared, the data are substituted for the parent's equity method revenues in constructing the parent's GPLA income statement.

GAIN OR LOSS ON NET MONETARY ITEMS

Monetary gains will be a significant factor in the GPLA net income of many firms. For the Dow 30 in 1974, they raised the median firm from 63.5 percent of conventional net income to 87 percent (see Exhibit 9.2). For the other 44 companies reported on in Exhibit 9.3, monetary gains raised the median GPLA net income from 72 percent to 94 percent of conventional net income. For the public utilities, monetary gains raised GPLA net income to more than twice conventional net income, on average.

Clearly, the higher the debt ratio, the greater will be monetary gains as a percentage of GPLA net income. But these monetary gains do not produce cash inflows. (A portion of the gains do affect working capital, or funds, as discussed below.) The monetary gains on long-term items show the reduced economic significance of contractually fixed cash outflows that will have to be made later. Some, including the management of Indiana Telephone, which has published portions of GPLA financial statements for years, argue that this gain should not be recognized in current income. Only when the long-term debt is retired, they say, should gain be recognized. We disagree with this position and come to these arguments shortly. We do agree, though, that recognition of monetary gains in GPLA net income may enable a company to show adjusted profits even though its cash position is deteriorating. We suggest that with enough debt outstanding a firm can report GPLA profits right up to the time it becomes insolvent. For these reasons we strongly advocate that the analyst construct a GPLA funds statement, or statement of changes in financial position.

GPLA Statement of Changes in Financial Position

The FASB does not require a GPLA statement of changes in financial position, but constructing one is relatively easy and provides meaningful insights into current liquidity. Exhibit 10.2 shows conventional and GPLA working capital, or funds, from operations sections of statements of changes in financial position for General Electric, Alcoa, and Shell for 1974. The GE and Alcoa funds statement excerpts are constructed from our estimates reported in Exhibits 7.1 and 9.1. The Shell GPLA statement excerpt is constructed from information given in its 1974 annual report and our estimates of Shell's reported purchasing-power gain on deferred tax items (see note at Exhibit 10.1).

The GPLA funds statement starts with net income, which includes the effect of gain or loss on monetary items in the GPLA columns of Exhibit 10.2. Next come the various addbacks and subtractions for items not producing or using working capital. The monetary gains (or losses) on long-term debt must be subtracted from (added to) GPLA net income because these gains or losses do not affect current funds. Similarly, the undistributed income (loss) of unconsolidated subsidiaries must be subtracted (added), because it also does not affect current funds.[2] The monetary gain (or loss) for net current monetary items is included in GPLA funds from operations. Current liabilities less cash, receivables, and certain marketable securities do affect current funds. These current monetary items are components of working capital in virtually all definitions of *funds* except the one defining *funds* as cash only. Gain or loss in purchasing power for these items directly affects the current funds position of the firm.

Most firms are net borrowers of monetary items in total. Many firms, however, are net lenders of *current* monetary items and suffer losses in current purchasing power during inflation. These are the firms whose quick, or acid-test, ratios are greater than one. Alcoa and Shell are net lenders of current monetary items. GE is a net borrower of current monetary items. Shell's case points up another place where the analyst will want to be careful. Shell's published GPLA income statement, Exhibit 10.1, shows purchasing-power gains on "long-term debt" and losses on "other monetary items." But included in these "other" items is the gain on

---

[2] A review of the funds statement with a detailed treatment of the effect of the equity method is contained in Appendix 19.1 of Sidney Davidson, James S. Schindler, and Roman L. Weil, *Fundamentals of Accounting*, 5th ed., The Dryden Press, Hinsdale, Ill., 1975.

EXHIBIT 10.2

PARTIAL STATEMENTS OF CHANGES IN FINANCIAL POSITION FOR THE YEAR ENDED DECEMBER 31, 1974

	General Electric Company (GE)[a]		Aluminum Company of America (Alcoa)[b]		Shell Oil[c]	
	Conventional	GPLA	Conventional	GPLA	Conventional	GPLA
Sources of working capital						
From operations:						
Net income (including in GPLA columns the effect of monetary items)	$ 608.1	$ 569.7	$173.1	$224.1	$ 620.5	623.4
Add back expenses that did not use working capital:						
Depreciation, depletion, etc.	376.2	545.3	164.7	271.3	502.9	654.2
Income taxes deferred by timing differences	26.0	27.5	27.2	28.8	16.4	17.1
Other	—	—	.9	1.0	—	
	$1,010.3	$1,142.5	$365.9	$525.2	$1,139.8	$1,294.7

176

Subtract (add) revenues (losses) that did not produce (use) working capital:						
Equity in earnings (losses) retained by unconsolidated subsidiaries:						
Net earnings (losses) including monetary items in GPLA columns	$42.7	($23.9)	($3.3)	$24.7	—	—
Less dividends received	(34.0) $ 8.7	(35.9) ($ 59.8)	— ($ 3.3)	— $24.7	—	—
Gain (losses) on holdings of *long-term* monetary items:						
Foreign	—	$ 1.0	—	$ 2.1	—	—
Domestic	—	59.6^d	—	105.1^c	107.2	$153.8^f $ 153.8
Less (plus) total subtractions (additions) for revenues (losses) not producing (using) working capital	$ 8.7	$ 0.8	($ 3.3)	$131.9	—	$ 153.8
Total sources from operations	$1,001.6	$1,141.7	$369.2	$393.3	$1,139.8	$1,140.9

[a]See Exhibits 7.1 and 7.2.

[b]See Exhibit 9.1.

[c]See Exhibit 10.1.

[d]See footnote d of Exhibit 7.1 or 8.5, where the gain on foreign and long-term debt is identified.

[e]See footnote f of Exhibit 9.1, where the gain on foreign and long-term debt is identified.

[f]$117.0 on long-term debt and $36.8 on deferred taxes treated as monetary items. See Exhibit 10.1. The gain on deferred taxes was estimated as 11.8 percent of the average balance, computed as one-half the sum of beginning and ending balances, in the deferred tax account during the year.

177

treating deferred taxes as monetary ($36.8 million, our estimate) netted against losses on current lendings of $41.9 (= −$5.1 − $36.8) million. The extent of Shell's loss of current liquidity is masked in its GPLA income statement. The GPLA funds statement makes the loss clearer.

Converting Working Capital Funds to Quick Asset Funds. If you are concerned with very short-term liquidity, you may not want to use working capital (= current assets less current liabilities) as your definition of funds. You may prefer to concentrate on net quick assets (= cash, receivables, and marketable securities less current liabilities). To convert a funds statement from a working capital basis to a quick asset basis merely requires, for most firms, that the increase in inventories be subtracted from the increase in working capital.[3] Calculations of the GPLA increase in inventories is a relatively straightforward process. We show the results of such calculations for GE, Alcoa, and Shell in Exhibit 10.3.

FIFO INCREASE IN GPLA INVENTORIES. As indicated by the analysis in Chapter Eight, FIFO GPLA inventories increase by a percentage equal to the percentage increase in GPLA cost of FIFO goods sold over conventional cost of FIFO goods sold less one-half year of general price change. More precisely, the percentage increase in FIFO inventories is

$$\frac{\text{GPLA cost of FIFO goods sold/conventional cost of FIFO goods sold}}{1 + \text{rate of price change for one-half year}} - 1$$

LIFO INCREASE IN GPLA INVENTORIES. In the usual case where inventories amounts increase, LIFO GPLA inventories increase by a percentage equal to the percentage increase in GPLA cost of LIFO goods sold over conventional cost of LIFO goods sold plus one-half year of general price change. This percentage will usually be slightly under one full year of price change. More precisely, the percentage increase to derive LIFO inventories is[4]

[(1 + percentage increase in cost of LIFO goods sold to GPLA basis) × (1+ rate of price change for one-half year)] − 1

---

[3]The amount of current prepayments is also included in working capital, but for most firms its amount is so small, relatively, that it can be ignored. Of the three companies illustrated in Exhibits 10.2 and 10.3, only Alcoa separately classifies the increase in current prepayments. Alcoa's increase in current prepayments is $48,000, whereas the total working capital from operations is $369.2 million.

[4]When LIFO inventory amounts decrease, the GPLA inventory decrease is the conventional inventory decrease increased by a percentage equal to about 2 years (or sometimes more— see footnote 5 of Chapter Eight) of price change.

EXHIBIT 10.3

CONVERSION OF FUNDS FROM OPERATIONS ON WORKING CAPITAL BASIS TO QUICK ASSET BASIS

	GE (80%, LIFO, 20% FIFO)		Alcoa (LIFO)		Shell Oil (LIFO)	
	Conventional	GPLA	Conventional	GPLA	Conventional	GPLA
Total sources of working capital from operations (Exhibit 10.2)	$1,101.6	$1,141.7	$369.2	$393.3	$1,139.8	$1,140.9
Less (increase) or plus decrease in inventories:						
LIFO stock	(216.6)[a]	(241.7)[c]	(114.2)[e]	(127.2)[f]	(121.7)[g]	(135.8)[h]
FIFO stock	(54.2)[b]	(55.7)[d]	—	—	—	—
Total sources of quick assets from operations	$ 830.8	$ 844.3	$255.0	$266.1	$1,018.1	$1,005.1

[a] See Exhibit 8.5; $1,805.6 − $1,589.0 = $216.6.

[b] See Exhibit 8.5; $451.4 − $397.2 = $54.2.

[c] $216.6 × 1.056 × 1.057 = $216.6 × 1.116 = $241.7.

[d] $54.2 × 1.087/1.057 = $54.2 × 1.028 = $55.7.

[e] From Alcoa 1974 annual report.

[f] $114.2 × 1.054 × 1.057 = $114.4 × 1.114 = $127.2.

[g] From Shell 1974 annual report.

[h] $121.7 × 1.056 × 1.057 = $121.7 × 1.116 = $135.8.

For none of these companies is the difference between quick assets from operations on the conventional basis, as opposed to the GPLA basis, as great as 5 percent.

Gain or Losses on Long-Term Monetary Items

Should purchasing power gains or losses on long-term monetary items, which will not flow through the cash account until the distant future in many cases, be currently recognized in GPLA net income? We think so. First, we argue that the firm always has the option, at the margin, of issuing more equity securities and using the proceeds to retire debt, so that the gain can be realized currently. That the firm chooses not to do so does not affect its opportunity. Second, we argue that if depreciation, which does not use current funds, is recognized as a current expense, then gains on long-term items can analogously be recognized as current income.[5] Third, we argue (see Chapter Seven) that the gain on monetary items is in a real sense an offset to reported interest expense. Interest expense incorporates the inflation expected by both the borrower and the lender at the time the loan is made.[6] In conventional financial statements, the income statement is based on the accrual concept whereas the statement of changes in financial position reports on current funds flows. Analogously, we think the GPLA income statement should be based on the accrual concept whereas a GPLA statement of changes in financial position can report changes in current purchasing power. We advocate that a GPLA statement of changes in financial position be used by the analyst in the same way he or she uses a conventional one. Purchasing power gains on long-term debt are excluded from sources of funds in the GPLA funds statement.

What About Deferred Tax Items? Shell, in conflict with generally accepted accounting principles, reported a purchasing-power gain on deferred tax items, treating them as a long-term monetary liability. Shell's

---

[5]The counterargument here is that depreciation is a current expense for past outflows of funds, whereas gains on long-term debt would be a current income for future inflows of funds. This argument about past outflows applies only to the unadjusted historical-cost portion of depreciation. The GPLA depreciation adjustment is exactly analogous to the gain on long-term monetary items in this respect.

[6]We would prefer to show the gains on long-term debt from anticipated inflation as an offset to reported interest expense and the remainder, positive or negative, as an unanticipated purchasing power gain or loss. As Chapter Seven points out, who benefits after the fact depends on whether the actual rate of inflation exceeded the anticipated rate when the loan was made (borrower gains) or whether the actual rate falls short of that anticipated when the loan was made (lender gains).

auditors, Price Waterhouse, noted the divergence from GAAP and concurred with it.[7]

In making comparisons of GPLA net incomes across firms, the analyst will want to ensure that the treatment of deferred income taxes and deferred investment tax credits as monetary or not is the same for the firms being compared. If not, appropriate adjustments should be made.

GAIN OR LOSS ON FOREIGN MONETARY ITEMS

The gain or loss on foreign monetary items will usually be included in published GPLA income before gain or loss on domestic monetary items. The amount of gain or loss on foreign items is not likely to be specifically labeled. Although we compute it as the change in prices for the year multiplied by the average net foreign monetary balance for the year, it is not technically computed that way. (The technical computation, as Chapters Six and Seven point out, involves a write-down of GPLA foreign items to market if such an adjustment is called for.) We believe that debt is debt, independent of the country of borrowing, so that in making comparisons across firms, the presentation of the gain or loss on foreign monetary items within the income statement should be treated the same as gain or loss on domestic monetary items.[8] The analyst who agrees with us may want to estimate the foreign gain or loss, subtract it from GPLA income before monetary gain or loss, and add it in with reported gain or loss on monetary items. In any case, the analyst who wants to construct a GPLA funds statement must estimate purchasing-power gain (or loss) on foreign long-term debt so that it can be subtracted (or added) in computing funds from operations.

RAPIDLY GROWING VERSUS SLOWLY GROWING COMPANIES

General price level adjustments tend to decrease GPLA income before monetary items for rapidly growing companies less than for slowly growing companies. Put another way, rapidly growing companies have, on the

---

[7]So do we. We also argue that comprehensive tax allocation is not good accounting on conventional financial statements. See Sidney Davidson, James S. Schindler, and Roman L. Weil, *Fundamentals of Accounting*, 5th ed., The Dryden Press, Hinsdale, Ill., 1975, chap. 15; A logically complete argument as to why deferred taxes are monetary is presented by John K. Shank and Richard F. Vancil, "Are Deferred Taxes Monetary? Matching Revisited," *The Accounting Review*, 51, 1976.

[8]The inflation rate (domestic or foreign) to be used in computing gain or loss on foreign items is an open theoretical issue. See the discussion in Chapter Twelve on the rate to be used in computing gain or loss on domestic monetary items.

average, newer plants, and the upward adjustment of depreciation expense is smaller for them than for most slowly growing companies. The effect on net income, including gain or loss on monetary items, is compounded if, as is likely to be true, the rapidly growing company has a larger portion of its capitalization made up of debt and thus a larger monetary gain.

For believers in the desirability of economic growth, GPLA financial statements may have a serendipitous effect. The more rapidly growing companies are likely to show an improved GPLA earnings picture relative to more slowly growing companies. Whether one believes this will affect the cost of capital to them depends on whether, and to what extent, one believes in the efficiency of capital markets.

EFFECTS OF DIFFERENT RATES OF INFLATION

A more rapid rate of inflation will in almost all cases reduce GPLA income before monetary gains as a percentage of reported income. The effects of more rapid inflation on GPLA net income, including monetary gains, are more difficult to predict in general. Clearly it depends on the relative importance of greater monetary gains compared with higher cost of goods sold and higher depreciation expenses. For public utilities, with insignificant cost of goods sold, we are reasonably confident of the effects of different rates of inflation on GPLA net income. Chapter Nine presents the model for predicting the GPLA net income of public utilities for different rates of inflation.

EFFECTS OF MORE EXTENSIVE LEASE CAPITALIZATION

One of the topics under consideration by the FASB is more extensive lease capitalization. If leases that are now accounted for as operating leases by lessees become, under new rules, accounted for as financing leases, there will be an increase in reported long-lived assets (the leasehold) and an increase in reported long-term debt (the present value of the liability for lease payments). Both the dollar difference between reported and adjusted depreciation and the amount of monetary gains would be increased by such broader capitalization. In the typical case, the increase in monetary gain is likely to exceed—usually by a substantial amount for a growing firm—the additional amortization charges. The difference between the two depends on the inflation rate this year compared to that of earlier years, the length of the leases, and where in the life cycle of the leases this year falls.

Precisely those growing companies that will have their reported conventional earnings most adversely affected by lease capitalization will have the greatest boost to GPLA earnings from that capitalization. Perhaps this consideration may diminish some of the opposition to broader lease capitalization.

Illustration of Lease Capitalization on Net Income, Conventional and GPLA

By SEC requirement, companies must disclose the effect on net income of capitalizing financing leases, as defined by the SEC, if the effect is material. In this section, we work through sample calculations of the effect of lease capitalization on GPLA income for Sears Roebuck and for UAL (United Air Lines). UAL's annual report discloses all the information about components of capitalized lease expense (interest and amortization expenses). Sears' annual reports disclose all the information required to derive the components of capitalized lease expense. Exhibit 10.4 shows the calculations. Interest expense is shown, or derived, on line (8), and amortization expense on line (11). GPLA amortization calculations require knowing the average age of the assets being amortized. In our GPLA depreciation calculations, we use accumulated depreciation divided by depreciation for the year. We do not know, however, the accumulated amortization of the implied leasehold assets. For Sears, we judge that its leases are primarily for stores and depreciation is primarily for fixtures in the stores. Hence we conclude that the leases are on average at least as old as the depreciable assets. For both Sears and UAL, we adjust the amortization for leases by the same percentage as we adjust the conventional depreciation charges. In doing so we expect that we are more likely to be underadjusting than overadjusting Sears' implied amortization charges for the lease. All of the calculations for Sears and UAL are shown in Exhibit 10.4. In general, lease capitalization reduces conventional income but, in times of rising prices, increases GPLA income. The comparisons between the GPLA results for the years of 1973 and 1974 indicate that as the inflation rate increases, GPLA income resulting from lease capitalization increases for these two companies. In conventional statements, Sears' 1974 (1973) pretax income would be reduced by $3.7 ($2.9) million if leases are capitalized. In the GPLA statements, Sears' 1974 (1973) pretax income would be increased by $9.4 ($3.7) million if leases are capitalized. Under lease capitalization, UAL shows even more dramatic changes in pretax income from conventional to GPLA statements as the rate of inflation increases from about 7.5 percent in 1973 to about 12 percent in 1974.

EXHIBIT 10.4

EFFECTS OF LEASE CAPITALIZATION ON CONVENTIONAL AND GPLA NET INCOME FOR SEARS, ROEBUCK & COMPANY, AND UAL (UNITED AIR LINES)

($ Amounts in Millions)

	Sears — For year ended January 31				UAL — For year ended December 31			
	1974[a]		1975[d]		1973[f]		1974[i]	
	Conventional[b]	GPLA	Conventional[b]	GPLA	Conventional[b]	GPLA	Conventional[b]	GPLA
(1) Lease expense as reported under operating method	$ 67.0	$70.0	$ 76.0	$80.0	$100.2	$103.8	$112.0	$118.4
Assuming Capitalization of Leases								
(2) Average interest rate used in capitalization as of the start of the year	NA		5.6%		NA		NA	
(3) Present value of lease obligations as of the start of the year	$386.0		$351.0		$681.4		$815.2	
(4) Average interest rate used in capitalization as of the end of the year	5.6%		5.8%		NA		NA	
(5) Present value of lease obligations as of the end of the year	$351.0		$426.0		$815.2		$882.0	
(6) Average interest rate used in capitalizing lease obligations, .5 × [(2) + (4)]	5.6%		5.7%		6.71%		6.92%	
(7) Average lease obligation during year, .5 × [(3) + (5)]	$368.5		$388.5		$748.3		$848.6	
(8) Interest expense on lease if capitalized, (6) × (7)	$ 20.6	$21.5	$ 22.1	$23.3	$ 51.2	$ 53.1	$ 58.8	$ 62.2
(9) Decline in net income if leases were capitalized (from annual report footnotes)	$ 1.5		$ 1.9		$ 7.8		$ 6.9	
(10) Decline in income before taxes if leases were capitalized, assuming marginal income tax rate of 48 percent, (9)/(1 − .48)	$ 2.9		$ 3.7		$ 15.0		$ 13.4[j]	

	(1)	(2)	(3)	(4)	(5)	(6)	(7)	(8)
(11) Amortization expense of leasehold for year, (1) – (8) + (10)	$ 49.3	$72.8[c]	$ 57.6	$89.6[c]	$ 64.0	$ 93.4[h]	$ 66.6	$ 98.8[c]
(12) Purchasing-power gain on lease obligation, (7) × price increase for year, see footnotes a, d, f, i.		$33.5		$42.3		$ 55.4		$100.1
(13) Increase (decrease) in pretax income, (1) – (8) – (11) + (12)	($ 2.9)	$ 9.2	($ 3.7)	$ 9.4	($ 15.0)	$ 12.7	($ 13.4)	$ 57.5

NA, not given in annual report.

[a] Prices increased by 9.1 percent in 12 months ending January 31, 1974, or 4.5 percent for one-half that period.

[b] (1), (2), (3), (4), (5), and (9) for "conventional" columns taken from annual reports.

[c] Sears' depreciable assets were 8.63 years old as of year-end; prices increased by 47.6 percent in the 8.63 years preceding 1/31/74. We assume that leased assets were of same age: 1.476 × $49.3 = $72.8.

[d] Prices increased by 10.9 percent in 12 months ending January 31, 1975, or 5.3 percent for one-half that period.

[e] Sears' depreciable assets were 8.00 years old as of year-end; prices increased by 55.6 percent in 8.00 years preceding 1/31/75. We assume that leased assets were of same age: 1.556 × 56.6 = $87.9.

[f] Prices increased by 7.4 percent in the 12 months preceding 12/31/73; one-half year of price change is 3.64 percent.

[g] All information, except rows (10) and (.3), in this column is explicitly given in the UAL annual report.

[h] UAL's depreciable assets were 5.6 years old, on average, as of year-end; prices increased by 46.0 percent in the 5.6 years preceding 12/31/73. We assume that leased assets were of same age: 1.146 × $64.0 = $93.4.

[i] Prices increased by 11.8 percent during 1974 and by 5.7 percent for one-half a year.

[j] By actual division, this number is $13.3 $13.4 is shown to make additions for line (11) exact.

[k] Adjusted for 6.8 years (same as for depreciation charges) of price change, or 48.4 percent: 1.484 × $66.6 = $98.8.

Note: The analysis in this exhibit has been extended to six companies over two years by Sidney Davidson and Roman L. Weil in "Lease Capitalization and Inflation Accounting," *Financial Analysts Journal*, 31, 6(November/December 1975), pp. 22–29, 57.

RATIO ANALYSIS AND SENSITIVITY TO GNP DEFLATOR

The analyst often wants to compare financial ratios across firms. In our opinion, the two most useful ratios for measuring performance are the rate of return on all capital and the rate of return on stockholders' equity. The former measures management performance and the latter measures the return to owners. When these measures are based on GPLA statements, they can be misleading. The main problem arises from using the GNP Deflator for adjusting plant amounts on the GPLA balance sheet and consequently for adjusting depreciation amounts on the GPLA income statement. As discussed earlier, the rates of price change for a given firm's plant assets are likely to be quite different from the rate of change in general prices measured by the GNP Deflator. If, for example, the rate of change in a given firm's plant costs exceeds the rate of general price increase, then the GPLA amount of plant and depreciation are understated relative to current costs. Thus the income shown in the numerator of the rate of return calculations is too large relative to current values because too little depreciation is subtracted from revenues in computing net income. Furthermore, the denominator of the calculations is too small because the current cost of plant is understated. These two biases work in the same direction to overstate the implied rates of return. Similarly, if a given firm's plant costs increase less rapidly than general prices, then the effect is doubly to bias the rate of return downwards.

A difference of a given size in relative rates of price increase makes larger differences in the rate of return calculations. Exhibit 10.5 illustrates this phenomenon. We have taken information from the GPLA statements of Shell, Exhibit 10.1, and show four sets of ratios:

1. those based on the conventional statements,

2. those based on published GPLA statements,

3. those based on published GPLA statements assuming that Shell's plant costs have increased by 10 percent more than the GNP Deflator, and

4. those based on published GPLA statements assuming that Shell's plant costs have increased by 10 percent less than the GNP Deflator.

The ratios shown in Exhibit 10.5 differ somewhat from those shown by Shell in Exhibit 10.1 because we use end-of-year balances and slightly different definitions of the ratios. For these purposes, we define the rate of return on all capital as

$$\frac{\text{Net income + aftertax interest expense}}{\text{End-of-year balance of total assets}}$$

and the rate of return on stockholders' equity as

$$\frac{\text{Net income}}{\text{End-of-year balance of stockholders' equity}}$$

In general, rates of return calculated from GPLA amounts are less than those calculated from conventional statements. Notice, by comparing the ratios in Columns (3) and (4) with those in Column (2), how much more sensitive to assumptions about relative rates of price change are the rates

EXHIBIT 10.5

ILLUSTRATION OF SENSITIVITY OF RATE OF RETURN ESTIMATES TO ASSUMPTIONS ABOUT RELATIVE PRICE CHANGES

Information taken from, or based on, 1974 GPLA Statements of Shell Oil Company (see Exhibit 10.1)

(Dollar Amounts in Millions)

	Conventional	GPLA	Specific price level adjusted statements Assuming that plant costs change at a rate different from the GNP Deflator and the results of using specific prices, to reflect current costs, are wanted. Assumption about plant costs: Plant costs change at a rate equal to 10 percent	
			More than Deflator	Less than Deflator
Depreciation, depletion, etc.	$ 502.9[a]	$ 654.2[a]	$ 719.6[b]	$ 588.8[c]
(N1) Net income plus aftertax interest expense ..	652.1[d]	656.4[e]	591.0[f]	721.8[g]
Properties, plant, and equipment (net)	3,905.3[a]	5,146.6[a]	5,661.3[b]	4,631.9[c]
(D1) Total assets	6,128.9[a]	7,480.1[n]	7,994.8[h]	6,965.4[i]
ALL CAPITAL EARNINGS RATE (RETURN ON TOTAL CAPITAL)= N1/D1	10.6%	8.8%	7.4%	10.4%
(N2) Net income	$ 620.5[a]	$ 623.4[a]	$ 558.0[j]	$ 688.8[k]
(D2) Shareholders' equity	3,559.7[a]	4,910.9[a]	5,425.6[l]	4,396.2[m]
RATE OF RETURN ON SHAREHOLDERS' EQUITY = N2/D2	17.4%	12.7%	10.3%	15.7%

[a]Given in Shell's report, Exhibit 10.1.   [b]110 percent of amount in Column (2).   [c]90 percent of amount in Column (2).

[d]$620.5 + (1 − .48) × $60.8 = $652.1.   [e]$623.4 + (1 − .48) × $63.5 = $656.4.   [f]$656.4 + $654.2 − $719.6 = $591.0.

[g]$656.4 + $654.2 − $588.8 = $721.8.   [h]$7,480.1 + $5,661.3 − $5,146.6 = $7,994.8. $7,480.1 + $4,631.9 − $5,146.6 = $6,965.4.

[j]$623.4 + $654.2 − $719.6 = $558.8.   [k]$623.4 + $654.2 − $588.8 = $688.8. $4,910.0 + $7,994.8 − $7,480.1 = $5,425.6.

[m]$4,910.9 + $6,965.4 − $7,480.1 = $4,396.2.

of·return than are the net income figures. Our assumptions about relative price changes cause *specific* price level adjusted plant and depreciation amounts to change by 10 percent. These assumptions cause changes in specific price level adjusted income and in the specific price level adjusted amount of assets. These two changes, in turn, cause changes in specific price level adjusted rates of return of from 16 to 24 percent of the GPLA ratios.

EXHIBIT 10.6

ESTIMATING THE GPLA BALANCE SHEET

General Electric Company

As of December 31, 1974

($ Amounts in Millions)

	Conventional	Adjustment factor	GPLA
Assets			
Monetary assets			
Current	$2,908.3	None	$ 2,908.3
Noncurrent	522.2	None	522.2
Inventories	2,257.0	Note *a*	3,092.4
Plant and equipment ...	2,615.6	1.449[b]	3,790.0
	$8,303.1		
All other assets	1,066.0	1.20[c]	1,279.2
Total assets	$9,369.1		$11,592.1
Equities			
Monetary liabilities			
Current	$3,879.5	None	$ 3,879.5
Noncurrent	1,195.2	None	1,195.2
Other liabilities and minority interest	590.1	1.20[c]	708.1
Total liabilities	$5,664.8		$ 5,782.8
Stockholders' equity	3,704.3	Plug[d]	5,809.3
Total equities	$9,369.1		$11,592.1

Estimating the GPLA Balance Sheet and GPLA Ratios

Computing financial ratios requires balance sheet, as well as income statement, data. Chapter Eight shows how to estimate a GPLA income statement. The GPLA ratios for Shell were constructed from Shell's GPLA balance sheet. Analysts who want to estimate ratios prior to the publication of "official" GPLA balance sheets or for interim reports must estimate their own balance sheets. Any reader who has followed us this far will find it relatively easy to estimate a GPLA balance sheet. The steps are explained below and illustrated in Exhibit 10.6 for the General Electric Company's balance sheet as of December 31, 1974.

Monetary Items. All monetary assets and liabilities are shown on the GPLA balance sheet as of the end of the period in the same amounts as are shown on the conventional balance sheet. The amounts shown for monetary items as of the beginning of the period should be restated in end-of-year dollars.

Note *a:*

Cost of goods sold (excluding depreciation) .	$ 9,761.4
Ending inventory (LIFO)	2,257.0
Beginning inventory (LIFO)	(1,986.2)
Purchases	$10,032.2

	Beginning inventory	Ending inventory
As shown in published balance sheet .	$1,986.2	$2,257.0
Excess of FIFO valuation over LIFO valuation (adjustment to convert all inventory to FIFO basis; as shown in notes to annual report)	429.7	783.7
Implied FIFO valuation of inventory .	$2,415.9	$3,040.7

$$\frac{\text{Ending implied FIFO inventory}}{\text{Purchases}} = \frac{\$3,040.7}{\$10,032.2} = 30.3 \text{ percent}$$

Price change for 15.2 (= 30.3/2) percent of year when prices increased by 11.8 percent for the year = $(1.118)^{.152} - 1 = 1.7$ percent. $1.017 \times$ implied FIFO ending inventory = $1.017 \times \$3,040.7 = \$3,092.4$, which is the ending inventory on a GPLA basis.

[b] See Exhibit 7.1 for depreciation of 44.9 percent.

[c] Two years of price change assumed: $1.074 \times 1.118 - 1 = 20$ percent.

[d] $11,592.1 - \$5,782.8 = \$5,809.3$.

Inventories. GPLA inventories are easy to estimate when a FIFO flow assumption is used. Conventional ending FIFO inventory consists only of the last few purchases made during the year. The purchases that make up ending FIFO inventory, assuming that all purchases occur fairly evenly throughout the year, took place in the last part of the year equal to the following fraction of a year:

$$\frac{\text{Ending inventory}}{\text{purchases}} = \frac{\text{ending inventory}}{\text{cost of goods sold} + \text{ending inventory} - \text{beginning inventory}}$$

Conventional FIFO ending inventory is adjusted by one-half the above fraction of a year's price change to estimate GPLA FIFO ending inventory.

If a LIFO flow assumption is used, then the notes of the annual report show what conventional beginning and ending inventories would be under FIFO. Convert the conventional LIFO beginning and ending inventories to FIFO and adjust that amount for a fraction of a year's price change equal to

$$\frac{1}{2} \times \frac{\text{FIFO derived ending inventory}}{\text{purchases}}$$

Plant Assets. All depreciable assets are shown on the GPLA balance sheet at an amount equal to their conventional balances increased by a percentage that is the same as the percentage increase in estimated GPLA depreciation charges for the year over conventional depreciation charges for the year. Land is increased, in the same percentage, under the assumption that the land on which depreciable assets sit is about as old as the depreciable assets themselves. (If you think it appropriate, land balances can be increased by the price change for an additional 5 or so years.)

All Other Assets and Liabilities. We estimate the GPLA balance of all other assets and liabilities by increasing their conventional balances by a percentage equal to 2 years of price change. This relatively arbitrary assumption is used only for a small fraction of a given company's balance sheet amounts, and any other reasonable amount of price change could be used as well.

MINORITY INTERESTS. We treat minority interests in consolidated subsidiaries as part of "Other liabilities," rather than as stockholders' equity. Theorists argue about the proper placement of minority interest on the consolidated balance sheet. Whatever its placement on the consolidated balance sheet, its amount is clearly not part of the stockholders' equity of the parent and thus in computing rates of return on the parent's equity, minority interest should be counted with liabilities, not with stockholders' equity. If the balance sheet being analyzed includes minority interest with stockholders' equity, then minority interest should be reclassified for these purposes as "Other liabilities." The "Other liabilities" are adjusted by 2 years of price change in our illustrative calculations for GE (Exhibit 10.6).

Stockholders' Equity. GPLA stockholders' equity is GPLA assets less GPLA liabilities. The accountant, in preparing "official" GPLA statements, has an independent check of this derived, or plugged, amount. In making estimates, we do not.

PART **III**

ACCOUNTING FOR CHANGING PRICES

Chapter Eleven

METHODS OF ACCOUNTING FOR CHANGING PRICES: CONCEPTS, METHODS, AND USES

T HIS CHAPTER DESCRIBES SEVERAL METHODS that have been suggested for accounting for changing prices. There are essentially two different kinds of accounting for changing prices: current value accounting and uniform dollar accounting. A third method, best in our opinion, combines the most useful aspects of both. This chapter presents and discusses the following three methods: current value accounting, general price level adjusted (uniform dollar) accounting, and current value accounting combined with general price level adjustments. The first and the last of these [illustrated in Columns (2) and (4) of Exhibits 11.1 and 11.2] are similar methods because the balance sheet totals are identical. Reported net income differs, however, and the balance sheet items are classified in different ways.

The first major section of this chapter presents rudiments of the three different methods of accounting for changing prices and compares them with conventional accounting. Then, we discuss the conceptual merits and practical difficulties of the several methods. Chapter Twelve presents the criticisms of GPLA accounting.

METHODS OF ACCOUNTING FOR CHANGING PRICES

Three methods of accounting for changing prices are illustrated in Exhibits 11.1 and 11.2. Even though the examples are based on simple assumptions, they incorporate virtually all of the complications and issues of accounting for changing prices.

Revenues, Inventory, Cost of Goods Sold, and Holding Gains or Losses

Exhibit 11.1 shows transactions for a hypothetical company for a year in which the general price level increased by 32 percent (20 percent in the

EXHIBIT 11.1

CONVENTIONAL ACCOUNTING COMPARED WITH CURRENT VALUE AND

Balance Sheet as of January 1, 19XX

Cash....$100   Contributed capital....$100

	Transactions During 19XX		
Date	January 1, 19XX	June 30, 19XX	December 31, 19XX
GNP Deflator	100 ——(20% increase)→	120 —(10% increase)→	132
Cost of one widule ..	$50	$80	$90
Transaction	Buy 2 widules at $50 each, $100	Sell 1 widule for $120	Close books and prepare statements

	Historical dollars		Uniform dollars dated 12/31/XX	
Cost basis	Acquisition	Replacement	Acquisition	Replacement
Usual name	GAAP	current value	GPLA	current value & GPLA
	(1)	(2)	(3)	(4)
Income Statement, Year of 19XX				
Revenues	$120	$120	$132[a]	$132[a]
Cost of goods sold	50	80	66[b]	88[c]
Operating income	$ 70	$ 40	$ 66	$ 44
Realized holding gains	—	30[d]	—	22[e]
Gain (loss) on monetary items	—	—	(12)[f]	(12)[f]
Realized income	$ 70	$ 70	$ 54	$ 54
Unrealized holding gains	—	40[g]	—	24[h]
Net Income	$ 70	$110	$ 54	$ 78
Balance Sheet, December 31, 19XX				
Assets				
Cash	$120	$120	$120	$120
Inventory	50	90	66[b]	90
Total assets	$170	$210	$186	$210
Equities				
Contributed capital	$100	$100	$132	$132
Retained earnings	70	70	54	54
Unrealized holding gains	—	40	—	24
Total Equities	$170	$210	$186	$210

(1)Traditional.   (2)Easy to explain, hard to audit.   (3)Hard to explain, easy to audit.   (4)Hard to explain, hard to audit.

[a]$120 × 1.10.   [b]$50 × 1.32.   [c] $80 × 1.10.   [d]$80 − $50.   [e]($80 − 1.20 × $50) × 1.10.   [f]$120 × (−10%).   [g]$90 − $50.   [h] $90−((\$50 × 1.32).

first 6 months and 10 percent in the second 6 months—1.20 × 1.10 = 1.32). The market value of inventory units (widules) was $50 per unit on January 1, $80 on June 30, and $90 on December 31. (It is not at all unusual, of course, for some specific price changes to differ substantially from the change in the general price level. Realistic cases of even more substantial differences than those used in the example are easily found.)

The company starts the year with $100 cash and $100 of contributed capital, as shown in the January 1 balance sheet. The company buys two widules (inventory) on January 1 for $50 each and sells one on June 30 for $120.

Historical Dollar, Conventional Accounting. Column (1) of Exhibit 11.1 shows how these transactions are accounted for in conventional financial statements. Revenues are $120, cost of goods sold is $50, and net income is $70.

Current Value Accounting. Column (2) of Exhibit 11.1 shows how the transactions would be accounted for under current value, or replacement cost, accounting. Revenues are still $120. The cost of the unit sold, at the time it was sold, is $80, so the operating income is $40. In addition, there a realized holding gain on that item sold of $30 (equal to current value at time of sale of $80 less acquisition cost of $50). Furthermore, there is an unrealized holding gain of $40 (equal to current value of $90 at end of year less acquisition cost of $50). Thus net income is $110 (= $40 + $30 + $40). The December 31 balance sheet shows all assets and liabilities at current values as of December 31.

General Price Level Adjusted Accounting Based on Historical Costs. Column (3) of Exhibit 11.1 shows the income statement and balance sheet that would be reported in general price level adjusted accounting as described in this book. All costs are historical, but financial statement data are restated to dollars of constant purchasing power. In the illustration, the dollars of uniform purchasing power are dated December 31, 19XX.

Revenues of $120 realized on June 30 are the equivalent of $132 of December 31 purchasing power. Prices increased by 10 percent between June 30 and December 31, so it takes $132 on December to buy the same general market basket (as represented by the GNP Deflator) as could have been bought on June 30 for $120.

The cost of goods sold of $50 in historical dollars is restated to $66 (= 1.32 × $50) in terms of December 31 purchasing power, because the goods were acquired on January 1.

Because the company held cash, $120, from June 30 through December 31, when the purchasing power of the dollar declined by 10 percent, there is a loss on holdings of monetary items of $12 (= .10 × $120).

The balance sheet shows the historical cost of inventory restated to dollars dated December 31. The amount of capital contributed by owners was $100 in terms of January 1 purchasing power. This amount is equivalent to $132 of December 31 purchasing power because prices increased by 32 percent during the year. Hence contributed capital is shown on the balance sheet in terms of December 31 purchasing power as

$132. The retained earnings amount shown on the balance sheet is transferred from the income statement.

Current Values Adjusted for General Price Level Changes.

Column (4) of Exhibit 11.1 shows the accounting when the principles of current value accounting are combined with the principles of stating all amounts in uniform dollars. This approach has received acceptance among many theorists as the best possible approach, but is not likely to be required in the foreseeable future.[1]

Revenues are translated to end-of-year dollars as in Column (3). Cost of goods sold in current values is $80 as of June 30. But these are dollars of June 30 purchasing power. Translated to dollars of December 31 purchasing power, cost of goods sold is 10 percent more than $80, or $88.

The realized holding gain is measured as follows. In terms of June 30 purchasing power, the holding gain is the difference between current value on June 30 and acquisition cost restated to dollars of June 30 purchasing power. The acquisition cost of $50 on January 1 is the equivalent of $60 (= 1.20 × $50) of June 30 purchasing power. Hence the realized holding gain is $20, the $80 (current value as of June 30) less $60 (cost in June 30 dollars). This holding gain of $20 is measured in dollars of June 30 purchasing power and must be restated to $22 (= 1.10 × $20) of December 31 purchasing power.

The unrealized holding gain is somewhat easier to compute: the current value of one widule on December 31 is $90. It cost $50 on January 1, which is equivalant to $66 (= 1.32 × $50) of December 31 purchasing power. The unrealized holding gain is $24 (= $90 − $66).

Cash was held during the second half of the year when prices increased by 10 percent, so there is a loss on holdings of monetary items of $12, calculated as before.

The balance sheet shows inventory at current values as of December 31 and the amount of contributed capital in terms of December 31 purchasing power. Notice that the balance sheet totals in Column (4) are the same as in Column (2). This is no coincidence. The only basic difference between current value accounting and current value accounting with general price level adjustments is that net income is reported differently. When the effects of changing prices are incorporated into current value accounting, we get a separation of real holding gains from nominal holding gains. The $32 difference between the net incomes reported in Columns (2) and (4) reflects the fact that the contributed capital in

---

[1]Perhaps the best argument for this combined approach is given by Robert R. Sterling, "Relevant Financial Reporting in an Age of Price Change," *Journal of Accountancy*, February 1975, pp. 42–51.

December 31 dollars is exactly $32 more than contributed capital in January 1 purchasing power. That $32 represents a shift from income to contributed capital in price level adjusted current value accounting, but is not recognized in historical-dollar current value accounting.

Long-Lived Assets and Accounting for Changing Prices

Accounting for long-lived assets and depreciation in schemes designed to reflect changing prices requires some special techniques. These are explained in this section and in Exhibit 11.2. The assumptions for the illustration are as follows:

1. A new machine is purchased on 1/1/X1 for $10,000.

2. It is estimated that the machine will have a 10-year service life and zero salvage value at retirement.

3. Depreciation is computed on a straight-line basis at 10 percent of cost per year.

4. The GNP Deflator increased by 40 percent between 1/1/X1 and 12/31/X4.

5. The GNP Deflator increased by 10 percent between 1/1/X4 and 12/31/X4.

6. A new machine of exactly the same type as the one purchased in (1) costs $20,000 on 1/1/X4 and $25,000 on 12/31/X4.

7. Used machines just like the ones purchased in (1) have current values equal to book values as shown in Column (2) at 1/1/X4 and 12/31/X1.

Current Value Accounting. At the start of 19X4, the current value (new) of the asset is $20,000 and it is 30 percent "gone," so accumulated depreciation must be $6,000 and the book value must be $14,000. During the year, 10 percent of the asset's cost is allocated to depreciation charges for the year. The asset's average replacement cost new during the year is $22,500 = ($20,000 + $25,000)/2. Thus the depreciation charge for the year, based on 10 percent of this "cost," is $2,250.

During the year, however, the current value of a similar, but new, asset increased from $20,000 to $25,000. Thus the owner of the asset has a holding gain. The gain on an unused asset would have been $5,000, but on average, our asset was only 65 percent new during the year. (It was 70

EXHIBIT 11.2

ILLUSTRATION OF DEPRECIATION COMPUTATIONS, GENERAL PRICE LEVEL ADJUSTMENTS, AND RELATED HOLDING GAINS FOI LONG-LIVED ASSETS

Assumptions

1. Machine purchased new on 1/1/X1 for $10,000.
2. Machine estimated to last 10 years and have zero salvage value at retirement.
3. Depreciation computed on a straight-line basis at 10 percent of cost per year.
4. GNP Deflator increased by 40 percent between 1/1/X1 and 12/31/X4.
5. GNP Deflator increased by 10 percent between 1/1/X4 and 12/31/X4.
6. New machine of exactly the same type as the one purchased in (1) costs $20,000 on 1/1/X4 and $25,000 on 12/31/X4.
7. Used machines just like the ones purchased in (1) have current values equal to book values as shown in Column (2) of this Exhibit at 1/1/X4 and 12/31/X1.

	Historical dollars		Uniform dollars dated 12/31/X4	
	GAAP (1)	Current value (2)	GPLA (3)	Current value & GPLA (4)
Balance Sheet, 1/1/X4				
Asset "cost"	$10,000	$20,000	$14,000[a]	$22,000[b]
Less accumulated depreciation[c]	(3,000)	(6,000)	(4,200)	(6,600)
Book value (30% depreciated)	$ 7,000	$14,000	$ 9,800	$15,400
Income Statement for 19X4				
Depreciation (10% of average "cost" during year)	(1,000)	(2,250)[d]	(1,400)[e]	(2,350)[f]
Holding gain	—	3,250[g]	—	1,950[h]
Balance Sheet, 12/31/X4				
Book value (40% depreciated)	$ 6,000	$15,000	$ 8,400	$15,000
Asset "cost"[i]	$10,000	$25,000	$14,000	$25,000

[a] $10,000 × 140/110 = $10,000 × 1.40.

[b] $20,000 × 110/100 = $20,000 × 1.10.

[c] Asset is 30 percent depreciated at January 1; 30 percent of "cost."

[d] 10 percent of average cost of new asset during year; .10 × ($20,000 + $25,000)/2 = $2,250.

[e] 10 percent of adjusted cost of $14,000.

[f] 10 percent of average cost [= .5 × ($22,000 + $25,000)] of new asset expressed in dollars dated December 31, 19X4.

[g] Gain on "unused" asset during year is $5,000. On average, our asset was 65 percent new during the year; .65 × $5,000 = $3,250.

[h] Gain on "unused" asset during year in constant dollars dated December 31, 19X4, is $3,000 = $25,000− 1.10 × $20,000. On average, our asset was 65 percent new during the year; 65 × $3,000 = $1,950.

[i] Asset is 40 percent depreciated as of December 31.

percent new at the start of the year and 60 percent new at the end of the year.) Thus our holding gain is only 65 percent of $5,000, or $3,250.[2]

General Price Level Adjustments for Long-Lived Assets. Column (3) of Exhibit 11.2 shows the accounting for the long-lived asset with general price level adjustments. During the 4 years since the asset was acquired, the general price level increased by 40 percent. The December 31 balance sheet would show the asset's cost at $14,000, which is equal to the original cost of $10,000 restated to December 31, 19X4, dollars. At the start of the year the asset is 30 percent depreciated, so the book value at the start of the year is .70 × $14,000 = $9,800 of December 31, 19X4, purchasing power.

Depreciation charges for the year are 10 percent of cost stated in December 31 dollars, or $1,400. As of the end of the year, the asset is 60 percent gone.

Of all the adjustments in general price level accounting, the depreciation adjustment is likely to show the largest change from the traditional statements. Furthermore, it is likely to be the least representative of current economic conditions. Only when the current value, or replacement cost, of assets similar to the ones being depreciated have changed at the same rate as general prices have changed, will the adjustment reflect relevant information.

Current Value Adjusted for General Price Level Changes. Column (4) of Exhibit 11.2 shows the accounting when the techniques of Column (2) for current values and Column (3) for general price level adjustments are combined.

The current value of the asset at the beginning of 19X4 was $20,000, but that amount is equal to $22,000 of December 13, 19X4, purchasing power. Because the asset is 30 percent depreciated at the start of 19X4, its

---

[2]Notice that Exhibit 11.2, unlike Exhibit 11.1, does not separate the holding gain into realized and unrealized portions. Theorists disagree about how much of that holding gain should be considered to be realized. At one extreme are those who think that holding gains should be realized only as depreciation is charged. These theorists would recognize $1,250 of holding gain during the year, which is equal to 10 percent of the $10,000 increase in current value since the asset was acquired through the start of 19X4 plus $250 of depreciation on the average increase in value during 19X4. See E. O. Edwards and P. W. Bell, *The Theory and Measurement of Business Income,* University of California Press, Berkeley and Los Angeles, 1961, pp. 189–197. At the other extreme are those who would recognize $5,000 of holding gain, which is equal to the entire amount of the increase in the value of a new asset during the year. They would also have to show larger depreciation charges so that the book value at the end of the year is correctly stated as shown in Exhibit 11.2. This is the treatment used by many French accountants in the early 1950's in preparing tax returns for long-lived assets based on then-current values. The resolution of this issue is not important to our discussion. (We tend to agree with Edwards and Bell.)

book value is $15,400, or 70 percent of $22,000, in December 31 purchasing power.

The depreciation charge for the year is 10 percent of the average value of the new asset expressed in December 31, 19X4, dollars. The average value during 19X4 is $23,500 [= .5(1.10 × $20,000 + $25,000)]. Hence the depreciation charge for the year is 10 percent of $23,000, which is $2,350.

The holding gain for the year is computed as follows. A new asset increased in value by $3,000 (= $25,000 − 1.10 × $20,000) of December 31 purchasing power. On average our asset was 65 percent unused during 19X4, so the holding gain is 65 percent of $3,000, or $1,950.[3] It is no coincidence that the net book values of the asset to be shown on the December 31 balance sheet are the same in Columns (2) and (4) of Exhibit 11.2.

CURRENT VALUE ACCOUNTING

In recent years, the focus in financial reporting has shifted increasingly from providing historical reports on managements' stewardship to providing information that is helpful in making rational investment decisions. In keeping with this trend, many accountants have proposed that accounting measurements rely more heavily on measures of current prices of specific items. This is not a new idea, but the frequency of such proposals, the zeal of their advocates, and the widespread support the proposals have received, particularly among academicians, is a relatively recent development.

Among the asserted advantages of the use of current prices of specific items are (1) a more meaningful statement of financial position, (2) an improved measure of the results of primary, recurring operating activities, (3) the recognition of gains and losses resulting from holding assets during the periods the specific prices of those assets change, and (4) the segregation of the results of ordinary operations from holding gains and losses.

AAA Committee's Analysis

The underlying considerations have been set forth by a Concepts and Standards Committee of the American Accounting Association in its consideration of accounting for long-lived assets:[4]

---

[3]Again, there is the problem of separating the holding gain into the realized and unrealized portions. The issues are the same as those discussed in the previous footnote.

[4]Committee on Concepts and Standards—Long-lived Assets, "Accounting for Land, Buildings, and Equipment," *The Accounting Review,* 39, July 1964, pp. 693–694.

Basic Considerations. 1. The allocation of investor capital within the economic system is heavily influenced by the cumulative effect of investor decisions. The firm's reported net income and financial position are among the primary quantitative measurements affecting these decisions. . . .

Specifically, the purpose of financial statements is to assist the investor in making his own qualitative judgments about a firm. Among the major attributes of financial statements which facilitate this process are the following:

a. *The measurement and reporting of current income should provide a basis for the prediction of future earnings.* To facilitate the predictive process, reported current income should include: (1) the result of ordinary operations, (2) catastrophic losses and discovery of assets, and (3) holding gains and losses.

Income from ordinary operations is measured by matching current revenues and current cost expirations including depreciation. Holding gains and losses relating to long-lived assets result from holding such assets during periods of value change (other than value change resulting from depreciation). . . .

The three components of current income referred to above should be reported separately. Because these components result from different causes, they are likely to exhibit different patterns of behavior. As a consequence, separate reporting of these items makes the income statement a more effective basis for income prediction.

b. *The statement of financial position discloses asset composition and capital structure.* Such information is relevant to the appraisal of the firm's stability and the soundness of its financial policies. The statement of financial position also furnishes a measure of resources for which management is responsible and which it uses in the earning of income. In computations such as the calculation of rates of return, it is equally as important to have a currently relevant economic quantity for the denominator (usually some measure of resources employed) as for the numerator (usually some measure of current earnings).

At the same time, another American Accounting Association Committee on Concepts and Standards was arriving at essentially the same conclusions with respect to inventories.[5]

Accountants have long recognized holding losses as an essential part of proper inventory measurement. However, such losses have not been reported separately except in unusual cases where substantial

---

[5]Committee on Concepts and Standards—Inventory Measurement, "A Discussion of Various Approaches to Inventory Measurement," *The Accounting Review,* 39 (July 1964), pp. 705–706.

losses have occurred. Price (holding) gains are rarely, if ever, reported explicitly. Neither FIFO nor LIFO spotlights price gains or losses. For example, when prices rise, FIFO buries price gains in the regular income figure; LIFO excludes the effects of price changes from the income statement:

				LIFO			FIFO
Sales, 5,000 @ $.20				$1,000			$1,000
Beginning inventory	1,000 units	@ $.10 =	$100			$100	
Purchases	5,000 units	@ $.15 =	750			750	
Available for sale			$850			$850	
Ending inventory	1,000 units	@ $.10 =	100	750	1,000@ $.15	150	700
Gross margin				$ 250			$ 300

The $50 price gain (which is attributable to the 1,000 units in ending inventory @ $.05) is ignored in the $250 LIFO gross margin figure and is submerged in the $300 FIFO gross margin figure.

In contrast, in this simplified case the use of replacement cost will spotlight price gains as follows:

Sales, 5,000 @ $.20	$1,000
Cost of goods sold—at current replacement cost, 5,000 units @ $.15	750
Gross trading or transaction margin	$ 250
Price or holding gain, 1,000 units @ $.05	50
Gross trading margin plus price gain	$ 300
Inventory balance, 1,000 units @ $.15	$ 150

When meaningful measurement can be made, it seems evident that the segregation of price or holding gains or losses (from inventory planning and control decisions) and trading or transaction gains or losses (from exchange of goods and services at replacement price levels) will be more helpful than their usual combination into one gross margin measure.

Distinctions between trading and price facets of operations can be important in evaluating business performance and prospects. Managers must make decisions on inventory commitments, decisions on when and how much to buy and on how much to carry. Such decisions inevitably entail risks with respect to price changes. These decisions sooner or later affect reported net income; they also have an important bearing on financial position.

Inventory management decisions should be accounted for more clearly so that the user of the financial statements may readily focus on management's success or failure in dealing with the problem of inventory price changes. For example it is not uncommon for speculative inventory build-ups to occur because managers believe a price cycle has neared bottom, or because managers fear an impending strike or other disruption of supply. If prices soar, the possession of a large inventory acquired at lower than current replacement prices may be of immense significance to present and prospective investors.

Of course, this significance also holds for the opposite case, where management guesses wrong. CPAs are on guard to see that management reports these price losses, these opportunity losses or declines in expectations. But reports of price gains are usually delayed until sale, and then they are submerged in an income figure that fails to isolate trading gains and price gains—gains that usually arise from different types of decisions. The ignoring or burying of price losses and gains hinders timely and accurate measurement of organizational performance.

Current Costs and Operating Income

The use of current prices is based on a particular concept of income and a particular view of the way in which income measurements are used by investors. The AAA Committee on Long-Lived Assets explained this view as follows:[6]

> Income from ordinary operations should represent an amount, in current dollars, which, in the absence of catastrophic loss or discovery of assets, is available for distribution outside the firm without contraction of the level of its operating capacity; or, stated in another way, the amount which, by retention, is available for expansion of operating capacity. Measurement of this concept of income from ordinary operations can be accomplished only if the expiration of service potential is measured in terms of current cost. That is, in order to continue operations without contracting the level of operating capacity, exhausted services must be restored; the relevant cost of expired services is the current cost of restoration.
>
> For example, a firm may maintain some level of basic raw material inventory in order to continue operations at a given level. In the measurement of income from ordinary operations, the relevant expired cost when that material is utilized is the cost of replenishing the inventory. The number of dollars paid sometime in the past for the particular units of material used this period is not relevant.
>
> The identical concept applies to depreciation; that is, depreciation must be based on the current cost of restoring the service potential consumed during the period. The measurement problems are greater

[6]Committee on Concepts and Standards—Long-Lived Assets, *op. cit.,* pp. 695–697.

in the case of depreciation, however. The physical exhaustion of inventories is subject to actual count or weight; the expiration of the intangible service emanating from plant assets is subject only to rough, subjective evaluation. In addition, the determination of current cost may be more easily accomplished for inventories than for plant assets. Despite these measurement problems, the conceptual need for current-cost depreciation in the determination of income from ordinary operations cannot be denied.

Income from ordinary operations is important to investors in making investment decisions. This amount, when compared with cash dividends, is relevant to an appraisal of the intent of the management to contract or expand the operating capacity of the firm. Secondly, it facilitates prediction of future income from ordinary operations, assuming that costs other than depreciation are also stated in current terms. Third, interfirm income comparability is improved by universal measurement of depreciation on the basis of current cost. Finally, insofar as depreciation represents a reduction in the stock of assets for which management is responsible, this reduction is more clearly indicated by current-cost depreciation on all assets than by depreciation based on unmodified historical cost.

The *total* net income of the period is the maximum amount which, in the absence of stockholder capital transactions during the period, could be distributed outside the firm without contraction of the amount of stockholder equity at the beginning of the period. This is in contrast with *operating* income, which was defined earlier in terms of maintaining operating capacity.

Where holding gains and losses are reported, it is presumed that evidence meeting the specified tests of objectivity and verifiability is available. Under these conditions, holding gains and losses should be treated as increases and decreases in the measurement of net income for the period during which the gain or loss occurs.

Holding gains and losses resulting from unanticipated changes in technology or demand are necessarily directly reflected as changes in the equity of the stockholders. A favorable change in market conditions, for example, improves the position of the enterprise relative to other enterprises not subject to the change. However, such gains are not distributable without contraction of operating capacity and therefore do not enter into the measurement of income from ordinary operations. Similarly, such losses do not necessarily reduce operating capacity and therefore are not deducted in arriving at income from ordinary operations. Nevertheless, such value changes do represent changes in the equity of the stockholders and must be recognized in the overall measurement of total net income for the period during which such changes occur.

It should be understood that, over the life of the firm, the measurement of total net income based on current prices of specific items will be identical with that based on historical acquisition costs. The differences are solely a matter of timing and information—no mean considerations in view of the number of transactions occurring daily that involve an exchange of ownership and that are influenced significantly by accounting measurements. The use of current prices recognizes changes in value when the changes take place rather than only when the value changes happen to be realized in exchanges for liquid assets. In the process, the measurement of operating income is said to be improved and a more meaningful statement of financial position is said to be provided.

Concepts of Current Prices

Several different kinds of current prices have been proposed: for example, the price at which an identical asset could currently be purchased, the price at which equivalent service potential could currently be purchased, and the price at which the asset could currently be sold outside the firm.

Current Price of Replacing an Identical Asset. Imperial Tobacco Company of Canada has used current replacement costs in measuring fixed assets and depreciation in its published financial statements. Imperial Tobacco Company based its current prices of fixed assets on cost of replacement in kind, even though it is recognized that many of the assets involved would never be exactly duplicated. According to one report:[7]

> The company did not use the current market price of an asset as replacement cost except when that asset was an exact duplicate of the asset owned by the company. Imperial officials believed that machinery and equipment currently available might well represent greater efficiency than did existing equipment and that acquisition of greater efficiency, as opposed to mere replacement, was a matter of investing new capital, not the preservation of existing capital. . . . The definition of replacement cost used by Imperial was the amount of money required to exactly duplicate any particular asset without regard to the factor or factors which caused the change from the historical cost of the asset in question.

Edwards and Bell[8] also advocate the use of the current cost of identical assets:

[7]D. R. Ladd and J. F. Graham, Imperial Tobacco Company of Canada, Limited, ICH 8C1, Intercollegiate Case Clearing House, Boston, 1963.

[8]Edgar O. Edwards and Philip W. Bell, *op. cit.*

It must be remembered that it is not the current cost of equivalent services provided by the fixed asset over some time period which we wish to measure, but the current cost of using the particular fixed asset which the entrepreneur chose to adopt and is still using. It is that particular decision that the entrepreneur wishes to evaluate on the basis of accounting data. It may well be that he then may wish to compare these data with opportunity cost data relating to selling and/or replacing the fixed asset, but in order to make this decision about the future, he must have information about the actual present and past.

Current Price of Replacing Equivalent Service Potential. The AAA Long-Lived Assets Committee favors the use of entry prices—specifically, the price at which equivalent service potentials could currently be purchased.[9]

> At the acquisition date of an asset, the value of its service potential is presumed to be at least as great as its purchase price. If this were not the case, the asset presumably would not have been purchased. In most cases, purchase price provides the only objective evidence of the value of the service potential embodied in the asset. . . .
>
> The current cost of obtaining the same or equivalent services should be the basis for valuation of assets subsequent to acquisition, as well as at the date of acquisition.

A distinction is sometimes made between reproduction cost and replacement cost. Reproduction cost refers to the cost of identical property, as advocated by Edwards and Bell and used by Imperial Tobacco Company; replacement cost refers to the cost of equivalent property as advocated by the Long-Lived Assets Committee. Paton and Paton[10] offer support for the latter in this way:

> It should be understood that the significant replacement cost is the cost of providing the existing capacity to produce in terms of the most up-to-date methods available. Thus it's largely a waste of time to estimate the cost of replacing an obsolete or semiobsolete plant-unit literally in kind; such an estimate will neither afford a basis for a sound appraisal of the property nor furnish a useful measure of current operating cost. The fact of interest is what it would cost to replace the capacity represented in the existing asset with a machine of

---

[9]Committee on Concepts and Standards—Long-Lived Assets, *op. cit.,* pp. 694–695.

[10]William A. Paton and William A. Paton, Jr., *Asset Accounting,* Macmillan Company, New York, 1952, p. 325.

modern design. To put the point in another way, cost of replacing in kind is a significant basis on which to measure the economic importance of property in use only in the case of standard, up-to-date facilities.

Current Price at Which Asset Could Be Sold. Raymond J. Chambers is probably the leading advocate of the use of exit prices, that is, the prices at which assets could currently be sold. He explains:[11]

> At any *present* time all past prices are simply a matter of history. Only present prices have any bearing on the choice of an action. The price of a good ten years ago has no more relation to this question than the hypothetical price twenty years hence. As individual prices may change even over an interval when the general purchasing power of money does not, and as the general purchasing power of money may change even though some individual prices do not, no useful inference may be drawn from past prices which has a necessary bearing on present ·capacity to operate in a market. Every measurement of a financial property for the purpose of choosing a course of action—to buy, to hold, or to sell—is a measurement at a point of time, in the circumstances of the time, and in the units of currency at that time, even if the measurement process itself takes some time.

> Excluding all past prices, there are two prices which could be used to measure the monetary equivalent of any nonmonetary good in possession, the buying price and the selling price. But the buying price, or replacement price, does not indicate capacity, on the basis of present holdings, to go into a market with cash for the purpose of adapting oneself to contemporary conditions, whereas the selling price does. We propose, therefore, that the single financial property which is uniformly relevant at a point of time for all possible future actions in markets is the market selling price or realizable price of any or all goods held. Realizable price may be described as *current cash equivalent*. What men wish to know, for the purpose of adaptation, is the numerosity of the money tokens which could be substituted for particular objects and for collections of objects if money is required beyond the amount which one already holds.

Selecting the Appropriate Current Price Concept. Whether the current replacement cost or the current selling price of assets and equities is the appropriate current price concept depends on the uses made of financial statement information. Because the information needs of various

---

[11]Raymond, J. Chambers, *Accounting, Evaluation, and Economic Behavior,* Prentice-Hall, Inc., Englewood Cliffs, N.J., 1966.

users may differ, the relevant current price concept may also differ. Revsine offers support for this view as follows:[12]

> Observation suggests that the audience for financial reports is quite diverse. One characteristic of this diversity is that there are probably differences in the objectives of various categories of users. These differences in objectives imply there could be differences in the decision models used to achieve these disparate objectives. If the decision models vary among groups of users, then it is also possible that the information needed to satisfy the respective decision models varies among groups. That is, diversity in decision models implies (but does not necessarily guarantee) diversity in needed information. As a consequence of this potential diversity in information needs, accounting reports prepared under one measurement basis may be relevant for the information needs of one group and irrelevant to other groups.

Revsine[13] suggests that financial statements based on current replacement costs may be particularly relevant to users interested in predicting future operating flows of a firm and future distributable operating flows to investors in the firm. The current replacement cost of assets serves as an estimate of the future cash flows required in replacing assets' services used up during the period. These estimated future cash flows will affect the availability of resources for maintaining or increasing operating capacity and for making distributions to investors.

McKeown[14] suggests that financial statements based on current selling prices, or exit values, may be particularly useful in assessing the liquidity of a firm because exit-value statements measure assets at the net amount that could be realized from their disposal within a short time of the balance sheet date.

The Study Group on the Objectives of Financial Statements concluded that different valuation bases may be relevant *within* a particular set of financial statements.[15]

---

[12]Lawrence Revsine, "Replacement Cost Accounting: A Theoretical Foundation," in *Objectives of Financial Statements*, Vol. 2, edited by Joe J. Cramer, Jr., and George H. Sorter, AICPA, 1974, p. 179.

[13]*Ibid.*, pp. 182–192.

[14]John C. McKeown, "Usefulness of Exit-Value Accounting Statements in Satisfying Accounting Objectives," in *Objectives of Financial Statements*, Vol. 2, *op. cit.*, p. 162.

[15]Accounting Objectives Study Group, *Objectives of Financial Statements*, New York, AICPA, 1973, pp. 41–43.

The Study Group believes that the objectives of financial statements cannot be best served by the exclusive use of a single valuation basis. The objectives that prescribe statements of earnings and financial position are based on user's needs to predict, compare, and evaluate earning power. To satisfy these information requirements, the Study Group concludes that different valuation bases are preferable for different assets and liabilities. That means that financial statements might contain data based on a combination of valuation bases. . . . Current replacement cost may be the best substitute for measuring the benefits of long-term assets held for use rather than sale. Current replacement cost may be particularly appropriate when significant price changes or technological developments have occurred since the assets were acquired. . . . Exit value may be an appropriate substitute for measuring the potential benefit or sacrifice of assets and liabilities expected to be sold or discharged in a relatively short time.

Edwards, in 1975, again addressed the problem of entry versus exit prices as "current prices."[16] We agree with his argument for a combination of entry and exit prices, depending upon whether the exit price is determined from a market in which the owner is usually a seller:

A firm that values its assets at exit prices derived from markets in which the firm is normally a buyer reports *unusual* values—those which would obtain in a liquidation situation, at least so far as the assets being so valued are concerned. To employ such values when liquidation is not contemplated is surely misleading. . . .

I am not convinced of the merit of adopting as a normal basis for asset valuations in the going concern, exit prices in buyer markets. These are unusual values suitable for unusual situations. . . .

The point at issue, of course, is not *whether* to value by current entry or exit prices, but *when* to shift from entry to exit values. . . .

. . . [T]he principle . . . that all assets and liabilities of the going concern should be valued at current entry prices except for those that the firm normally sells . . . would come close to a rule of "replacement cost or net realizable value, whichever is higher," . . . [except for] a firm which is temporarily selling at a loss. . . .

In selecting the appropriate valuation basis for financial statements, it is clear that the information needs of financial statement users must first be identified. This identification process is essentially an empirical one toward which much research effort needs to be directed.

[16]Edgar O. Edwards, "The State of Current Value Accounting," *The Accounting Review*, 50, (April 1975), pp. 235–245.

Determining Current Prices

One of the major criticisms leveled at proposals to use current prices in accounting is the difficulty of determining such prices for many kinds of items. A variety of possibilities has been suggested.

In the American Accounting Association's *A Statement of Basic Accounting Theory*,[17] it is argued that the techniques already utilized in accounting practice in the process of applying the lower-of-cost-or-market rule to inventories, where market is defined as current replacement cost, should be equally acceptable for determining replacement costs that are in excess of historical cost.

> The current replacement cost of merchandise inventories can usually be secured from the supplier's current catalogue. . . . In manufacturing situations, market is deemed to be replacement cost based upon current prices for materials and labor and customary overhead costs.

The matter of determining current replacement costs of manufactured inventories also received the attention of the American Accounting Association's 1964 Inventory Committee:[18]

> Although in most situations the determination of replacement cost can be accomplished with a high degree of objectivity, difficult problems may arise, particularly in manufacturing situations. In the case of a merchandising enterprise, the determination of replacement cost should be easier, because extensive reliance can be placed on recent invoice prices. Sometimes it will be necessary to obtain quotations from suppliers as of the inventory pricing date. These quotations should be compatible with the company's usual purchasing procedures for the particular item in regard to quantities, discount terms, and method of shipment. A similar situation should prevail in the case of the raw material inventory of a manufacturing concern.

> Calculation of the replacement cost of the finished product or work in process inventory of a manufacturer will not be such a simple process. It will be necessary to determine the current (replacement) cost of each element of the total cost of the inventory units. In many cases the current cost of raw materials and labor should be determinable with tolerable precision by employing current wage rates and material costs multiplied by the actual (or standard) quantity of labor or material related to the partially or fully completed product. In the case of indirect manufacturing costs, adjustment of historical cost to current

[17]American Accounting Association, *A Statement of Basic Accounting Theory*, Evanston, Ill., 1966, p. 74.

[18]Committee on Concepts and Standards—Inventory Measurement, *op. cit.*, p. 710.

cost by the use of index numbers which give effect to changes in the price level of indirect cost factors may be the best available procedure.

As a practical matter, currently attainable standard costs of manufactured goods should suffice in many instances. In most other situations, the divergence of replacement cost from acquisition cost will largely be traceable to volatile prices for the raw material components rather than to significant changes in direct labor or factory overhead.

In *A Statement of Basic Accounting Theory,* a number of possibilities are also suggested for determining the current replacement cost of equipment: (1) Where the same item, or a service equivalent, is available, purchase price, new, on the current market, adjusted for depreciation; (2) acquisition price of items similar to those held in the current used market; (3) in the case where current market prices are available only for items reflecting technological improvements, current purchase price, new, with a downward adjustment to reflect obsolescence; (4) by applying specific price indexes for equipment of the broad classification within which equipment falls.

These suggestions and the other suggestions made in the *Statement* for particular kinds of assets (e.g., long-term investments, buildings, land, and various intangibles) are consistent with those of the earlier Long-Lived Assets Committee:[19]

> Where there is an established market for assets of like kind and condition, quoted prices provide the most objective evidence of current cost. Such prices may be readily available for land, buildings, and certain types of standard equipment. Where there is no established market for assets of like kind and condition, current cost may be estimated by reference to the purchase price of assets which provide equivalent service capacity. The purchase price of such substitute assets should be adjusted for differences in operating characteristics such as cost, capacity, and quality. In other cases, adjustment of historical cost by the use of specified price indexes may provide acceptable approximations of current cost. Appraisals are acceptable only if they are based on the above methods of estimating current cost. Whenever there is no objective method of determining the current cost of obtaining the same or equivalent services, depreciated acquisition cost should continue as the basis of valuation.

Based on its study of the index number problem, the staff of the Accounting Research Division of the AICPA concluded:[20]

[19]Committee on Concepts and Standards—Long-Lived Assets, *op. cit.,* p. 695.

[20]Staff of the Accounting Research Division, "Reporting the Financial Effects of Price-Level Changes," *Accounting Research Study No. 6,* AICPA, New York, 1963, pp. 113–114.

Changes in the prices of specific commodities can be reflected in financial reports by the use of appropriate price series for the individual accounts that appear in those reports. Fortunately, . . . a wealth of price data is collected and published by various agencies of the Federal Government. Some of these prices have been converted into indexes, others have not. The nonindexed price series are easily converted into indexes. . . . The subindexes of the Wholesale Price Index would supply many of the needed indexes. The most troublesome area would be finding good indexes to adjust building values, due to the inadequacies in construction cost indexes currently compiled; however, the solution is in process.

Feasibility of Financial Statements Based on Current Prices

Part of the research undertaken by the Study Group on the Objectives of Financial Statements was an empirical test of the feasibility of preparing replacement cost and exit-value financial statements for an actual firm engaged in the production of electronic equipment.

Revsine summarizes the results of efforts to prepare the firm's financial statements on a replacement cost basis as follows:[21]

Very few implementation problems were encountered during the course of the study. In those cases where data were initially absent, it was usually possible to reconstruct the missing information or to develop some surrogate approach. One might reasonably expect that even these occasional problems would diminish were market based measures widely adopted for reporting purposes.

This study has indicated that the test company was already employing what is essentially a replacement cost system for internal inventory accounting. This itself indicates the practicality of the replacement cost inventory procedures more forcefully than any academic study ever could.

With regard to fixed assets, the results were less equivocal but still essentially favorable. Market prices for 62 percent of the manufacturing equipment (as a percentage of original historical cost) were readily available. While the remaining portion of the equipment was valued by index adjustment, this was largely dictated by time constraints. It is possible that some portion of these assets could also have been valued directly.

Land was valued directly, although conservatively, by reference to a rejected offer that the test company had recently received. While cost

[21]Revsine, *op. cit.*, pp. 241–244.

considerations led to an index adjustment for the building, direct appraisal is a preferable, and obviously available, alternative in realistic circumstances.

On the basis of these results, it would appear defensible to conclude that the data necessary to prepare replacement cost financial statements were generally available. Thus, this case study did not disclose any obstacles which would impede the implementation of replacement cost reports. Whether this conclusion can be generalized to other situations is a subject for future research.

McKeown summarizes the results of efforts to prepare exit-value financial statements for the same electronic equipment manufacturer as follows:[22]

> Preparation of two exit-value balance sheets and an exit-value income statement for X Company demonstrated that in this case readily available market prices could be determined at very little cost for the land and building and most of the equipment. Market prices for the rest of the equipment (mainly metal furniture) were estimated again at nominal cost by use of general guidelines suggested by used furniture dealers. A more accurate estimate for these items might have been obtained by employing an appraiser. However, the cost of appraisal of these items would have been significant (five percent of appraised value) and would probably be incurred every three or five years if at all. This procedure of relatively infrequent appraisals should yield accurate estimates because, according to the used furniture dealers, the resale price is determined mainly by the type and quality of the asset rather than the age. Thus, barring major changes in the used asset market, an appraisal of a particular item (possibly adjusted by a specific price index) should be valid for several years.

> Measurements of items other than fixed assets were readily computed at nominal cost. The only way management would have had any effect on the exit-value figures reported would have been solicitation of special offers for particular assets. Although this activity could be called manipulation, the economic fact remains that management could realize the offered amount. Further, the effect of these offers could easily be segregated. Other than the solicitation of special offers, management cannot manipulate the exit-value figures because the measurements are taken from the markets rather than management estimates. This provides less opportunity for manipulation of profit figures than is available under conventional accounting procedures (alternative depreciation methods, sale of particular fixed assets to realize an available gain or loss, etc.).

[22]McKeown, *op. cit.*, p. 227.

The conclusion must be reached that critics of exit value who base their opposition on lack of feasibility of implementation will find no evidence to support their position in this case. Preparation of exit-value statements for X Company was possible at a reasonable cost.

CURRENT PRICES OF SPECIFIC ITEMS AND ADJUSTMENTS FOR CHANGES IN THE GENERAL PRICE LEVEL

By combining general price-level adjustments with the use of current prices of specific items, all of the asserted advantages of both can be obtained. The major impact of the use of general price level adjustments is the measurement of price level gains on net monetary working capital and long-term debt. Indeed, it will be recalled that the measurement of price level gains and losses is the unique product of price level adjustments. The major impact of the use of current prices of specific items is the measurement of holding gains and losses on nonmonetary items, particularly inventory and fixed assets. The major incremental information supplied by combining general price level adjustments with the use of current prices for specific items is the disaggregation of holding gains and losses into "real" and "nominal" components.

To illustrate the measurement of "real" and "nominal" holding gains and losses, assume that a quantity of raw material was acquired on January 1, Year 1, for $10,000 cash. The same batch of raw material was sold on December 31, Year 1, in the form of the company's finished product. The index of the general price level increased 8 percent during the year, indicating that in terms of general purchasing power, $10,800 was the December 31, Year 1 equivalent of $10,000 on January 1, Year 1. Because of an increasing demand for the limited supply of raw material, however, it cost $12,500 to replace that quantity of raw material on December 31, Year 1. Assuming that the finished product was sold at a price in excess of the current cost of production, conventional operating income (sale revenues less cost of goods sold and other operating expenses) would implicitly include an $800 "nominal" profit (= $10,800 − $10,000) due to the 8 percent general price inflation and a $1,700 "real" holding gain (= $12,500 − $10,800) attributable to the increase in the raw material specific price in excess of the increase in the general price level. The reporting of the real and nominal components of holding gains and losses is the unique product of financial statements adjusted for changes in both the general price level and for changes in the prices of specific items.

The principal advantages of recognizing both general and specific price changes may be summarized as follows:

1. The balance sheet at the end of the period reports assets and liabilities, both monetary and nonmonetary, at their current prices at the end of the period.

2. The comparative balance sheet for the beginning of the period reports all assets and liabilities at their beginning-of-the-period prices but restated into dollars of end-of-the-period general purchasing power. The comparative balance sheets, therefore, reflect a common measuring unit.

3. The income statement separates the results of operating activities from holding activities. Operating income is the difference between revenues recognized and expenses reported. Expenses are measured in terms of the current prices of goods and services at the time of their sale or use. Both revenues and expenses are restated, though, into dollars of end-of-the-period general purchasing power. Changes in the prices of nonmonetary assets up until the end of the period (or to the time of sale if sold during the period) are recognized as holding gains and losses. These holding gains and losses are disaggregated into their "nominal" component (change in specific prices equal to the change in the general price level) and "real" component (change in specific prices greater or less than the change in the general price level). Net income also includes a general price level gain or loss from holding monetary items during a period when the "specific price" of monetary items (i.e., the general purchasing power of the dollar) changes.

Special Problems

Several different concepts of "current price" have been advocated, and a variety of ways of determining current prices have been suggested. These matters were discussed earlier in this chapter. The addition of general price level adjustments does not affect those considerations.

Two special problems discussed in connection with the adjustment of historical amounts for changes in the general price level—manufactured inventories and measurements based on net realizable value—are essentially unchanged by the use of current prices. But, the rule of cost or market, whichever is lower, has no counterpart when using current prices of specific items. In effect the rule is *always use market,* whether higher or lower.

Clearly, the critical problem in using current prices is their objective determination, whatever concept of current price is adopted and whether general price level adjustments are made. Nothing further can be added to the earlier discussion until more experience with the use of current prices has accumulated.

SUMMARY

This chapter discusses three methods of accounting for inflation. In comparing each of the three methods with conventional financial statements, we draw the following conclusions. GPLA financial statements change the amounts, but not the timing, of revenues, expenses, gains, and losses. They are objective and verifiable, but do not disclose relevant current economic data except for the gain or loss on holdings of monetary items. Current value statements, without price level adjustments, change the timing, but not the ultimate amounts, of revenue, expenses, gains, and losses. These statements reflect changes in economic conditions as they occur but they may require subjective, and hence hard-to-audit, estimates of current values. These statements do not separate real from nominal holding gains. If we had to choose between one of these two methods of accounting for inflation, we would prefer the latter, which is based on current values. The two choices are not mutually exclusive, however, and a combination of current values and general price level adjustments is best in our view. Such statements change both the amounts and timing of revenue, expenses, gains, and losses when compared to conventional statements (but balance sheet totals are the same as on current value balance sheets). Such statements are, perhaps, the most useful because they provide information that is meaningful and comparable over time. They may require subjective estimates of current values, and many readers may find them complex.

Chapter Twelve

CRITICISMS OF GENERAL PRICE LEVEL ADJUSTED ACCOUNTING

DISAGREEMENTS ABOUT THE DESIRABILITY of adjusting financial statements for general price level changes have existed for many years. It is important that users of these statements understand just what they do and do not represent. The more important criticisms of general price level accounting are discussed in the following sections.

Briefly, the criticisms can be summarized as follows:

1. GPLA provides an inappropriate standard for measuring earnings performance. Because it does not measure current (opportunity) costs, it does not measure the economically significant factors in decision making.

2. The benefits to investors of general price level adjustments may not exceed the substantial costs of providing them.

3. Even if general price level adjustments are sought, the general price indexes are not sufficiently reliable for use in accounting reports.

GENERAL PRICE LEVEL ADJUSTED ACCOUNTING PROVIDES AN INAPPROPRIATE STANDARD FOR MEASURING EARNINGS PERFORMANCE

The major criticism of general price level adjusted accounting is closely related to one of its chief claimed advantages. What general price level adjusted accounting measures, it measures relatively objectively. But does it measure the economically significant factors in measuring earnings performance? The critics say *no*.

General price level adjusted accounting, as we have seen from the earlier chapters, basically involves applying a government-supplied price index to conventional historical cost financial statement data. The resulting GPLA numbers are as objective and auditable as traditional accounting data.[1] But traditional historical cost data do not disclose current values, and GPLA adjustments similarly do not disclose current values. If current value information is what is needed for assessing economic performance and making sound economic decisions, general price level adjusted accounting will not provide it.

The Financial Accounting Standards Board, in the Preface to the Exposure Draft, put the point clearly:[2]

> Expressing financial information in units of general purchasing power [general price level adjustments] should not be confused with the proposal that financial statements reflect changes in specific prices ("current values") of goods held or obligations owed by an enterprise while they are held or owed. . . . Some advocate the adoption of current value accounting rather than general purchasing power accounting, and general purchasing power accounting has sometimes been suggested as a means of approximating current values. Although both the general level of prices and most specific prices tend to move in the same direction in a period of inflation or deflation, general purchasing power accounting and current value accounting are proposals with different objectives, and each should be evaluated on its own merits.

In Chapter One we listed the major objectives of general price level adjusted accounting as being:

1. To make the results of arithmetic operations using accounting measurements more meaningful.

2. To make interperiod comparisons more meaningful.

3. To improve the meaning and measurement of income.

4. To provide explicit information about the impact of inflation across firms.

These are laudable objectives, and GPLA meets each of them to some degree. It is most successful in meeting the first objective of improving the

[1]There may be some question about the reliability of the index, but all those preparing and auditing GPLA data will be using the same index, reliable or not.

[2]Financial Accounting Standards Board, "Financial Reporting in Units of General Purchasing Power," Proposed Statement of Financial Accounting Standard, Stamford, Connecticut, 1974.

rationality of the arithmetic operations. With regard to the other three objectives, GPLA accounting suffers from applying a single uniform adjustment for changing prices to all firms, despite the fact that they may be experiencing different rates of price change in the activities that are important to them. In most cases GPLA accounting will go some way toward meeting these latter objectives, but usually not as well as would current value accounting if the data were available.

Perhaps the best way to sum up this criticism of applying a uniform price adjustment to firms operating under divergent conditions is to cite a portion of the president's letter in the annual report of Wedgewood, Ltd., the British firm that makes Wedgewood china, among other products. The English accounting institute has issued a tentative recommendation for publication of general price level adjusted financial statements. The president of Wedgewood stated that GPLA accounting statements were included in the annual report:

> . . . to give effect to the recommendations of the Institute of Chartered Accountants of England and Wales but for no other reason. The results of using the retail price index to adjust a widely varying range of revenue and capital items in divergent industries in different parts of the country over widely extended periods of time will provide no sensible basis of comparative performance. Any investment analyst who forms a view of Wedgewood from these statements will almost certainly arrive at a misleading verdict.

If the objective is to present financial information that will provide an appropriate standard for measuring earnings performance or evaluating economic decisions, general price level adjusted data do not meet the test. This is certainly true with regard to measuring the earnings performance of investments in nonmonetary assets. It is also true with regard to monetary assets.

The point concerning monetary assets may be illustrated by a simple example. Assume that on January 1 a firm lends $100,000 of excess cash it will not need for a year to one of its suppliers. The loan bears interest at 10 percent. At the end of the year, the firm's reported return on this loan will be measured in general price level adjusted accounting by the difference between the interest earned and the monetary loss (assuming inflation) recognized from being in a creditor position. This net return will then be compared with some desired earnings standard. But recognizing the monetary loss by using a measure of general purchasing power does not measure this firm's purchasing-power loss, for the general price index measures price changes for too wide a variety of goods and services. Of more importance to this firm is its ability to maintain purchasing power for the types of goods and services it normally purchases. A firm in the steel industry, for example, is not likely to be particularly concerned with maintaining the purchasing power of its current funds for the wide range of consumer goods and services included in the GNP index. The steel company is more likely to be concerned with its ability to maintain purchasing power for the various raw materials and productive facilities used in manufacturing steel.

General price level adjusted costs for nonmonetary assets clearly do not measure the opportunity cost of their use. What is needed is some measure of the current value of the specific items used if current economic profitability is to be assessed. Because the general price level index represents the weighted average of all price movements, it would be most coincidental for it to depict the change in current value of any specific asset.

The discussion of the previous chapter, especially the citations from the Committee on Concepts and Standards—Long-Lived Assets of the American Accounting Association,[3] spelled out the significance of current values for assets, liabilities, and expenses in economic decision making. GPLA data do not provide that information.

THE BENEFITS OF COMPREHENSIVE RESTATEMENT MAY NOT EXCEED THE COSTS

With respect to the benefits of general price level adjusted financial statements to statement users, several surveys of financial analysts and other statement users suggest that the statements contain little useful information.[4] Additionally, the costs of designing and maintaining accounting systems for generating GPLA statements are significant. Also significant are the costs to be incurred in educating financial statement users as to the meanings of the statements and as to the types of interpretations which should and should not be made from them.

Others, who feel that general price level adjusted statements may have some information value after an extensive educational effort, argue that there is sufficient information in the conventional statements for users to make desired adjustments for the effects of inflation. Several studies, for example, have indicated that a high degree of association exists between

---

[3]See especially Chapter Eleven, pp. 202–207.

[4]Ralph W. Estes, "An Assessment of the Usefulness of Current Cost and Price-Level Information by Financial Statement Users," *Journal of Accounting Research,* Autumn 1968, pp. 200–207; Thomas R. Dyckman, "Investment Analysis and General Price-Level Adjustments," *Studies in Accounting Research,* No. 1, American Accounting Association, Evanston, Ill., 1969; Don E. Garner, "The Need for Price-Level and Replacement Cost Data," *Journal of Accountancy,* September 1972, pp. 94–98.

the rate of return on stockholders' equity in historical dollars and the rate based on statements adjusted for general price changes.[5] Given the historical dollar measure, the price level adjusted measure can be easily estimated, as we show in Chapter Eight. Our procedures, which also rely on information from the historical dollar financial statements, give specific consideration to the inventory and depreciation methods used by a particular firm. Thus, it is possible to estimate various components of general price level adjusted net income, such as sales revenue, gross margin, and monetary gains and losses, at relatively modest cost.

Another possible use of GPLA financial statements might be to help investors predict future cash flows. Several theoretical and empirical studies have suggested that conventionally reported earnings are used by investors primarily as an aid in predicting future cash flows to them. This helps to explain the importance to investors of the funds statement as prepared in historical cost accounting. If GPLA data are presented, emphasis should similarly be placed on funds flows. The FASB proposal does not call for preparation of GPLA funds statements. Such statements are relatively easy to prepare from GPLA balance sheet and income statement data, as Chapter Ten demonstrates. However, the significance of funds flows, and especially the nonfunds nature of gains on long-term monetary liabilities, would be emphasized if formal statements were prepared. The cost/benefit ratio would certainly be improved by the inclusion of such statements if GPLA reports are required.

THE GENERAL PRICE INDEXES ARE NOT SUFFICIENTLY RELIABLE FOR USE IN ACCOUNTING REPORTS

Criticisms have been directed at some of the procedures followed in preparing general price indexes, creating uncertainty about their reliability and accuracy.

One criticism is directed at the use of posted prices for some items, rather than the prices of actual transactions, in index construction. Stigler and Kendahl have documented many[6] cases where posted prices were used despite significant differences from the prices of actual transactions.

[5]Russell J. Peterson, "Interindustry Estimation of General Price-Level Impact on Financial Information," *Accounting Review,* January 1973, pp. 34–43; John K. Simmons and Jack Gray, "An Investigation of Differing Accounting Frameworks on the Prediction of Net Income," *Accounting Review,* October 1969, pp. 757–776; and Lawrence Revsine and Jerry J. Weygandt, "Accounting for Inflation: The Controversy," *The Journal of Accountancy,* October 1974, pp. 72–78.

[6]George J. Stigler and James K. Kendahl, *The Behavior of Industrial Prices,* National Bureau of Economic Research, No. 90, General Series, 1970.

A second criticism of the procedures is that the goods and services included in the "market basket" and the weights applied to aggregate individual price changes in the price index are not updated on a sufficiently timely basis.[7] As a result, it is questionable whether the GNP index measures changes in the prices of goods and services actually being purchased during a particular period and in the proportions suggested by the weights used in the index.

A third criticism of the price index compilation procedures is the treatment of quality changes. To measure pure price changes adequately, any portion of an actual price change attributable to quality changes in the good or service must first be identified. Triplett[8] and Barzel,[9] among others, have found significant bias in certain components of the GNP index as a result of the failure in the construction methods to account adequately for quality changes.

Critics of general price level accounting argue that these and other defects of the compilation procedures raise serious questions about the propriety of using this index to adjust historical dollar financial statements. These critics counter the usual response that "all firms use the same indexes and any misstatement across firms will be equal" by suggesting that varying degrees of index accuracy through time do create differences across firms depending on the age and kinds of their assets and equities.

SUMMARY

In concluding this chapter and this book, we quote from an article by John C. Burton, Chief Accountant of the SEC.[10]

> Under the assumption that there is some utility to the accountants' work product, we must consider ways in which it can be changed to make it most useful under inflationary conditions. The first step is to understand the way inflation affects business entities. The impact of inflation falls with dramatic differences on different types of businesses and on different classes of assets within a business. The price of different goods rise at substantially different rates.

[7]For several examples, see Clyde P. Stickney and David O. Green, "No Price Level Adjusted Statements, Please (PLEAS)," *The CPA Journal,* January 1974, pp. 28–29.

[8]Jack E. Triplett, "Quality Bias in Price Indexes and New Methods of Measurement," in *Price Indexes and Quality Change,* edited by Zvi Griliches, Harvard University Press, Cambridge, Mass., 1971, p. 198.

[9]Yoram Barzel, "Productivity and the Price of Medical Services," *Journal of Political Economy,* 77 (November-December 1969), pp. 1014–1027.

[10]John C. Burton, "Accounting That Allows for Inflation," *Business Week,* November 30, 1974, pp. 12–14.

In addition, the ability of companies to raise prices at the same rate as costs rise will vary significantly. Some may be able to raise selling prices even more rapidly than costs increase. Others will be unable to increase prices to recover higher costs for fear of substantially reducing volume. In some cases, businesses may face government controls or social and government pressures to keep prices down.

Under such conditions, it seems apparent that the accountant's measurement of earning power must reflect current economic phenomena. On the sales side of the ledger, this presents no great problem. If prices are changing extremely rapidly within a single accounting period, an index of physical volume and the presentation of data for very small time segments might be required. In general, however, revenue recognition at the point of sale satisfactorily shows current market conditions.

If the matching process is to produce a measure of current earning power, costs must similarly reflect market conditions at the time of sale. This argues strongly for a measurement system based on the current economic costs. Under such an approach, expenses would be based on the current cost of replacement of the particular assets sold or used. . . .

Current value accounting is easy to explain and meaningful, but hard to audit. It requires estimates of the current values of all assets and liabilities. More often than not, prices for "used" assets are hard to get. Auditors would be required to make substantial judgmental decisions in implementing current value accounting. But we live in a litigious age, and auditors are reluctant to exercise judgment in such situations because, occasionally, subsequent events might not bear out these judgments, and costly and embarrassing lawsuits may result.

Other problems of current value accounting have not yet been settled by theorists. When there is a "bid–asked" spread for an asset—the replacement cost is higher than the current selling price (or net realizable value)—which of these numbers should be used? Those who believe in replacement costs are called "entry-value" theorists, and those who believe in net realizable values are called "exit-value" theorists. We think that exit value should be used only for those assets that the firms usually sells.

GPLA financial statements are easy to audit and are objective.[11] Two auditors given the same historical records and the same data for the GNP Deflator are likely to derive the same general price level adjusted statements.

---

[11]Moreover, some accountants think that GPLA accounting would significantly improve the income statement information over conventional statements. See, for example, Paul Rosenfield, "GPP Accounting—Relevance and Interpretability," *Journal of Accountancy*, August 1975, pp. 52–59.

In our opinion, the gain or loss on holdings of monetary items is the part of general price level adjusted accounting that results in adjustments that are both large and meaningful. The general price level adjustments for revenues and all expenses except cost of goods sold and depreciation are likely to be small and modestly meaningful. The adjustment for depreciation is large and may be misleading unless the prices of the particular long-lived assets being depreciated have changed just as the GNP deflator has changed. The percentage adjustment in cost of goods sold may be relatively small, but the dollar effect on net income may be large. Here again the effect may be misleading unless the firm's inventory costs move in unison with the general price level. Other than information on monetary gains or losses, in our opinion, general price level adjustments do not convey much useful information. Still, these are the statements that we think are likely to be required, and all analysts and investors will have to understand where they have meaning and where they do not.

Accounting that incorporates both current values and price level changes is, in our opinion, the best solution to the problem of accounting for changing prices. Such accounting reports holding gains and losses on all assets and the recognition of gain or loss on holdings of monetary items. It is, however, both hard to explain and hard to audit, and is unlikely to receive much acceptance in practice in the foreseeable future.

SELECTED BIBLIOGRAPHY

Alexander, Michael O., Ed., *Accounting for Inflation: A Challenge for Business,* Maclean-Hunter Ltd., Toronto, 1975.

Aliber, Robert Z., and Clyde P. Stickney, "Accounting Measures of Foreign Exchange Exposure: The Long and Short of It," *The Accounting Reveiw,* 50 (January 1975), pp. 44–57.

American Accounting Association (AAA), Committee on Concepts and Standards—Inventory Measurement, "A Discussion of Various Approaches to Inventory Measurement," *The Accounting Review,* 39 (July 1964), pp. 700–714.

American Accounting Association (AAA), Committee on Concepts and Standards—Long-Lived Assets, "Accounting for Land, Buildings, and Equipment," *The Accounting Review,* 39 (July 1964), pp. 693–699.

American Accounting Association (AAA), Committee on External Reporting, "An Evaluation of External Reporting Practices," *The Accounting Review* (Committee Reports Supplement to Volume XLIV, 1969), pp. 79–123.

American Accounting Association (AAA), Committee to Prepare a Statement of Basic Accounting Theory, *A Statement of Basic Accounting Theory,* American Accounting Association, Sarasota, Fla., 1966.

American Institute of Certified Public Accountants (AICPA), "Financial Statements Restated for General Price Level Changes," *Statement of the Accounting Principles Board No. 3,* June 1969.

American Institute of Certified Public Accounts (AICPA), Accounting Objectives Study Group, *Objectives of Financial Statements,* AICPA, New York, 1973.

American Institute of Certified Public Accountants (AICPA), Accounting Research Division, *Reporting the Financial Effects of Price-Level Changes,* Accounting Research Study No. 6, AICPA, New York, 1963.

American Institute of Certified Public Accountants (AICPA), Study Group On Business Income, *Changing Concepts of Business Income,* Macmillan Company, New York, 1952.

Backer, Morton, *Current Value Accounting,* Financial Executives Research Foundation, New York, 1973.

Backer, Morton, *Financial Reporting for Security Investment Credit Decisions,* NAA Research Studies in Management Reporting No. 3, National Association of Accountants, New York, 1970.

Barzel, Yoram, "Productivity and the Price of Medical Services," *Journal of Political Economy,* 77 (November–December 1969), pp. 1014–1027.

Bedford, Norton M., *Income Determination Theory: An Accounting Framework,* Addison-Wesley Publishing Co., Reading, Mass., 1965.

Bierman, Harold, Jr., "Effect of Inflation on the Computation of Income of Public Utilitites," *The Accounting Review,* 31 (April 1956), pp. 1349–1378.

Bonbright, James C., *Principles of Public Utility Rates,* Columbia University Press, New York, 1961.

Bonbright, James C., "Public Utility Rate Control in a Period of Price Inflation," *Land Economics,* February 1951, pp. 16–23.

Boulding, Kenneth E., "Economics and Accounting: The Uncongenial Twins," in *Studies in Accounting Theory,* 3rd ed., edited by W. T. Baxter and Sidney Davidson, Sweet & Maxwell, London, 1976.

Burton, John C., "Accounting That Allows for Inflation," *Business Week,* November 30, 1974, pp. 12–14.

Calder, J. A., "How the Replacement Cost Concept Came to Imperial Tobacco Company," *Canadian Chartered Accountant,* August 1970, pp. 89–94.

Chambers, R. J., "Edwards and Bell on Business Income," *The Accounting Review,* 40 (October 1965), pp. 731–741.

Chambers, Raymond J., *Accounting, Evaluation, and Economic Behavior,* Prentice-Hall, Englewood Cliffs, N.J., 1966.

Cooper, W. W., "Index-Number Adjustments of Financial Statements," *Illinois Certified Public Accountant,* September 1950, pp. 15–23.

Coopers & Lybrand, *Financial Reporting in an Era of Inflation,* New York, 1974.

Corbin, Donald A., "Case Study of Price-Level Adjustments," *The Accounting Review,* 30 (April 1955), pp. 268–281.

Corbin, Donald A., "The Impact of Changing Prices on a Department Store," *Journal of Accountancy,* April 1954, pp. 430–440.

Coughlan, John W., "Applicability of the Realization Principle to Money Claims in Common Dollar Accounting," *The Accounting Review,* 30 (January 1955), pp. 103–113.

Coutts, W. B., "Accounting for Inflation," *Canadian Chartered Accountant,* December 1962, pp. 619–625.

Coutts, W. B., "Accounting for Price Level Changes—An Appraisal of Theoretical Techniques," *Canadian Chartered Accountant,* January 1961, pp. 60–65.

Coutts, W. B., "An Adoption of Replacement Value Depreciation," *Canadian Chartered Accountant,* May 1962, pp. 478–482.

Davidson, Sidney, James N. Kelly, and Roman L. Weil, "How Inflation-Adjusted Accounting Would Pare Banks' Net," *Banking,* 57 (July 1975), pp. 31–33, 90, 94.

Davidson, Sidney, James S. Schindler, Clyde P. Stickney, and Roman L. Weil, *Accounting: The Language of Business,* 2nd ed., Thomas Horton & Daughters, Glen Ridge, N.J., 1975.

Davidson, Sidney, James S. Schindler, Clyde P. Stickney, and Roman L. Weil, *Financial Accounting: An Introduction to Concepts, Methods, and Uses,* The Dryden Press, Hinsdale, Ill., 1976, chaps. 11, 14.

Davidson, Sidney, James S. Schindler, and Roman L. Weil, *Fundamentals of Accounting,* 5th ed., The Dryden Press, Hinsdale, Ill., 1975.

Davidson, Sidney, Samy Sidky, and Roman L. Weil, "Inflation Accounting: How Well Do General Price Level Adjustments Reflect Current Costs of Inventory?" *Proceedings of the*

First Topical Research on Accounting Conference, The Vincent C. Ross Institute of the College of Business and Public Administration, New York University, 1975.

Davidson, Sidney, and Roman L. Weil, "Inflation Accounting: Public Utilities," *Financial Analysts Journal,* 31, 3 (May/June 1975), pp. 30–34, 62.

Davidson, Sidney, and Roman L. Weil, "Inflation Accounting: Some 1974 Income Measures," *Financial Analysts Journal,* 31, 5(September/October 1975), pp. 42–54.

Davidson, Sidney, and Roman L. Weil, "Inflation Accounting: What Will General Price Level Adjusted Income Statements Show?" *Financial Analysts Journal,* 31, 1 (January/February 1975), pp. 27–31 and 70–81.

Davidson, Sidney, and Yasukichi Yasuba, "Asset Revaluation and Income Taxation in Japan," *National Tax Journal,* March 1960, pp. 45–58.

Dean, Arthur H., "Impact of Changing Price Levels on Rate Making," *Public Utilities Fortnightly,* December 3, 1953, pp. 817–836.

"Depreciation and the Price Level," a symposium by James L. Dohr, W. A. Paton, Maurice E. Peloubet, William H. Bell, Howard C. Greer, and Eric L. Kohler, *The Accounting Review,* 23 (April 1948), pp. 115–136.

Dyckman, Thomas R., "Investment Analysis and General Price-Level Adjustments," *Studies in Accounting Research,* No. 1, American Accounting Association, Sarasota, Fla., 1969.

Edwards, E. O., "The State of Current Value Accounting," *The Accounting Review,* 50 (April 1975), pp. 235–245.

Edwards, E. O., and P. W. Bell, *The Theory and Measurement of Business Income,* University of California Press, Berkeley and Los Angeles, 1961.

Edwards, James Don, and Carl S. Warren, "Price-Level Adjustments: U.S. Viewpoints," *The Accountant's Magazine,* May 1975, pp. 174–177.

Edwards, Ronald S., "The Nature and Measurement of Income," edited version in *Studies in Accounting Theory,* 3rd ed., edited by W. T. Baxter and Sidney Davidson, Sweet & Maxwell, London, 1976.

Estes, Ralph W., "An Assessment of the Usefulness of Current Cost and Price-Level Information by Financial Statement Users," *Journal of Accounting Research,* Autumn 1968, pp. 200–207.

Falkenstein, Angela, *"Full Disclosure in an Inflationary Environment, Summary and Conclusions,* Legg Mason Washington Service, Washington, D.C., July 1974.

Fertig, Paul E., "Current Values and Index Numbers: The Problem of Objectivity," in *Research in Accounting Measurement,* edited by Robert K. Jaedicke, Yuji Ijiri, and Oswald Nielsen, American Accounting Association, Menasha, Wisc., 1966, pp. 137–149.

Financial Accounting Standards Board, "Financial Reporting in Units of General Purchasing Power," Proposed Statement of Financial Accounting Standard, Stamford, Conn., 1974.

Financial Accounting Standards Board: "Reporting the Effects of General Price-Level Changes in Financial Statements," *FASB Discussion Memorandum,* February 1974.

Gainsbrugh, Martin R., and Jules Backman, *Inflation and the Price Indexes,* materials submitted to the Subcommittee on Economic Statistics of the Joint Economic Committee, Congress of The United States, 89th Congress, 2nd Session, U.S. Government Printing Office, Washington, D.C., 1966, reprinted as "Studies in Business Economics, No. 94," National Industrial Conference Board, New York, 1966.

Garner, Don E., "The Need for Price-Level and Replacement Cost Data," *Journal of Accountancy,* September 1972, pp. 94–98.

Gordon, Myron J., *The Cost of Capital to a Public Utility,* Michigan State University, East Lansing, Mich., 1974.

Gordon, Myron J., "Scope and Method of Theory in Research in the Measurement of Income and Wealth: *The Accounting Review,* 35 (October 1960), pp. 603–618.

Grady, Paul, "Tax Effect Accounting When Basic Federal Income Tax Rate Changes," *Journal of Accountancy,* April 1964, pp. 25–27.

Gynther, R. S., "Accounting for Price-Level Changes," *Accountancy,* July 1962, pp. 560–564.

Gynther, R.S., *Accounting for Price-Level Changes; Theory and Procedures,* Pergamon Press, London, 1966.

Hanna, John R., *Accounting Income Models: An Application and Evaluation,* Special Study No. 8, The Society of Industrial Accountants, Hamilton, Ont., 1974.

Harmelink, Philip J., and Philip L. Kintzele, "Price Level Adjustments on Electric Utility Statements," *Public Utilities Fortnightly,* 95, 4 (February 13, 1975), pp. 30–33.

Hawkins, David F., "Accounting's Contribution to Greater Earnings Volatility and Possible Lower Multiples: A Look at the Future Through the Present," Accounting Bulletin 2, Drexel Burnham & Co., New York, 1975.

Hendricksen, Eldon S., *Price-Level Adjustments of Financial Statements—An Evaluation and Case Study of Two Public Utility Firms,* Economic and Business Studies, Bulletin No. 35, Washington State University: Bureau of Economic and Business Research, Pullman, Wash., June 1961.

Horngren, C. T., "Security Analysts and the Price Level," *The Accounting Reveiw,* 30 (October 1955), pp. 575–581.

Ijiri, Yuji, "Theory of Accounting Measurement," Studies in Accounting Research No. 10, American Accounting Association, Sarasota, Fla., 1975.

Imperial Tobacco Company of Canada, *Annual Reports,* 1961–1967, Imperial Tobacco Company of Canada, Montreal, annual.

Indiana Telephone Corporation, *Annual Reports,* 1973 and 1974, Indiana Telephone Corporation, Indianapolis, Ind.

Institute of Chartered Accountants in England and Wales, Accounting Standards Steering Committee, *Accounting for Changes in the Purchasing Power of Money,* Exposure Draft No. 8, Institute of Chartered Accounts in England and Wales, London, July 31, 1973.

Jones, Ralph Coughenour, *Effects of Price Level Changes on Business Income, Capital, and Taxes,* American Accounting Association, Sarasota, Fla., 1956.

Jones, Ralph Coughenour, *Price Level Changes and Financial Statements—Case Studies of Four Companies,* American Accounting Association, Sarasota, Fla., 1955.

Kirkman, Patrick R. A., *Accounting Under Inflationary Conditions,* George Allen & Unwin, London, 1974.

Ladd, D. R., and J. F. Graham, Imperial Tobacco Company of Canada, ICH 8C1, Intercollegiate Case Clearing House, Boston, 1963.

Largay, James A., III, and J. Leslie Livingstone, *Accounting for Changing Prices: Replacement Costs and General Price Level Adjustments,* Wiley/Hamilton, Santa Barbara, Ca., 1976.

Ma, Ronald, "A Comparative Review of Some Price Level Accounting Systems," *Abacus,* August 1965, pp. 107–130.

Mason, Perry, *Price-Level Changes and Financial Statements—Basic Concepts and Methods,* American Accounting Association, Sarasota, Fla., 1971.

McKeown, John C., "Usefulness of Exit-Value Accounting Statements in Staisfying Accounting Objectives," in *Objectives of Financial Statements,* Vol. 2, edited by Joe J. Cramer, Jr., and George H. Sorter, AICPA, 1974.

Moonitz, Maurice, "Chambers on the Price Level Study," *Abacus,* August 1967, pp. 55–61.

Moonitz, Maurice, *Changing Prices and Financial Reporting,* Stipes Publishing Co., Champaign, Ill., 1974.

Mullen, Louis E., "Are You Ready for Inflation Accounting?" *Journal of Accountancy,* June 1975, pp. 91–95.

Paton, William A., "Measuring Profits Under Inflation Conditions: A Serious Problem for Accountants," *Journal of Accountancy,* January 1950, pp. 16–27.

Paton, William A., and William A. Paton, Jr., *Assets—Accounting and Administration,* Roberts & Roehl, Detroit, 1971.

Petersen, Russell J., "An Examination of the Effects of Changes in the General Price Level on Published Financial Statements," Doctoral Dissertation, University of Washington, June 1971.

Petersen, Russell J., "Interindustry Estimation of General Price-Level Impact on Financial Information," *The Accounting Review,* 48 (January 1973), pp. 34–43.

Pomeranz, Felix, and John MacDonald, "Price-Level Accounting—Quo Vadis?" *Proceedings of the First Topical Research on Accounting Conference,* The Vincent C. Ross Institute of the College of Business and Public Administration, New York University, 1975.

Revsine, Lawrence, *Replacement Cost Accounting,* Prentice-Hall, Englewood Cliffs, N.J., 1973.

Revsine, Lawrence, "Replacement Cost Accounting: A Theoretical Foundation," in *Objectives of Financial Statements,* Vol. 2, edited by Joe J. Cramer, Jr., and George H. Sorter, AICPA, 1974.

Revsine, Lawrence, and Jerry J. Weygandt, "Accounting for Inflation: The Controversy," *Journal of Accountancy,* October 1974, pp. 72–78.

Rosen, L. S., *Current Value Accounting and Price-Level Restatements,* The Canadian Institute of Chartered Accountants, Toronto, 1972.

Rosenfield, Paul, "Accounting for Inflation—A Field Test," *Journal of Accountancy,* June 1969, pp. 45–50.

Rosenfield, Paul, "GPP Accounting—Relevance and Interpretability," *Journal of Accountancy,* August 1975, pp. 52–59.

Ross, Howard, *The Elusive Art of Accounting,* The Ronald Press Company, New York, 1966.

Ross, L. S., *Current Value Accounting and Price-Level Restatements,* Canadian Institute of Chartered Accountants, Toronto, 1972.

Shell Oil Company, *1974 Annual Report Statistical Supplement,* Shell Oil Company, Houston, Texas, 1974.

Shepherd, William G., "Financial Statements Gone Awry," *Business Week,* September 14, 1974, p. 96.

Siegel, Irving H., "Index-Number Differences: Geometric Means," *Journal of the American Statistical Association,* June 1942, pp. 271–274.

Simmons, John K., and Jack Gray, "An Investigation of Differing Accounting Frameworks on the Prediction of Net Income," *The Accounting Review,* 44 (October 1969), pp. 757–776.

Solomons, David, "Accounting for Changing Price Levels: Recent British Views," *Journal of Accountancy,* June 1954, pp. 702–707.

Sprouse, Robert T., "Adjustments for Changing Prices," in *Handbook of Modern Accounting,* Sidney Davidson, editor-in-chief, New York: McGraw-Hill Book Company, New York, 1970, chap. 30.

Sterling, Robert R., "Relevant Financial Reporting in an Age of Price Changes," *Journal of Accountancy,* February 1975, pp. 42–51.

Sterling, Robert R., *Theory of the Measurement of Enterprise Income,* The University Press of Kansas, Lawrence, Kansas, 1970.

Stickler, Alan D., and Christina S. R. Hutchins, *General Price-Level Accounting: Described and Illustrated,* Canadian Institute of Chartered Accountants, Toronto, 1975.

Stickney, Clyde P., and David O. Green, "No Price Level Adjusted Statements, Please (PLEAS)," *The CPA Journal,* January 1974, pp. 28–29.

Stigler, George J., and James K. Kendahl, *The Behavior of Industrial Prices,* National Bureau of Economic Research, No. 90, General Series, 1970.

Study Group on the Objectives of Financial Statements, *Objectives of Financial Statements,* Vols. I and II, AICPA, October 1973 and May 1974.

Sweeney, Henry, *Stabilized Accounting,* Harper & Brothers, New York, 1936. Reissued by Holt, Rinehart and Winston, New York, 1964.

Thomas, Arthur L., "The Allocation Problem in Financial Accounting Theory," Studies in Accounting Research No. 3, American Accounting Association, Sarasota, Fla., 1969.

Thomas, Arthur L., "The Allocation Problem: Part Two," Studies in Accounting Research No. 9, American Accounting Association, Sarasota, Fla., 1974.

Toledo Edison, *General Price-Level Financial Statement Study,* Toledo Edison, Toledo, Ohio, 1974.

Triplett, Jack E., "Quality Bias in Price Indexes and New Methods of Measurement," in *Price Indexes and Quality Change,* edited by Zvi Griliches, Harvard University Press, Cambridge, Mass., 1971.

Vatter, William J., "Fund-Theory View of Price-Level Adjustments," *The Accounting Review,* 37 (April 1962), pp. 189–207.

Weidenbaum, Murray L., "The Future of the Electric Utilities," Reprint No. 31, *Challenge,* January/February 1975.

Wilcox, Edward B., and Howard C. Greer, "Case Against Price-Level Adjustments in Income Determination" (with comments by George O. May), *Journal of Accountancy,* December 1950, pp. 492–505.

Wilk, L. A., *Accounting for Inflation,* Sweet and Maxwell, London, 1960.

Young, Arthur, & Company, *Measuring and Reporting the Impact of Inflation Through Price-Level Accounting, A Management Briefing,* Arthur Young & Company, New York, 1975.

Zeff, Stephen A., ed., *Asset Appreciation, Business Income and Price-Level Accounting, 1919–1935.* Arno Press, New York, 1975.

Zeff, Stephen A., and Hugo Ovando Z., "Inflation Accounting and the Development of Accounting Principles in Chile," *The Accountant's Magazine,* June 1975, pp. 212–214.

Zimmerman, Jerold, "Price-Level Restatements: A Technical Note," *Journal of Accounting Research,* 12, 2 (Autumn 1974), pp. 372–382.

INDEX